Understanding Language Series

Series Editors: Bernard Comrie and Greville Corbett

Understanding Semantics

Sebastian Löbner

Professor of General Linguistics, University of Düsseldorf

A member of the Hodder Headline Group
LONDON
Distributed in the United States of America by
Oxford University Press Inc., New York

First published in Great Britain in 2002 by
Arnold, a member of the Hodder Headline Group,
338 Euston Road, London NW1 3BH

http://www.arnoldpublishers.com

Distributed in the United States of America by
Oxford University Press Inc.,
198 Madison Avenue, New York, NY10016

The advice and information in this book are believed to be true and
accurate at the date of going to press, but neither the author nor the publisher
can accept any legal responsibility or liability for any errors or omissions.

British Library Cataloguing in Publication Data
A catalogue record for this book is available from the British Library

Library of Congress Cataloging-in-Publication Data
A catalog record for this book is available from the Library of Congress

ISBN 0 340 73197 4 (hb)
ISBN 0 340 73198 2 (pb)

2 3 4 5 6 7 8 9 10

Production Editor: Rada Radojicic
Production Controller: Bryan Eccleshall
Cover Design: Terry Griffiths

Typeset in 10/12pt Palatino by Phoenix Photosetting, Chatham, Kent
Printed and bound in Great Britain by MPG Books Ltd, Bodmin, Cornwall

What do you think about this book? Or any other Arnold title?
Please send your comments to feedback.arnold@hodder.co.uk

Contents

PART II THEORETICAL APPROACHES   123

7 Meaning components   125

8 Meaning and language comparison   153

Preface

For a long time this book was to be co-authored with Bernd Kortmann (University of Freiburg, Germany). Bernd was the one who wrote the book proposal for the publishers, the sample chapter, first versions of two more chapters and, not least importantly, who asked me to join him as a co-author. Even when it turned out that, for a number of reasons, Bernd had to resign from this project, he continued to serve as a critical reader of the various stages through which the chapters in this book went. If it were not for Bernd's initiative and the original plan of writing it together, I probably would not have written this book.

The title of the book, *Understanding Semantics*, is taken seriously. This textbook is not only meant to be an introduction to the major fields of the discipline, but also to the dominant approaches that shape semantics in its current state of the art. I have been striving to open the view on linguistic meaning from different perspectives. These include the language internal level of meaning relations, the cognitive level of meanings as concepts in our minds and the 'objective' level of truth and reference. As for the phenomena discussed, the book offers a balanced treatment of lexical meaning and sentence meaning. To a certain extent, it also opens the dimension of language comparison. In addition, I have tried to widen the view by including subjects like non-descriptive meaning and processes of interpretation beyond compositional meaning.

The result is not an introduction to Löbner semantics. If you work your way through the book, you will be able to continue your studies in various directions. I have done my best to give a correct and balanced account of the phenomena and theories presented. Whenever possible, standard terminology has been used. The way in which the complex matter is organized and presented is, however, certainly my particular way. When reading through the second part, you will find me rather critical in places of each of the approaches described. On the one hand, my criticisms were the natural result of the attempt to present a consistent and comprehensive picture: different theories cover different aspects of the whole and neglect others; sometimes they contradict each other in central points. On the other hand, a critical approach to scientific matters is essential from the very beginning. Therefore, transparency of notions and argumentation was one of my primary objectives. If you are my ideal reader, you will read the book carefully and completely and thereby gain a complex and coherent view of meaning in language; you will get an idea of what kind of a communicational instrument language is; you will acquire the background for going deeper into the matter by reading more advanced semantic literature and you will develop a critical eye for judging, and maybe some day participating in, the scientific discussion. You need not know much about linguistics in order to understand this introduction. All you need is an interest in language and scientific thinking.

There is a web page for this book (http://www.phil-fak.uni-duesseldorf.de/~loebner/und-sem/) with useful information: correction of errors, answers to frequently asked questions, comments, reviews, etc. My email address is given there. Any feedback is welcome!

Acknowledgements

There are quite a few people to whom I want to express my sincere gratitude for their help and support. Bernd's role has already been mentioned. He and two members of his department, Verena Haser and Lieselotte Anderwald, provided detailed comments on the greater part of the book. Four persons accompanied the manuscript from the first to the last line, not only commenting on it in detail but, much more importantly, constantly encouraging me. These were the editors, Bernard Comrie and Greville Corbett, my Berlin colleague Ewald Lang and my partner Ruth Ropertz. Further thanks go to Volker Beeh for commenting on Chapter 4, and to Tünde Vallyon for providing the Hungarian and Russian data. My daughter Saskia Löbner volunteered as a test reader. Finally, I want to thank Nick Quaintmere for helping with my English, and the Düsseldorf Department for General Linguistics for paying him.

Sebastian Löbner
Düsseldorf
August 2001

Part

I

BASIC CONCEPTS AND PHENOMENA

This book consists of two parts: Part I introduces basic concepts and central phenomena investigated in semantics. On this basis, Part II treats the essentials of three major theoretical approaches: structuralist semantics, cognitive semantics and logical ('formal') semantics.

The first step is to mark out what semantics is about. Being the theory of linguistic meaning, the discipline does not concern meaning in the widest sense of the word, but the meaning of linguistic expressions. Chapter 1 will help to delineate the relevant notion of meaning and the major fields of semantics. In Chapter 2, the notion of meaning is further refined: descriptive meaning (responsible for factual information) is distinguished from social meaning and expressive meaning. We will see how descriptive meaning is connected to truth and reference. Chapter 3 addresses the ubiquitous phenomenon of ambiguity from two perspectives: as a phenomenon related to lexical meaning, and as the result of meaning manipulations that occur when utterances are interpreted in context. Chapter 4 describes the basics of the logical approach to meaning: notions such as entailment, equivalence and incompatibility are defined on the basis of truth and reference and their relevance is discussed for the analysis of meaning. A short Chapter 5 follows, which deals with common meaning relations such as hyponymy and oppositions. Chapter 6 on predication concludes the first part. It explores the essentials of sentence meaning by addressing the way in which the different words in a sentence contribute to its meaning.

Meaning and semantics

1

Semantics is the part of linguistics that is concerned with meaning. While this is the kind of definition which may satisfy, say, your friend who happens to see you with this book in your hands and asks what it is about, the author is of course faced with the task of explaining to you more precisely what the object of semantic study is. 'Meaning' is a notion with a wide range of applications, some of which belong to the field of semantics while others lie beyond it. Meaning is always the meaning *of* something. Words have meanings, as do phrases and sentences. But deeds may have meaning too. If a government pursues a certain policy, we may ask what the meaning is of doing so. The 'meaning' of an action or a policy is what sense it makes or what purpose it serves or what it is good for. More generally, we apply the notion of meaning to all sorts of phenomena that we try to make sense of, asking what is the 'meaning' of it all.

The first thing to be stated is that semantics is exclusively concerned with the meanings of linguistic entities such as words, phrases, grammatical forms and sentences, but not with the meanings of actions or phenomena. Given that semantics is treated here as a part of linguistics, this is a trivial restriction. One exception to the exclusion of actions is verbal actions, i.e. utterances of linguistic material, ranging from phrases and sentences to dialogues and texts. The meanings of words and sentences cannot be studied independently of how they are actually used in speech.[1] After all, it is language use that provides the data for semantics. Therefore the meanings of linguistic utterances also matter to semantics.

1.1 Levels of meaning

Even if we restrict the study of meaning to words and sentences, the notion of meaning has to be further broken down into different levels at which we interpret words and sentences.

1.1.1 Expression meaning

Let us get started by looking at a simple example that will illustrate what semantics is about:

(1)   *I don't need your bicycle.*

This is an ordinary English sentence. Without even noticing, you have already recognized it as such, you have interpreted it and you are probably imagining a situation where you would say it or someone would say it to you. A characteristic semantic question is: what is the meaning of this sentence? Since you understand the sentence, you know what it means. But knowing what the sentence means is one thing, describing its meaning is another. The situation is similar with almost all our knowledge. We may exactly know how to get from one place to another, yet be unable to tell the way to someone else. We may be able to sing a song by heart, but unable to describe its melody. We are able to recognize tens of thousands of words when we hear them but the knowledge that enables us to do so is unconscious. Uncovering the knowledge of the meanings of words and sentences and revealing its nature are the central objectives of semantics.

Let us now try to determine the meaning of the sentence in (1). A plausible procedure is to start from the meanings of the words it contains. The main verb in a sentence occupies a key role in its meaning. So, what is the meaning of the verb *need*? Actually, there are two verbs *need*: an auxiliary verb (as in *I need not go*) and a full verb. In (1) we have the full verb. It is used with a direct object (*your bicycle*) and roughly means ⟩require⟨.[2] We 'need' something if it is for some reason or purpose necessary or very important for us. In our example, what is needed is described as 'your bicycle', i.e. by an expression composed of the possessive pronoun *your* and the noun *bicycle*. The noun means some sort of vehicle, with two wheels and without a motor – we need not take the trouble of attempting a precise definition. The two words *need* and *bicycle* are the main carriers of information in the sentence, so-called **content words**. *To need* is one of thousands of other verbs that could fill this position in the sentence. It differs semantically from all the others and is thus a very specific item. Even more nouns could be inserted in *I don't need your ___* . In this sense, the noun *bicycle* too is a very specific word with a meaning that distinguishes it from a very great number of other nouns.

All the other elements in our sentence are different in that they represent items from a very limited choice of expressions of the same kind. Such words are called **function words** and include articles, pronouns, prepositions, conjunctions and other 'small' words. The subject expression *I* is one of seven personal pronouns in English (*I, you, he, she, it, we* and *they*).[3] The pronoun has three case forms (*I, me, mine*). The form *I* is the nominative case and is required by the rules of standard English grammar if the pronoun fills the subject position, as it does in (1). What is the meaning of *I*? If Mary says the sentence in (1), it is Mary who is said not to need the bicycle. If John says (1), it is John. In other words, *I* is used for the one who says it, more technically: for the one who produces a token of this pronoun. The technical term for using an expression for something is **reference**. The function of the pronoun *I* is reference to the speaker of the sentence: when people use *I*, they **refer** to themselves. The entity referred to by an expression is called its **referent**. So the referent of *I* is always the speaker. The meaning of the pronoun can thus be described as follows: *I* indicates reference to the speaker. Similarly, the pronoun *you* indicates reference to one or more addressees.

For each personal pronoun there is a corresponding possessive pronoun: *I–my, you–your*, etc. *Your* in (1) indicates that the bicycle referred to is that of the addressee(s). If we think about the kind of relation that links the bicycle to the addressee(s), we realize that a broad variety of relations is possible. Possession in the sense of ownership is only one option: *your bicycle* may refer to the bicycle that belongs to the addressee(s), but also to the bicycle they are just riding, or cleaning, or repairing, or even the bicycle they have been talking about for the last ten minutes. Possessive pronouns, and other possessive constructions, indicate some sort of relation that allows us to identify the 'possessed' entity (here: the *bicycle*) by linking it to the 'possessor' (here: the addressee(s)). So the meaning of *your* can roughly be described as ⟩linked to the addressee(s)⟨.

The form *don't* is a contraction of the auxiliary verb *do* and the negation particle *not*. *Don't* contributes two things to the meaning of the sentence. First, it negates the verb *need* and thereby turns what the verb means into its contrary (roughly speaking). Second, it contributes present tense. *Didn't* or *won't* would instead contribute past or future tense. What is tense? It is the indication that the situation the sentence describes is related to a particular time. This too is covered by the term *reference*. The time actually referred to depends on when the sentence is used. Due to the present tense in (1), we will relate the situation described to the 'present' time, i.e. the time when the sentence is being uttered.[4] If (1) is uttered on 31 July 2002, 3 p.m., it conveys that the bicycle is not needed at that particular time. Combining these two components of *don't*, we may say: the meaning of *don't* is an indication of reference to the time when the sentence is said and it turns the situation expressed by the main verb into the contrary.

So far this has been an attempt to determine the meaning of each word in the sentence *I don't need your bicycle*. This is typical work of a semanticist. As you will have noticed, it is far from trivial. For a content word, the description of its meaning must be specific enough to distinguish it from all other words with different meanings. For example, it would not suffice to describe the meaning of *bicycle* merely as ⟩vehicle with two wheels⟨. At the same time, the description must be general enough to cover all cases in which this word could be used. Since one usually imagines a particular context when one tries to think of a word and its meaning, one tends to take the meaning too specifically, disregarding other cases in which the word can also be used. As for function words like pronouns and auxiliaries, their meanings may seem at first view elusive but it is possible to account for their meanings too, as our little discussion may have illustrated.

If we put all the pieces together, we can describe the meaning of the sentence as a whole. It can be roughly formulated as: ⟩for the speaker, the two-wheeled vehicle of the addressee(s) is not necessary, or very important, at the time when this is being uttered⟨.

It is very important to realize that the sentence as such, as well as the words in it, leaves open who the speaker and the addressee(s) are, what particular time is referred to and which bicycle. This is not part of the sentence's meaning. Such questions can only be settled if the sentence is actually used on a concrete occasion. What is, however, determined by the meaning of the sentence is the way how the answers to these questions depend on the occasion when the sentence is used. First, if it is actually used, it is necessarily used by someone who produces the sentence (speaks it, writes it, signs it, etc.). With *I* in subject position, the sentence 'tells' us that it is the speaker who does not need the bicycle. The use of *I* functions like an instruction: find out who produced this sentence, this is the referent of *I*. Second, the use of *your* presupposes that there are one or more addressees of the utterance. The meaning of the sentence describes the bicycle as linked to them. Third, if a sentence is used, it is necessarily used at a certain time. This time serves as the reference time for determining what is present, past or future. The present tense part of the meaning of the sentence conveys the instruction: attribute the situation described to the time when the sentence is said. Thus the meaning of the sentence specifies the way in which its reference is determined *if and when* it is used at some occasion.

The meanings of words, phrases and sentences, taken as such, i.e. out of any particular context, in their general sense, constitute the level of meaning which will henceforth be called **expression meaning**. *Expression* is just a general term for words, phrases and sentences. The term *expression meaning* covers, in particular, word meaning and sentence meaning. The level of expression meaning constitutes the central subject of linguistic semantics. It studies the material, or equipment, as it were, that languages provide for communication. As you have noticed, the determination of expression meaning requires an abstraction from the use of the expressions in concrete contexts. Rather, what one tries to capture is the *potential* of the expressions. Expressions such as *I* illustrate the point: due to its meaning, it has the potential of referring to whoever is the speaker of an utterance. Similarly, the noun *bicycle* has the potential of referring to whatever exhibits those characteristic properties that make up the meaning of the word. In this sense, the notion of expression meaning itself is an abstraction and a theoretical construct. But it is justified in the way language is conceptualized not only in linguistics but likewise in common thinking: we do talk about the meanings of words and complex expressions as such, i.e. we do address this level of meaning. In the following, occasionally the subscript 'e' will be used in order to indicate that *meaning* is meant in the sense of *expression meaning*.

1.1.2 Utterance meaning

Let us now examine what happens when the sentence in (1) is actually used. We will consider two scenarios:

> Scenario 1
> 1 August 1996, morning. Mary has been planning a trip to town that afternoon. Two days before, she talked with her neighbour John about the trip and asked him to lend her his bike for the trip. She had lent her car to her daughter and did not know if she would get it back in time. Meanwhile her daughter is back and has returned Mary's car. Mary is talking with John on her mobile, telling him, embedded within the usual small talk: 'I don't need your bicycle.'

Used in this context, the sentence acquires a concrete meaning. References are fixed: the personal pronoun *I* refers to Mary, the possessive pronoun *your* establishes a relation to her neighbour John and time reference is fixed, too: in the given context, the present tense verb will be taken to refer not to the time when Mary utters the sentence, but to the afternoon of 1 August 1996. This is clear from the fact that Mary could have said: 'I don't need your bicycle this afternoon', without changing the meaning of her utterance. Furthermore, the reference of the grammatical object *your bicycle* is fixed: it is the bicycle Mary asked John to lend her, two days before.

This is a different level of meaning which will be called **utterance meaning**, or meaning$_u$ for short. It comes about when a sentence with its meaning$_e$ is actually used in a concrete context. First of all, utterance meaning involves reference. In addition to, and in connection with, reference another central notion comes into play, the notion of **truth**. If Mary says (1) in scenario 1, the sentence is true. But in a slightly different scenario it might be false. As long as the sentence (1) is not actually used with concrete reference, it fails to be true or false. The question of truth primarily concerns 'declarative' sentences such as the one under review. Only such sentences, when uttered, are true or false. But it matters also for interrogative and other types of sentences. For example, if John asked Mary 'Do you need my bicycle?', the use of the question form would convey that he wants to know from his addressee whether, from her perspective, *I need your bicycle* is true or false.

Scenario 2

Same time and place. John's five-year-old daughter Maggie is playing at home with her five-year-old friend Titus. They are playing with a game of cards that display all kinds of vehicles. Titus is in the possession of a card that shows a snowmobile. Maggie is eager to exchange this card for one of hers and offers Titus a card with a bicycle. Titus rejects the exchange: 'I don't need your bicycle.'

In this scenario, references of *I*, *your* and the present tense are fixed accordingly. What is interesting is that in such a context the word *bicycle* can be naturally interpreted as referring not to a bicycle but to a card carrying the picture of a bicycle. Are we to draw the consequence that the meaning$_e$ of the word *bicycle* must be taken as covering not only bicycles but also pictures of this kind of vehicle and things that carry such a picture? The answer is 'No'. What happens in such cases is that the word meaning$_e$ is shifted to fit the given context. Such shifts are quite common. The phenomenon will be discussed in 3.4 and 6.7.2. For current purposes it suffices to emphasize that expression meaning may be subject to certain kinds of meaning shifts which bear on reference and truth.

In the literature, the notion of utterance meaning is not used in a uniform way. In order to fix it here, we need a notion for what above was called *occasion*, *context* or *scenario*. The technical term for this is **context of utterance**. Roughly speaking, the context of utterance, or CoU for short, is the sum of circumstances that bear on reference and truth. The most important ones are the following aspects:

- the **speaker** (or producer) of the utterance;
- the **addressee(s)** (or recipients) of the utterance;
- the **time** at which the utterance is produced and/or received;
- the **place** where the utterance is produced and/or received;
- the **facts** given when the utterance is produced and/or received.

In certain cases, e.g. communication by mail, the time, place and facts may differ for the production of an utterance and its reception. For, example, if John writes in a letter to Mary *I will be with you tomorrow night*, Mary will have to figure out which day *tomorrow* refers to. In the following it is assumed, for the sake of simplicity, that production and reception are simultaneous.

As we have seen in connection with (1), it may matter for reference (e.g. of personal pronouns) who the speaker and the addressees are in a given CoU. The place where an utterance is made matters for the reference of expressions such as *here*, *there*, *upstairs*, *downtown*, etc. as well as for the truth of sentences like *It's raining*. Facts matter principally for truth as well as for reference. For example, Mary can only refer to John's bicycle in such CoUs where John, in fact, has a bicycle. CoUs may be real or fictitious. For example, if we read a work of fiction, the relevant facts and figures are those of the story.

Given this background **utterance meaning** can be defined as the meaning that results from using an expression in a given CoU. Utterance meaning derives from expression meaning on the basis of the particulars provided by the CoU. The only aspects of the CoU that matter are those that immediately bear on reference and truth of the expression.

When someone produces an utterance, the addressees usually make all kinds of inferences. For example, in scenario 1, John may infer that Mary is still planning to make the trip; that she would have asked him to lend her his bicycle if she could not have used her car; that, however, her daughter is back with the car and that Mary is not going to lend her the car again on that afternoon; he will infer that Mary will take the car for her trip; that she considers herself able to drive, etc. All this is not explicitly said with that sentence, and it need not be true under different circumstances. In the given scenario, these inferences can be considered to be communicated because Mary can rely upon John's understanding all this.

Although these inferences are somehow triggered in the addressee's mind when he interprets Mary's utterance, it is important to separate what is actually being *said* from what is inferred. Some authors prefer not to draw this distinction and adopt a very wide notion of utterance meaning. We will not do so. The investigation of such inferences, their role in communication and how they are related to the meaning$_u$ of what is actually said, is an important part of the linguistic discipline called **pragmatics**, the scientific study of, roughly speaking, the rules that govern language use. Within pragmatics, Paul Grice's theory of 'conversational implicatures' deals with inferences of this kind.

Utterance meaning is also of concern for semantics: it has to explain how reference and truth depend on the CoU. For example, a semantic theory of tense would have to describe and explain which relations to the time of utterance present, past and future tense forms can indicate. A further important subject, gradually gaining importance, is the analysis of the systematic meaning shifts that expression meanings may undergo (cf. the reference of *bicycle* to a picture of a bicycle in scenario 2).

1.1.3 Communicative meaning

Neither the level of expression meaning nor that of utterance meaning is the primary level on which we interpret verbal utterances. In an actual exchange, our main concern inevitably is this: what does the speaker intend with the utterance, in particular, what does the speaker want from me? Conversely, when we take on the speaking part, we choose our words in pursuit of a certain communicational intention. Verbal exchanges are a form of social interaction. They form an important part of our social lives. As such, they will always be interpreted as part of the whole social exchange and relationship entertained with the speaker.

One and the same sentence can be uttered with quite different communicative results. The utterance of (1) in scenario 1 will be taken as a statement, and thereby as a withdrawal of a former request. In scenario 2, the utterance of the same sentence constitutes the refusal of an offer. In other CoUs, uttering the sentence could serve still other communicative ends. A theory that addresses this level of interpretation is speech act theory, introduced in the 1950s by the philosopher John L. Austin (1911–60) and developed further by others, in particular John R. Searle. The central idea of speech act theory is that whenever we make an utterance in a verbal exchange we act on several levels. One level is what Austin calls the 'locutionary act'. A locutionary act is the act of using a certain expression (usually a sentence) with a certain meaning$_u$ in the given CoU. In doing so, we also perform an 'illocutionary act' on the level on which the utterance constitutes a certain type of 'speech act': a statement, a question, a request, a promise, a refusal, a confirmation, a warning, etc. For example, when Titus in scenario 2 says *I don't need your bicycle*, he performs the locutionary act of saying that sentence with the utterance meaning it has in the given context, including reference to the card with the picture of a bicycle. On the illocutionary level, he performs a refusal of Maggie's offer.

The speech act level will be referred to as **communicative meaning**, meaning$_c$. Unlike expression meaning and utterance meaning, communicative meaning lies outside the range of semantics. Rather, it is of central concern for pragmatics. Exceptions to this division are constituted by expressions that due to their expression meaning serve the performance of certain types of speech acts, e.g. *Thank you*. Its meaning is the indication of the speech act of thanking. Other such expressions are phrases for greeting or apologizing. They will be treated in more detail in 2.3.1.

Having distinguished three levels of meaning, we have at the same time established, albeit sketchily, what constitutes the field of semantics proper. The discussion can be summed up as follows:

> **Semantics** is the study of the meanings of linguistic expressions, either simple or complex, taken in isolation. It further accounts for the way utterance meaning, i.e., the meaning of an expression used in a concrete context of utterance, is related to expression meaning.

Table 1.1 gives a survey of the three levels of meaning and how they are defined. As we have seen, communicative meaning is built upon utterance meaning, and this in turn is built on expression meaning. In this sense, semantics provides the ground for pragmatic considerations.

Level of meaning	Definition
expression meaning	the meaning of a simple or complex expression taken in isolation
utterance meaning	the meaning of an expression when used in a given context of utterance; fixed reference and truth value (for declarative sentences)
communicative meaning	the meaning of an utterance as a communicative act in a given social setting

Table 1.1 Three levels of meaning

1.2 Sentence meaning and compositionality

We will now take a closer look at expression meaning, in particular, sentence meaning$_e$. It is a trivial fact that the meanings of words and sentences differ in one important point. Meanings of words must simply be known and therefore learned. In our minds, we carry a huge 'lexicon' where all the words we know and their meanings are stored and to our disposition. Stored meanings are therefore called **lexical meanings**. We do not, however, have ready-made, learned meanings of complete sentences stored in our minds.

Both statements are in need of qualification. On the one hand, there are many words we need not have learned and can yet understand. These are words that can be regularly derived from other words we know. For example, you would understand the verb *mousify* even if you have just encountered it for the first time, since you know the pattern in English for deriving verbs from nouns by attaching the suffix *-ify* roughly meaning ⟩make into a . . .⟨. Another possibility for forming new, but interpretable words is the combination of two words into one, such as *mouse food*. On the other hand, there are some complex expressions, including sentences that do have a fixed, learned meaning, such as proverbs: *The early bird catches the worm*. These too have lexical meanings. But by and large, sentences and words differ in that only the latter have lexical meanings.

Although we usually understand sentences without any conscious effort, their meanings must be derived from our stored linguistic knowledge. This process is technically called **composition**.[5] Complex expressions whose meanings are not stored in the lexicon are therefore said to have **compositional meaning**. In dealing with (1), we thought about the meanings of the words it contains, but somehow glossed over the way in which the meaning of the sentence comes about. You may wonder why this is a question at all. But as you will see immediately, the question is not that trivial.

1.2.1 Grammatical meaning

Just for a change, we will consider a new example:

(2)   *The dog ate the yellow socks.*

Let us assume that we have assessed the lexical meanings of the words in (2): *the, dog, eat, yellow* and *sock*. There are no larger units in the sentence with lexical meaning; the rest of the interpretation is composition. Still regarding the words, we may observe that they occur here in particular grammatical forms. The verb form *ate* is past tense, more precisely: simple past tense rather than progressive (*was eating*); it is in the so-called indicative mood rather than in the conditional (*would eat*), it is active rather than passive (*was eaten*), it is not negated (*did not eat*). The noun *socks* is plural; and, of course, although this is not especially marked on the word, *dog* is singular. The adjective *yellow* is neither comparative (*yellower*) nor superlative (*yellowest*) but in its basic form, called 'positive'. The forms of the words matter directly for their meaning, and consequently for the meaning of the whole sentence. The singular noun *dog* has a different meaning from the plural noun *dogs*: *dog* refers to a single creature of this kind, and *dogs* to more than one. Likewise, the meaning of present tense *eat(s)* is not the same as that of past tense *ate*. In our lexicon only one meaning of a word is stored, reasonably the singular meaning of nouns, a tenseless meaning of verbs and the 'positive' meaning of adjectives.[6] Therefore, the meanings of the words *in their given form* must be derived from their lexical meanings by rules. There are rules for deriving the plural meaning of a noun, the comparative meaning of an adjective or the simple past tense meaning of a verb, respectively. These rules are part of the apparatus we use in composition.

It must be noted that not all differences in the grammatical forms of words matter for their meaning. A certain form may be necessary just for grammatical reasons. In English this does not occur very often, but here are two examples:

(3) a. *I am angry with Ann.*
   b. *Ann is angry with me.*

In the variant of English applied here, the form of the first person pronoun in (3a) is grammatically necessary because the pronoun forms the subject. Being the object in (3b), it must take the form *me*. *Me am angry with Ann* or *Ann is angry with I* would be ungrammatical. Since the form of the pronoun is determined by grammar, there is no meaning difference between *I* and *me*. The analogue holds for the difference between *am* in (3a) and *is* in (3b). Both carry the same meaning of present tense indicative *be*. Thus differences in form only matter for meaning if they can be chosen freely, independently of the syntactic structure of the sentence.[7]

That word forms may matter for semantic composition is a first important point to establish.

- The grammatical form of a word, in so far as it is not determined by grammar, contributes to its compositional meaning.

Therefore the form itself, e.g. singular, plural, positive, comparative, simple past tense, progressive past tense, etc. has a meaning$_e$. Such meanings are called **grammatical meaning**.[8]

1.2.2 Syntactic structure and combination rules

As the next step of composition, the meanings of the words (in their given forms) are combined into a whole, the meaning of the sentence. This process is guided by the syntactic structure of the sentence (this is, for the most part, what grammar is good for: to guide the interpretation of complex expressions). Let us first determine which words in (2) belong together. The words *the dog* form a syntactic unit. This kind of unit, in this case consisting of the definite article and the noun *dog*, is called a **noun phrase, NP** for short. The words *the yellow socks* form another NP, containing an adjective in addition to the article and the noun. Actually, the adjective and the noun form another unit within the NP. The combination of words into larger syntactic units is governed by the rules of grammar. There is a rule for combining adjectives with nouns, and another rule for combining a noun, or an adjective-noun combination, with an article (the article comes first). Given such rules for forming larger syntactic units we need corresponding composition rules, for example:

- a rule for deriving the meaning of an adjective-noun combination (*yellow socks*) from the meaning of the adjective and the meaning of the noun;
- a rule for deriving the meaning of an article-noun NP (*the dog*) from the meaning of the article and the meaning of the noun.

We will not try to specify these rules now. Suffice it to say that this is not at all a trivial task; for example, combinations of adjectives and nouns are interpreted in many different ways.

Having assessed *the dog* and *the yellow socks* as larger units, we turn to the total structure of the sentence. It consists of these two NPs and the verb *ate*. Due to the rules of English grammar, these three parts are related as follows: the verb is the predicate of the sentence, the NP *the dog* is its subject and *the yellow socks* its direct object. From a syntactic point of view, the verb and the direct object form a unit, known as **verb phrase, or VP**, which is then combined with the subject to form the complete sentence. We therefore need two more composition rules:

- a rule for deriving the meaning of a VP (*ate the yellow socks*) from the meaning of the verb (*ate*) and the meaning of the direct object NP (*the yellow socks*);
- a rule for deriving the meaning of a sentence (*the dog ate the yellow socks*) from the meaning of the subject NP (*the dog*) and the meaning of the VP (*ate the yellow socks*).

Again, these rules are not trivial. Roughly speaking, the composition works as follows: the verb *eat* in its given 'active' form means an event, of eating, which necessarily involves two elements, an eater and something that is eaten; the subject NP contributes a description of the eater and the direct object NP a description of the object that is eaten.

1.2.3 The principle of compositionality

Let us sum up the general results we can draw from this example. The syntactic rules of a language allow the formation of complex expressions from what will be called basic expressions. (Basic expressions are expressions with a lexical meaning.) The meaning of complex expressions is determined by semantic composition. This mechanism draws on three sources:

1 the **lexical meanings** of the basic expressions;
2 the **grammatical forms** of the basic expressions;
3 the **syntactic structure** of the complex expression.

The general scheme in Figure 1.1 shows that semantic composition is thought of as a so-called **bottom-up** process:[9] it proceeds from the smallest units to the larger ones. The lexical meanings of the smallest units serve as input for the rules of grammatical meaning, whose output is the input for the combination rules. The converse of a bottom-up process is a top-down process. If semantic interpretation were conceived as a top-down process, this would mean that the meanings of words are derived from the meanings of sentences.[10]

As long as a complex expression is formed in accordance with the grammatical rules of the language, it can be interpreted compositionally. For every syntactic rule there is a corresponding composition rule – there *must* be, because otherwise grammar would produce strings of words that would be impossible to interpret. Along with the lexical knowledge, these rules belong to our linguistic knowledge.

That complex expressions receive their meaning by the process of composition, is the central idea underlying semantics. It is called the Principle of Compositionality:[11]

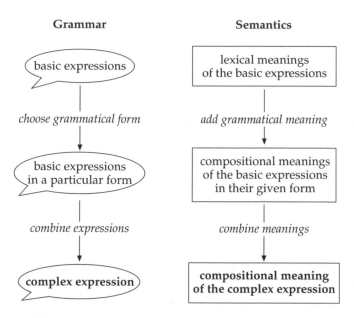

Figure 1.1 The process of composition

Principle of Compositionality
The meaning$_e$ of a complex expression is determined by the lexical meanings of its components, their grammatical meanings and the syntactic structure of the whole.

The principle implies that the meanings$_e$ of complex expressions are *fully* determined by the three sources mentioned, i.e. by the linguistic input alone. Thus, in particular, the process does not draw on extra-linguistic context knowledge. The principle as it stands can therefore be taken as an indirect definition of expression meaning: expression meaning is that level of meaning that can be obtained by the process of composition, i.e. on the basis of lexical meanings, interpretation rules for grammatical forms and semantic combination rules.

It must be noted that the principle does not hold for the level of utterance meaning. Utterance meaning can only be determined by bringing in non-linguistic knowledge about the given CoU. For example, part of the utterance meaning of (2) in a particular CoU might be that the yellow socks belong to John. This, of course, is an aspect of the meaning$_u$ of (2) that cannot be derived from the mere linguistic information provided by the sentence.

The Principle of Compositionality yields a convenient division of semantics into the following subdisciplines:

- **lexical semantics**: the investigation of expression meanings stored in the mental lexicon (*mouse*, *sock*);
- **compositional word semantics**: the investigation of the meanings of words that are formed by the rules of word formation (*mousify*, *mouse food*);
- **semantics of grammatical forms**: the investigation of the meaning contribution of grammatical forms that can be freely chosen, often understood as including the semantic analysis of function words such as articles, prepositions and conjunctions;
- **sentence semantics**: the investigation of the rules that determine how the meanings of the components of a complex expression interact and combine.

Often semantics is subdivided into two subdisciplines only: lexical semantics is then understood as also comprising compositional word semantics, and the semantics of grammatical forms is subsumed under sentence semantics.

A further domain is defined negatively, as it were, by the principle: the part of semantics that is concerned with utterance meaning, i.e. meaning beyond composition:

- **utterance semantics**: the investigation of the mechanisms (e.g. meaning shifts) that determine, on the basis of the compositionally derived expression meaning, the range of possible utterance meanings.

In this volume, we will be concerned mainly with lexical meaning (Chapters 2, 3, 4, 5, 6, 7, 8 and 9) and sentence meaning (Chapters 4, 6 and 10); utterance meaning, i.e. meaning shifts, will be discussed in Chapters 3 and 6. Neither compositional word meaning nor grammatical meaning will be dealt with in depth.

Checklist

levels of meaning
expression meaning
   content words
   function words
   lexical meaning
   sentence meaning
utterance meaning
   context of utterance, CoU
   reference
   truth
   meaning shifts

inferences
   Grice
communicative meaning
   speech act theory
   Searle, Austin
composition
   compositional word meaning
   grammatical meaning
   rules of meaning combination
   bottom-up
   Principle of Compositionality

Further reading

Lyons (1995, Chapter 1) on levels of meaning. Verschueren (1999, Chapter 1) on inferences and speech acts, Chapter 3 on the role of context in interpretation. Levinson (1983, Chapters 3 and 5) for a more comprehensive discussion of Grice's theory and speech act theory. Tallerman (1998, Chapters 2 and 3) on elementary syntax.

Notes

1 Following a common practice of simplification, I will talk about language and language use as though language were exclusively spoken language. Actually terms such as speech and speaker are to be taken as including language use in all possible media: spoken, written, signed, sent in Morse code or whatever.

2 〉 〈 quotes are used for meanings.

3 Alternatively one may assume that English has two personal pronouns *you*, a singular *you* corresponding to French *tu*, German *du* and former English *thou*, etc. and a plural *you* corresponding to French *vous* and German *ihr*. Whether English has two pronouns *you* or one which is neutral to the distinction between singular and plural ('grammatical number') is a difficult question we do not want to go into here. We will assume the latter alternative.

4 Present tense does not always refer to present time. For example, it is often used for reference to future time (cf. *I need your bicycle tomorrow*).

5 Incidentally, this is also the term for combining two words into one, such as *mouse* and *food* into *mouse food*. If necessary, the two cases are distinguished as *semantic* vs *morphological* composition.

6 In some cases, certain forms of words may have a special lexical meaning, such as the plural form of nouns, e.g. *glasses* as opposed to *glass*. Some nouns are only used in the plural (*trousers*), for others the distinction does not seem to matter (*logic, logics*).

7 Whether or not a particular choice, e.g. between singular or plural, is free, may depend on the grammatical construction. Usually the choice of grammatical number is free for nouns, but sometimes it is not, cf. the ungrammaticality of *he saved our life* (vs ... *lives*). Similarly some sentence types exclude certain tenses, although normally the tense of the verb can be freely chosen.

8 The term is somewhat misleading, because grammatical forms that are determined by grammar and therefore lack a meaning, nevertheless have a grammatical *function*, e.g. the indication of whether a pronoun is the subject or the object of a sentence. The term *grammatical meaning* could be misunderstood as referring to the grammatical function of such forms.

9 For better readability, the schema in Figure 1.1 depicts the process upside-down.

10 Actually this appears to be what happens when we encounter unknown words in context. In such situations we are often able to infer the meaning of the

unknown word if we can somehow grasp the meaning$_u$ of the whole utterance. But this does not mean that the process of interpretation in general is top-down. Clearly, unknown word meanings can only be inferred if the rest of the sentence meaning can be derived compositionally, i.e. bottom-up.

[11] The principle is attributed to the German philosopher, logician and mathematician Gottlob Frege (1845–1925), and sometimes called Frege's Principle. Although he obviously applied the principle, there is no passage in his publications that could serve as a quotation.

Descriptive, social and expressive meaning

2

This chapter will try to convey a more precise idea about expression meaning. In the first part about 'descriptive' meaning, we will consider the relationship between meaning, reference and truth. The second part is concerned with non-descriptive meaning, i.e. parts of the meaning that are relevant on the level of social interaction or for the expression of subjective attitudes and evaluations.

2.1 Meanings are concepts

In order to understand what kind of entities meanings$_e$ are, the best thing we can do is consider the role that meanings play in actual communication. We will consider another concrete example and assume a CoU that takes up scenario 1 from 1.1.2: Mary, just back from her trip, finds her daughter Sheila quite upset. Sheila has spent the time with Mary's dog Ken, and the two do not like each other. When asked what happened, Sheila answers:

(1)   *The dog has ruined my blue skirt.*

Let us suppose that what Sheila says is true and that Mary believes what Sheila says. Mary will then know something she did not know before: that Ken has ruined Sheila's blue skirt. She knows this because Sheila said (1) and because this sentence has the meaning it has. Let us take a closer look at how the transfer of information by such a sentence works, first for a single word and then for the whole sentence.

2.1.1 The meaning of a word

We assume that Sheila is referring to Ken. What enables Mary to recognize that? Sheila used the words *the dog*: the definite article *the* and the noun *dog*.

Both play an important role. The main information is conveyed by the noun. It specifies the referent as an entity of a certain kind, namely a dog. What entitles us to say so? It is the fact that the word *dog* means what it means. When you were asked to explain what the word *dog* means, you would probably say that dogs are a certain kind of medium-sized animals with four legs and a tail, that they are often kept as pets, that they bark, that they may bite, etc. In other words, you will most likely give a description of dogs. This is an adequate reaction: giving a description of dogs may well count as an explanation of the meaning of *dog*. At least roughly, the meaning of such words may safely be regarded as a description of the kind of thing the word can be used for.

Now, a very important point to realize is this: the word does not carry this description with it. This can be seen from the trivial fact that words which we do not know do not have any meaning to us. What a word in fact carries with it when it is spoken and heard is its sound *form* (or its spelling, if it is written). When Sheila says the word *dog*, she produces a certain sound pattern. And when Mary hears the word, she recognizes this pattern. The recognition, in turn, is only possible if the sound pattern is stored in Mary's mind as part of her linguistic knowledge.

The meaning of the word *dog*, i.e. the description of dogs, must also be something residing in Mary's mind. It must be information directly linked to the sound pattern of the word. The meaning is therefore a *mental* description. For mental descriptions in general, the term **concept** will be used. A concept for a kind, or **category**,[1] of entities is information in the mind that allows us to discriminate entities of that kind from entities of other kinds. A concept should not be equated with a visual image. Many categories we have words for, like *mistake, thought, noise, structure, mood* are not categories of visible things. But even for categories of visible things such as dogs, the mental description is by no means exhausted by a specification of their visual appearance. The dog concept, for example, also specifies the behaviour of dogs and how dogs may matter for us (as pets, watch dogs, guide-dogs, dangerous animals that may attack us, etc.).

We can now give a partial answer to the question of how Mary is able to recognize that Sheila is referring to Ken: Sheila acoustically produces the word *dog*; Mary recognizes the sound pattern; in her mind the pattern is linked to the meaning of the word *dog*, the concept 〉dog〈[2]; the concept is a mental description of a potential referent. So due to the use of the word *dog*, Mary knows what *kind* of entity Sheila is referring to.

That Mary has the concept 〉dog〈 linked to the sound pattern of *dog* in her mind is, of course, only part of the story. Sheila must have the same concept in her mind linked to the same sound pattern. More generally, a word can only be considered established if its form and meaning are linked in the minds of a great number of language users.

Still, we have not explained how Mary is led to assume that Sheila refers to this particular dog. The crucial clue to an explanation is the definite article *the*. Had Sheila used the indefinite article *a* instead, Mary would not have concluded that Sheila was referring to Ken. What is the meaning of the definite article? It does not provide a direct cue to Ken, but it signals that the description supplied by the following noun applies to an entity in the given CoU which the addressees are supposed to be able to sort out. Therefore the article will cause Mary to ask herself which entity in the given CoU fulfils these conditions.

This is how far the meanings$_e$ of the words *the dog* take us in reconstructing the communication between Sheila and Mary with respect to the reference to this dog Ken. For the conclusion that it is Ken which Sheila is referring to, Mary needs extra-linguistic context information. The fact that Sheila is using the definite article restricts the choice of candidate dogs to those Mary and Sheila both know. A further restriction is provided by what Sheila says about the dog: that it has ruined her blue skirt. In the given CoU this may then suffice to exclude all dogs but Ken.

2.1.2 The meaning of a sentence

In her mind, Mary has the forms and meanings of all words in (1) at her disposal. She also knows the grammatical meanings of the singular form, of the positive form of the adjective and of the indicative present perfect form of the verb (recall 1.2.1). Applying all this and her knowledge of grammar to the linguistic input, she will be able to compose the meaning$_e$ of the whole sentence (1.2). The result is one complex concept which combines all the elements of the sentence. Let us call this a concept for a kind of **situation**. The main component of the situation concept is the concept ⟩ruin⟨ contributed by the verb. It is of central importance because it connects all other elements.[3] As a concept for an event of the kind 'x ruins y' it involves three elements: the event itself, the ruiner x and the ruined object y. In the total situation concept, the event is described as one of ruining, the ruiner is described as a dog that is identifiable in the given CoU, the ruined object is described as a skirt, a blue one, linked to the speaker (recall 1.1.1 for the meaning of possessive pronouns like *my* and *your*); the present perfect tense contributes the specification that the situation at the time of utterance results from a previous event of the kind indicated. Thus the meaning of the sentence as a whole is a concept for a specific kind of situation. It can roughly be described as shown in the definition below. The description does not contain an explanation of the word meanings, but it makes explicit the contribution of the functional elements (1.1.1).

> ⟩the situation at the time of utterance results from a previous event in which a dog that can be uniquely determined in the CoU ruined a blue skirt which can be determined by its being linked to the speaker.⟨

What was said about the meanings of words and sentences can be summed up as follows:

- The **meaning of a word**, more precisely a content word (noun, verb, adjective), is a concept that provides a mental description of a certain kind of entity.
- The **meaning of a sentence** is a concept that provides a mental description of a certain kind of situation.

2.2 Descriptive meaning

In the previous section it was established that meanings$_e$ are concepts. Actually the discussion here and in Chapter 1 was confined to only a certain part of meaning, namely, that part which bears on reference and truth. It is called **descriptive meaning** or *propositional meaning*. We will elaborate on descriptive meaning now, making more explicit how it is related to reference and truth. Non-descriptive meaning will be turned to in the second half of the chapter.

2.2.1 Descriptive meaning and reference

Reference and the descriptive meaning of words

When dealing with reference, the first thing to be observed is that, strictly speaking, it is usually not simply words that have referents. If the sentence in (1) is true, it involves reference to five things: the dog (an object, in the widest sense), the speaker's blue skirt (another object), the speaker herself, the ruining of the skirt (an event) and the time of utterance (a time). Table 2.1 shows to which elements of the sentence the five referents belong. The subject NP and the object NP each have a referent, the possessive pronoun within the object NP has a referent of its own. The finite verb contributes reference to a certain kind of event and, due to its tense, to a certain time. The adjective *blue* has no referent of its own, but it contributes to the description of the referent of the NP *my blue skirt*. The example shows that the referring elements of the sentence can be phrases (e.g. NPs), words (the verb) or grammatical forms (tense).

Type	Referent	Referring element
object	the dog	NP *the dog*
object	the speaker's blue skirt	NP *my blue skirt*
object	the speaker	poss. pronoun *my*
event	ruining	verb *ruin*
time	utterance time	tense *has ___ed*

Table 2.1 Five referents of sentence (1)

All this notwithstanding, it makes sense to talk of the **potential referents** of content words. Since the referent of an NP is essentially described by the noun, we may loosely speak of it as the 'referent of the noun'. Analogously, we can talk of the 'referent of a verb'. Adjectives never have a referent of their own, but they always describe the referent of some NP (see 6.4 for details). Thus, still more loosely speaking, we may extend the notion of referent to adjectives, keeping in mind that their 'referents' are borrowed, as it were. If the notion of potential referent is extended to all content words, descriptive meaning can be defined in a way that relates it directly to reference:

DEFINITION
The **descriptive meaning of a content word** is a concept for its potential referents.

When a sentence is used in a particular CoU, the addressees will try to fix concrete referents that match the descriptions. However, and this is a very important point, it may be impossible to fix referents, if the sentence is not true. Consider the sentence in (2):

(2)   *There is a letter for you.*

Let us assume that Sheila says so to her mother, but that she is not telling the truth: there is no letter for Mary. There may be a letter, but not for Mary, or no letter at all. In any event, if the sentence is not true, the NP *a letter for you* lacks a referent. Usually, the finite verb of the sentence has a concrete event referent only if the sentence is true. For example, if (1) is false in some CoU, then the dog has not ruined the speaker's blue skirt and hence the verb *ruin*, in that CoU, fails to have a referent.

The descriptive meaning of sentences: propositions

There is no generally accepted notion for what a sentence as a whole refers to in a given CoU. For lack of a better term it will be called the **situation referred to**. It can be defined as the set of the referents of all referring elements of the sentence and how they are linked. For the sentence in (1), the situation referred to in the given CoU involved the five referents listed in Table 2.1.

The notion of the situation referred to only makes sense if the sentence is true: as we have seen, some elements of the sentence may lack a referent if it is not true. Thus, only in the case where a sentence is true in a particular CoU, does it properly refer to a situation of the kind it describes. Therefore, whenever the term *situation referred to* is used, it will be assumed that the sentence is true.

By analogy with the notion of potential referents we can talk of the *situations potentially referred to*. These are all those situations that fit the mental description provided by the meaning of the sentence, i.e. all the situations for which the sentence is true. The descriptive meaning of a sentence can now be defined as shown in the definition below. In accordance with common terminology, the descriptive meaning of a sentence is called its 'proposition'. Alternatively, the proposition of a sentence will be referred to as the 'situation expressed', or the 'situation described':

DEFINITION
The **descriptive meaning of a sentence**, its **proposition**, is a concept that provides a mental description of the kind of situations it potentially refers to.

As we have seen, it is not only content words that shape the descriptive meaning of the sentence. Functional elements such as pronouns and articles or tense, a grammatical form, contribute to the proposition as well (recall the description of the meaning of (1) given on p. 21). Making use of the definition above, we can give the following general definition:

DEFINITION
The **descriptive meaning of a word or a grammatical form** is its contribution to descriptive sentence meaning.

Expression (type)	Descriptive meaning (*definitions adopted from *The New Oxford Dictionary of English*)	Referent type
skirt (noun)	⟩a woman's outer garment fastened around the waist and hanging down around the legs⟨*	object
eat (verb)	⟩put (food) into the mouth and chew and swallow it⟨*	event
blue (adjective)	⟩of a colour intermediate between green and violet, as of the sky or sea on a sunny day⟨*	object [borrowed]
the [noun] (article)	the referent of the noun is uniquely determined in the given CoU	—
I (pronoun)	the referent is the speaker	object
The dog has ruined my blue skirt. (sentence)	see p. 21	situation

Table 2.2 Descriptive meaning

To sum up, the descriptive meaning of a sentence is a concept for a certain kind of situation. If the sentence is true in a CoU, such a situation actually exists and can be considered the referent of the sentence. The situation referred to contains the referents of all referring elements of the sentence. Table 2.2 gives a survey of different types of potentially referring expressions, their respective descriptive meanings and types of referents.

2.2.2 Denotations and truth conditions

Denotations

The descriptive meaning of a content word is a concept for its potential referents. As such it determines, or mentally describes, a category of entities. The meaning of *dog* is a concept that determines the category DOG[4] of all dogs, the concept ⟩ruin⟨ determines the category RUIN of all events of ruining. The category determined by the meaning of a content word is called its 'denotation'; a word is said to 'denote' this category:

> DEFINITION
> The **denotation** of a content word is the category, or set, of all its potential referents.

The denotation of a word is more than the set of all *existing* entities of that kind. It includes real referents as well as fictitious ones, usual exemplars and unusual ones, maybe even exemplars we cannot imagine because they are yet to be invented.[5]

The relationship between a word, its meaning and its denotation is often depicted in the **semiotic triangle**, a convenient schema which will be used in this volume in a variety of forms. Figure 2.1 gives the semiotic triangle for the descriptive meaning of content words. The arrow that connects the word with its denotation is drawn with a broken line. This is to indicate that a word is not directly linked to its denotation, but only indirectly via its descriptive meaning.

Truth conditions

There is no established term for what would be the denotation of a sentence. By analogy with the denotation of a content word it would be the

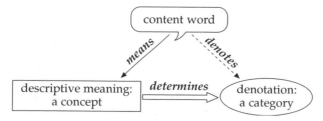

Figure 2.1 The semiotic triangle for content words

set, or category, of all situations to which the sentence can potentially refer, i.e. the category of all situations in which the sentence is true. There is, however, another notion that is quite common and directly related to the would-be denotation of a sentence: its so-called truth conditions:

> DEFINITION
> The **truth conditions** of a sentence are the conditions under which it is true.

If we know the truth conditions of a sentence, then we know which situations the sentence can refer to, i.e. the 'denotation' of the sentence. Conversely, if we know which situations a sentence can refer to, we know its truth conditions. Thus the notion of truth conditions can be considered the practical equivalent of the notion of the denotation of a sentence.

By analogy with Figure 2.1, the connection between a sentence, its proposition and its truth conditions can be put as follows: the descriptive meaning of the sentence is its proposition, and the proposition determines the truth conditions of the sentence. The resulting picture is given in Figure 2.2, another variant of the semiotic triangle.

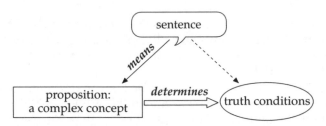

Figure 2.2 The semiotic triangle for sentences

2.2.3 Proposition and sentence type

So far in this discussion of sentence meaning one aspect has been neglected: the grammatical type of the sentence also contributes to its meaning, and this contribution is non-descriptive. Compare, for example, sentence (1) to its interrogative counterpart (3):

(1)   *The dog has ruined my blue skirt.*
(3)   *Has the dog ruined my blue skirt?*

The question describes exactly the same sort of situation. Hence it is considered to have the same proposition as (1). Yet the total meaning of (3) is, of course, different from the meaning of (1): (3) renders a question while (1) renders an assertion. The difference in meaning is due to the grammatical forms of the sentences or, technically speaking, to differences in grammatical **sentence type**. (1) is a so-called declarative sentence. Declarative sentences in English have a certain word order: the finite verb is in the second position of the sentence, usually after the subject. (3) is an interrogative sentence of the yes–no question type: the finite verb is in the initial position and has to be an auxiliary verb.

The semantic contribution of the grammatical sentence type is not part of the proposition. For declarative sentences it consists in presenting the situation expressed as actually pertaining. This sentence type is therefore used for making assertions, communicating information, etc. The interrogative sentence type, by contrast, leaves open whether or not the situation pertains. It is therefore the standard option to be chosen for asking questions.

The meaning contribution of grammatical sentence type is a first example of non-descriptive meaning. We will now consider two more types: social meaning and expressive meaning. The meaning of sentence type belongs to neither of them.

2.3 Meaning and social interaction: social meaning

Talking to others is social interaction, i.e. an activity exerted in co-ordination with others. Any verbal utterance will receive an interpretation as a communicative act (1.1.3) in the current social network, and in this sense it always has a *social function*. Language as such can be said to serve first and foremost social functions. (This does not contradict the view that language is primarily a means of communication: communication, in particular the communication of information, *is* of course a very important type of social interaction.)

2.3.1 Expressions with social meaning

The term **social meaning** does not refer to this general aspect of verbal interaction, and is thereby not to be confused with the communicative meaning of a verbal act. Rather, social meaning is on a par with descriptive meaning: it is part of the lexical meaning of certain words, phrases or grammatical forms. If an expression has social meaning, it has so independently of the particular CoU. Like descriptive meaning, social meaning is an invariable part of the expression meaning. Most expressions and grammatical forms do not have social meaning, but some do. Let us consider an example. Sheila is on the train in Germany and is addressed by the ticket inspector:

(4) a. *Ihre Fahrkarte, bitte! – Danke.*   (German)
   b. *Deine Fahrkarte, bitte! – Danke.*   (German)
   c. 'Your ticket, please! – Thank you.'

(4a) would be appropriate if Sheila is an adult and no acquaintance of the inspector. The third person plural form of the possessive pronoun, *Ihre*, literally 'Their' (the third person plural pronouns in this 'polite' use are written with a capital letter: *Sie* for *you*, *Ihr* for *your*), is required for the formal, or 'polite', style of speech used for addressing adults. (4b) contains the simple second person singular possessive pronoun *dein* and would be the proper, informal, form of address if Sheila were a child, a relative, or a close acquaintance of the ticket inspector. Otherwise, using (4b) would be considered rude. If the inspector addressed Sheila in English, (4c) would be adequate in all cases. But when speaking German, the inspector is forced to choose between the formal and the informal way of address (or to avoid the use of pronouns altogether). By the choice of the pronoun the speaker indicates his social relationship to the addressee(s).

The formal German pronoun *Sie*, when used as a term of address, has the same descriptive meaning as English *you*: it indicates reference to the addressee(s). But, in addition, it has a non-descriptive meaning which English *you* lacks. Correspondingly, the informal variants *du* (singular) and *ihr* (plural) have the same descriptive meaning as *Sie* (if one disregards the differentiation in number) but differ in social meaning. The distinction between the two kinds of relationship relevant for choosing either *Sie* or *du* in German is also relevant in other respects: it coincides with the use of surnames with title vs first names as vocative terms of address. For example the unmarked way of address and reference to the addressee would be (5a) or (5b), while the mixed variants in (5c) and (5d) are marked under normal circumstances:

(5) a. *Ist das Ihr Fahrrad, Herr Schmidt?*   formal
   b. *Ist das dein Fahrrad, Helmut?*   informal
   c. ?? *Ist das Ihr Fahrrad, Helmut?*   mixed
   d. ?? *Ist das dein Fahrrad, Herr Schmidt?*   mixed
     'Is that your bicycle Mr Schmidt/Helmut?'

(4a) and (4b) above contain two further expressions with social meaning: *bitte* ⟩please⟨ and *danke* ⟩thank you⟨. Unlike the German terms of address, these two expressions have exclusively social meaning, they are the first expressions we encounter which lack descriptive meaning altogether. (English *thank you*, containing *you*, might be considered as referring to the addressee(s). To this extent it also has descriptive meaning.) The sentences in (4) are elliptical: they lack anything but the direct object and could be spelt out as *geben Sie mir Ihre Fahrkarte, bitte* (lit. ⟩give you me your ticket, please⟨). At least they will be interpreted in this sense and can thus be considered defective imperative sentences with the proposition ⟩addressee gives speaker addressee's ticket⟨. The addition of *bitte* does not change the proposition. Rather, it marks the request as modestly polite. *Bitte*, in this use, is a mere formality marker, indicating, similar to the forms of address, a certain kind of social relationship between speaker and addressee(s).

Danke ›thank you‹ has no descriptive meaning either. It just serves as a slightly formal response that counts as an acknowledgement of a favour or service. Given different social rules, the ticket inspector might have bowed instead of saying anything. Since the utterance lacks a proposition, the question of truth does not arise. If someone says 'Danke' or 'Thank you', he automatically has thanked, regardless of whether or not he is actually thankful. He is observing the appropriate social rule simply by producing those conventionally prescribed words.

All languages have set phrases with a clear-cut social meaning, and no other: phrases of greeting (*Hi*) or saying goodbye, phrases of apologizing (*sorry*), acknowledging (*thank you*) or answering the phone. For each such phrase in each language, there is a social rule that defines the circumstances under which it is properly used and what it means. This is, in general, the defining criterion of expressions with social meaning: an expression or grammatical form has social meaning if and only if its use is governed by the social rules of conduct or, more generally, rules for handling social interactions. By contrast, the use of expressions with descriptive meaning is governed by rules of factual adequacy.

Expression (type)	Social meaning	Descriptive meaning
German *du* (pronoun of address)	informal relationship	the person addressed
German *Sie* (pronoun of address)	formal relationship	the person or persons addressed
English *you* (pronoun of address)	—	the person or persons addressed
Sheila (proper name as term of address)	informal relationship	the person called Sheila
Mr Murple (proper name as term of address)	formal relationship	the person called Mr Murple
please (adverb)	formal demand	—
Hi! (complete utterance)	informal greeting	—

Table 2.3 Social meaning

In 1.1, three levels of meaning were introduced. Expressions like *please* or *goodbye*, with exclusively social meaning, can be regarded as expressions with a lexically fixed communicative meaning (1.1.3). They constitute ready-made speech act devices. The social rules that govern their use are treated in Austin's speech act theory under the label 'felicity conditions' (i.e. conditions necessary for the speech act to actually come about; see Further Reading in Chapter 1 for references).

2.3.2 Social meaning in Japanese

In European and European-influenced societies, social differentiation of speech is only moderately reflected in the language system. Apart from set phrases, social meaning is essentially restricted to terms for reference to the addressee. Furthermore, the system of differentiation is usually restricted to two levels of formality, an informal and a more formal way of speaking. In other cultures, however, say those of Japan, Korea or non-socialist China, the differentiation of expressions pervades language to a much greater extent. In English or German, you do not find any formality markers in sentences which do not refer to the addressee. There would be no simple way of reformulating an utterance like *The dog ate the yellow socks* to express your relationship with the addressee along the lines relevant for the use of surname vs first name or the use of *Sie* vs *du* in German. (The only possibility would be to add a vocative to the sentence: *The dog ate the yellow socks, John/Mr Murple*). In Japanese, however, one would have to choose from among two or more levels of formality in any sentence whatsoever, because formality is obligatorily marked on the finite verb. In Japanese, the sentence *the dog ate the yellow socks* would correspond to either (6a) or (6b):

(6) a. | *inu* | *wa* | *kiiroi* | *sokkusu* | *o* | *tabe-ta*. |
	dog	TOP	yellow	socks	ACC	eat PT[6]
b.	*inu*	*wa*	*kiiroi*	*sokkusu*	*o*	*tabe-**mashi**-ta*.
	dog	TOP	yellow	socks	ACC	eat FORM PT

The plain past tense form of the verb in (6a) represents the informal way of talking which is only appropriate in rather intimate relationships like those within a family, between lovers or good friends. Normal formal talking, which is the standard between people of the same status, is expressed by inserting a formality marker, here in the form *-mashi-*, between the stem of the verb and its tense ending (6b). The resulting form is called the *masu-*form. The marker *-mashi-* has no descriptive meaning.

In addition to marking the level of formality on the finite verb, Japanese has rich differentiation among pronouns, or pronoun-like expressions, for the addressee as well as for the speaker. Instead of the single first person singular pronoun *I* in English, a Japanese speaker has to choose from among plain omission (usual and neutral), *boku* or *ore* (informal, men only), *watashi* (formal, standard), *watakushi* (very formal) and other, more special expressions. Furthermore, there are different nouns and verbs for things belonging to, or actions done by, oneself or others. Let us consider another example in order to get an idea of how the differentiation of formality works:

(7) a. *Uchi   ni i-ru.*
   b. *Uchi   ni i-mas-u.*
   c. *Uchi   ni ori-mas-u.*
      home IN be (present tense)

The sentences in (7) are typical colloquial Japanese sentences, lacking a subject term. The word *uchi* for someone's home is an informal term. The verb *iru* ⟩to be [temporarily]⟨ is used in its plain, informal form in (7a). (7b) is more formal, replacing plain *iru* with its *masu*-form *imasu*. In addition to the grammatical form, the choice of the verb itself matters for social meaning. The verb *iru* as such has no social meaning attached to it. In (7c), however, it is replaced by the verb *oru* in its *masu*-form *orimasu*. *Oru* also means ⟩to be/come/go⟨, but is ⟩humble⟨: by using it, its subject is socially lowered. There is also a variant of ⟩to be/come/go⟨ that raises its subject referent in social status, the verb *irassharu* with its *masu*-form *irasshaimasu*:

(7) d. *Otaku ni irasshai-mas-u.*

If, for the sake of simplicity, the meanings ⟩to go/to come⟨ of *oru* and *irassharu* are disregarded, the four sentences in (7) all have the same descriptive meaning: ⟩[someone not specified] is at home⟨. The term *uchi* for someone's home, is informal, while *otaku* is a formal term that marks the person whose home it is as superior. It is now interesting to see how the differences in social meaning restrict the use and interpretations of the sentences. The employment of terms with social meaning in Japanese is governed by two principles: (i) the addressee is never inferior, and (ii) the speaker is never superior. Given these principles, (7d), although it contains no subject, can only be used in the sense ⟩*you* are at home⟨ and (7c) always amounts to ⟩*I* am at home⟨. (7a) and (7b), however, can mean ⟩I/you/he/she/it/we/they are ... at home⟨ since the verb is neutral with respect to the social status of the subject.

2.4 Meaning and subjectivity: expressive meaning

Anything we say will also be taken as the expression of a personal emotion, opinion or attitude. When you imagine Sheila saying *The dog has ruined my blue skirt*, you will probably have assumed a manner of speaking that displays anger, indignation or frustration. But the sentence *can* also be spoken in a neutral manner or in a way that exhibits different emotions, for example desperation or concern, but also delight, amusement or relief. It could be pronounced in a mean or a kind manner. Or hastily, or particularly slowly. All these ways of shaping an utterance would serve the expression of Sheila's feelings and/or her attitudes towards the dog, or Mary, or the entire situation. But even if she chose a neutral way of speaking, Sheila would inevitably display certain traits of her personality, by choosing the term *ruin* for what the dog did to her skirt, by not calling the dog by its name, by reporting damage of her property to the dog owner, etc. In this sense, every utterance serves, consciously or not, the expression of personal feelings, evaluations and attitudes.

2.4.1 Expressive meaning

Again, this general aspect of language use, its *expressive function*, is not what is meant with the notion of **expressive meaning**. On a par with descriptive and social meaning, expressive meaning is part of the lexical meaning of certain expressions,[7] a semantic quality of words and phrases independent of the CoU and of the way they are being spoken. Let us call expressions with expressive meaning simply **expressives**. Again, there are two kinds of expressives, those with exclusively expressive meaning and others with both descriptive and expressive meaning. (For expressions with both social and expressive meaning, see 2.4.2.) We will first turn to the former.

The most typical instances of expressives with exclusively expressive meaning are words and phrases used for directly expressing an emotion, feeling or sensation, such as *ouch, wow, oh*. Such **interjections** are language-specific. Languages may differ in how many such expressions they have, and an expressive may have different meanings in different languages. Here are some interjections from Hungarian: *fuj* (disgust), *au* (sudden pain), *jaj* (sudden pain or fright), *jajaj* (sadness or concern), *hüha* (admiration, warning, fright), *hú* (admiration), *ejha* (astonishment). Other examples of expressives are exclamations of various sorts, such as English *Gosh!*, *Goddammit!*, *Jesus!*, *Oh my goodness!*, and so on.

At least some feelings, sensations, attitudes and evaluations can thus be expressed in two ways: subjectively and directly by means of expressives, and objectively by forming sentences with the respective descriptive meaning. The difference between, say, 'Ouch!' and 'That hurts!' is this: 'That hurts!' is a sentence with a regular descriptive meaning, consisting in the proposition that 'that hurts'; 'Ouch!' expresses sudden pain, as would a certain grimace. You can react to someone saying 'That hurts!' with 'Really?', 'That's too bad' or 'I don't believe that', which are replies relating to the proposition of the sentence. You cannot reply to 'Ouch!' in the same way because there is no proposition.

The rules governing the use of expressives are simple. Since all expressives serve to express personal feelings, attitudes or sensations, which are perceptible only to the holder, their correct use is just a matter of personal judgement. For instance, saying *ugh!* is generally taken as an expression of disgust. In order to decide whether the use of this expression is correct in a given CoU, the speaker only has to make up her mind whether or not she wants the addressee(s) to believe that she finds something disgusting.

Interjections and exclamations can be used as complete utterances. Other expressives such as *hopefully, (un)fortunately* or *thank God* can be inserted into a sentence in order to add a personal attitude to the situation expressed. These additions do not contribute to the proposition, as the following examples may illustrate:

(8) a. *Hopefully Bob will arrive tonight. – Really?*
    b. *I hope Bob will arrive tonight. – Really?*

The questioning reply 'Really?' is always directed at a proposition asserted before. In (8a), the remark can only be related to the proposition that Bob will arrive that night, not to the speaker's attitude expressed by *hopefully*. In (8b), however, the same attitude is *described* by the descriptive formulation *I hope . . .* and is hence part of the proposition of the sentence. Therefore the reply 'Really?' can be used to question the speaker's claim that she *hopes* that Bob will arrive, i.e. her attitude described. Alternatively, the reply 'Really?' can be related to the embedded proposition that Bob will arrive that night, which is identical to the proposition of the sentence in (8a).

More drastic cases of expressives are **swear words** such as those occurring in the following passages from the film *Pulp Fiction*:[8]

(9) J: But me, my eyes are wide *fuckin'* open.
     V: What *the fuck* does that mean?
     J: That's it for me. From here on in, you can consider *my ass* retired.

(10) Any of you *fuckin' pricks* move and I'll execute every *motherfuckin'* last one of you.

The adverbial insert *the fuck* in (9) serves the expression of an emotion that is probably neither necessarily positive (like joy) nor negative (like indignation) but just strong: it adds an emotional charge to the whole utterance. Other expressives, like *bloody* or the highly productive *fucking* add the same kind of emphasis to single components of the proposition. None of these expressives make additions to the propositional content. However, in our examples two other expressions with expressive meaning do: *my ass* in (9) is an emotionally charged term for reference to the speaker. It must have descriptive meaning because it is an NP in object position. Its descriptive meaning is just ⟩I⟨. Similarly, the expression *you fuckin' pricks* in (10) has the same descriptive meaning as the plain pronoun *you*, plus the specific expressive content of the rest of the phrase. The expression is not just emotionally charged but clearly offensive when used with reference to others.

In English and presumably most other languages, there exist many emotionally charged terms for persons, such as *idiot, bastard, motherfucker* or *ass-hole* for the offensive part, or *darling, baby, honey* as terms of affection. They all have the same unspecific descriptive meaning: ⟩person⟨. The phenomenon extends to expressions for men, women, children, body parts or other things of central importance in everyday life, such as certain animals, vehicles, housing, food, clothes, as well as to the most common activities: walking, talking, working, eating, drinking, sleeping or sexual activities. Most expressive terms add a negative attitude to the descriptive meaning, others are just emotional. Positive expressive meanings are rare. Many of these expressions have a neutral, purely descriptive, meaning variant besides the expressive one. For example, *paw* in its neutral meaning denotes the feet of certain animals. The expressive variant of the word means ⟩hand⟨ (of a person) for its descriptive meaning part while its expressive meaning part is an unspecific emotional emphasis.

Type	Expression	Expressive meaning	Descriptive meaning
interjection	*ouch*	sudden pain	—
adjective	*stupid*	dislike, contempt	—
adverb	*fortunately*	preference	—
noun	*bastard*	dislike	⟩person⟨
noun	*paw*	emotional emphasis	⟩hand⟨ (of a person)
verb	*cram*	emotional emphasis	⟩eat⟨

Table 2.4 Expressive meaning

2.4.2 Social versus expressive meaning

Many semanticists consider expressive meaning and social meaning not to be clearly separated. The distinction is, however, not as difficult as it might appear. The use of terms and forms with social meaning is governed by rules of social conduct. They define what kind of social circumstances make suitable occasions for using the expression and they define what its use is taken for: a greeting, an apology, a polite or intimate way of referring to other persons, etc. By contrast, the use of terms with expressive meaning is governed by different criteria which concern only the subjective adequacy of expressing one's personal feelings, attitudes, etc. Sure enough, there are rules of conduct constraining the expression of feelings or attitudes in certain social situations, and the use of expressive terms, in particular swear

Meaning part	Function	Criteria for correct use
descriptive meaning	*description of referents and situations*	agreement with facts
social meaning	*indication of social relations and performance of social acts*	social rules of conduct
expressive meaning	*immediate expression of personal sensations, feelings, attitudes or evaluations*	subjective choice

Table 2.5 Parts of meaning

words as terms of address, may have severe social consequences. But while there are clear social rules for the use of, say, the first name vs the surname plus title as terms of address, there is no such rule for addressing someone as an 'idiot' or 'motherfucker'.

Some expressions with predominantly social meaning can be considered a means of the socially ritualized expression of feelings and attitudes, e.g. terms of thanking, wishing well, congratulation, condolence or apologizing. Phrases such as *I'm sorry* or *nice to meet you*, which literally represent descriptions of attitudes, point in this direction. Still, these phrases are primarily social and not expressive. One's real subjective feelings are not, and cannot be, socially relevant. What counts is the actual expression of feelings and a behaviour consistent with having them.

2.5 Connotations

If an expression has descriptive meaning, any mention of it will activate not only the concept for its potential referents but together with it a host of further associations. Among the associations, some are conventional. They are called **connotations** and often considered to be something like a secondary meaning in addition to the primary lexical meaning. Connotations such as 'dirty' for pigs are neither part of the descriptive meaning of *pig* (clean pigs can perfectly be referred to as 'pigs') nor do they constitute expressive meaning (the word *pig* can be used in an expressively neutral way). Often the connotations of a word change, while its meaning remains the same. For example, the connotations of the word *computer* have changed considerably since the 1960s (when computers had the connotations of dangerous super-intelligent machines threatening to escape human control and take over), but the word still means the same. What has changed dramatically in the past 50 years is the actual denotation (recall note 5) of the word, and it is these changes which gave rise to the change of connotations. It is therefore more appropriate to consider connotations to be connected not to the word itself (like meaning) but rather to the actual denotation.

While a distinction is drawn in this volume between a word's meaning and the connotations associated with its actual denotation, it should be mentioned that expressive meaning, e.g. the negative attitude expressed by derogative terms, is called connotation by other authors. Indeed, connotations play a role for the semantic motivation of swear words. For example, the conventional attribute of dirtiness is the basis of the use of *pig* or German *Schwein* as an offensive term for people. But the attitude expressed by the swear word is not part of that meaning (neither descriptive nor expressive) of *pig*, in which it denotes the animal category, nor is the conventional attitude towards pigs identical with the expressive meaning conveyed by the swear word.

Negative connotations, together with social taboos, are responsible for what are called **euphemisms**: roughly, good or indirect terms for bad or tabooed things. Political language is full of euphemisms (just take the vocabulary of warfare), as are the semantic fields of death (*pass away* for *die*) or sexuality (cf. terms like *intercourse, sleep with someone, make love,* etc.) Negative connotations are also at issue in matters of political correctness. Certain 'labels' like *homosexual* are considered discriminatory due to their connotations and sought to be replaced by connotatively neutral terms or terms used by the members of the social group themselves. But as long as the discrimination itself persists in society, the new expressions will soon take on the old connotations. Due to this inflationary process, we are observing a rapid succession of 'politically correct' expressions for certain social groups (such as *disabled* being replaced by *handicapped* being replaced by *challenged*).

Checklist

descriptive meaning
reference
referent
situation referred to
proposition
truth
denotation
truth conditions
sentence type
   declarative sentence
   interrogative sentence
social meaning
social interaction

rules of social conduct
formality
terms of address
phrases with social meaning
expressive meaning
subjectivity
expressives
interjections
swear words
connotations
euphemisms
political correctness
taboos

Exercises

1 Try to define the descriptive meaning of the following words and compare your definition to the definition given in a monolingual English dictionary, e.g. *Oxford English Dictionary*: *fish*, *milk*, *red*, *pregnant*, *follow*.

2 What are the appropriate terms in English for (i) asking somebody to repeat something you did not understand; (ii) accepting an apology; (iii) answering the phone; (iv) New Year's greetings? What kind of meaning do these expressions have?

3 Try to find three interjections other than *ouch* and *ugh* and determine what they express.

4 Try to find expressives with the descriptive meaning ⟩mouth⟨, ⟩car⟨, ⟩child⟨, ⟩walk⟨, ⟩work⟨.

5 Try to find five examples of modern euphemisms.

6 Try to determine the presently politically correct terms for people who are politically incorrectly called 'blind', 'black' or 'fat'.

7 Discuss the role of words in communication.

8 Discuss the connection between descriptive meaning, reference and truth.

9 Most sentences of a natural language like English can be used in different CoUs to communicate different information, although their meaning remains the same. How is that possible?

10 Try to determine word by word the descriptive, social and/or expressive meaning of the expressions in the following dialogue:

A: *Hi, Velma. Are you going to that stupid lecture?*
B: *Well, yes. I'm sorry, Sweety.*

11 Discuss the relationship between expression meaning and connotations for words such as *pig*.

Further reading

Lyons (1977, Chapter 7) on reference, sense (his term for *meaning*) and denotation. Lyons (1995, Chapter 6.6–6.8, 7) on sentence type. Palmer (2001) for a comprehensive account of non-descriptive sentence meaning. Brown and Gilman (1960) for a classical study about pronouns of address. Brown and Levinson (1978) for a general account of social meaning. Suzuki (1978, Chapter 5) for a comparison of forms of address and self-reference in Japanese and English. Lyons (1995, Chapter 2.3), Cruse (1986, Chapter 12.2) for expressive vs descriptive meaning. Andersson and Trudgill (1990) and Hughes (1992) for comprehensive studies of swear words in English.

Notes

1   In Chapter 9 on cognitive semantics the notions *concept* and *category* will be treated in more depth and detail. For the present purposes you may take a category as a set of entities of the same kind.

2   This type of quotation mark will be used for concepts, and for meanings in general: 〉x-y-z〈 is the concept that constitutes the meaning of the expression x-y-z.

3   See Chapter 6 on predication.

4   SMALL CAPITALS are used for categories.

5   Yet the totality of existing exemplars of a category certainly is representative of the category and primarily shapes our concept for this kind of thing. We will occasionally use the term *actual denotation* for the subset of the denotation that is formed by its real existing members. The relationship between denotation and actual denotation will be discussed in 9.6.

6   TOP = topic marker ('as for . . .'), ACC = accusative case marker, FORM = formality marker, PT = past tense ending. In Japanese, particles follow the NP; there are no articles.

7   Be careful not to confuse the terms *expression meaning* and *expressive meaning*. Expression meaning is a general term for the meaning$_e$ of words, phrases, and sentences, since all these are expressions. Expressive meaning is a part of expression meaning, alongside with descriptive meaning and social meaning.

8   Quentin Tarantino, *Pulp Fiction* (London: Faber and Faber, 1994), pp. 140 and 13, respectively.

Meanings and readings

3

In dealing with different aspects of meaning in the previous two chapters, expressions were treated as though they had only one meaning (though possibly composed of different parts). This is, of course, not the case. Many words have more than one meaning and even complete sentences may allow for several readings. The technical term for this phenomenon is **ambiguity**: an expression or an utterance is ambiguous if it can be interpreted in more than one way. The notion of ambiguity can be applied to all levels of meaning: to expression meaning, utterance meaning and communicative meaning. This chapter has two parts. In the first, we will consider lexical ambiguity, i.e. the ambiguity of words at the level of expression meaning. The notion *word* will be replaced by the scientific term *lexeme* (3.1). We will then learn to distinguish between two forms of ambiguity: homonymy and polysemy (3.2). In 3.3 the notion of synonymy is defined. The second part of the chapter is concerned with different readings of sentences and words at the level of utterance meaning that result from meaning shifts (as briefly mentioned in 1.2.2). Several types of shifts, including metaphor and metonymy will be illustrated (3.4) and ascribed to the fact that the interpretation of words and sentences in their context obeys a 'Principle of Consistent Interpretation' (3.5). The chapter concludes with a brief reflection of the role which the meaning shifts mentioned play for polysemy.

3.1 Lexemes

As mentioned in 1.2, it is not only single words that carry lexical meaning, although single words represent the prototypical case. There are also composite expressions with a special meaning one has to learn, e.g. so-called **idioms** like *throw in the towel* meaning ›give up‹ or fixed combinations such as *white lie, broad bean* or *little finger*. An expression, simple or composite, carries a lexical meaning if this meaning cannot be compositionally derived but must be known, i.e. permanently stored in the mind. Expressions with a lexical meaning are called **lexemes** or **lexical items**. Composite lexemes need not be idioms[1] like the ones mentioned. Less spectacular cases are particle verbs such as *give up, fill in, look forward to, put on, figure out*, etc.

Lexemes constitute the **lexicon** of the language, a huge complex structure in the minds of the language users. Lexical meaning is not to be confused with the meaning you may find in a dictionary. Dictionaries describe the meanings of their entries by means of paraphrases. For example, you may find the meaning of *bird* described as 'feathered animal with two wings and two legs, usually able to fly' (*The New Oxford Dictionary of English*). In order to understand the description, you have to know what these other words, *feathered, animal*, etc. mean. If you look these up in turn, you will find yet other words used for their description. Dictionaries are in this sense circular. No matter how carefully they are compiled, they will always contain an irreducible set of words the meaning of which is not, in fact cannot be, explained in this way. By contrast, the lexical meanings we have in our mental lexicons are *not* just paraphrases. They are concepts. Whatever these are (this is a question for cognitive psychology), they are not words.

We have so far been considering expressions and their lexical meanings. But there is more to a lexeme than these two aspects. Above all, a lexeme is a linguistic entity within the language system; it can be built into phrases and sentences according to the grammatical rules of the language. Lexemes differ in their grammatical behaviour and are accordingly assigned to different **grammatical categories** such as verbs, nouns, adjectives, etc. Occasionally the informal term **word class** will be used instead of *grammatical category*. The grammatical category determines the way in which a lexeme can be used within a sentence. For example, a noun can be combined with an adjective, and the whole with an article to form an NP. The NP in turn can be combined as object with a verb to form a VP, and so on (cf. the discussion of (2) in 1.2.2).

In English, many expressions can be used as members of more than one category: for instance, *light* is used as a transitive verb (*light the candle*), a noun (*a bright light*) and an adjective (*a light colour*); *walk* may be a noun (*take a walk*), an intransitive verb (*walk in the park*) or a transitive verb (*walk the dog*); *too* may be a particle (›also‹) or an adverb (*too much*), and so on. Although these expressions may be very similar in meaning, they are considered different lexemes. There are (at least) three different lexemes *light*, three lexemes *walk* and two lexemes *too*. In general the same expression in different grammatical categories constitutes as many different lexemes.

The members of certain grammatical categories in a language may exhibit **inherent grammatical properties** such as gender. In German, Latin and Russian, any noun belongs to one of three gender classes: masculine, feminine or neuter. The gender of a noun is not a grammatical form it may take freely, but an inherent property of the lexeme which determines the form of the article and preceding adjectives (cf. German *der Computer* (masc.), *die Homepage* (fem.), *das Motherboard* (neut.)).

The grammatical category determines the range of **grammatical forms** a lexeme can take. Some categories do not exhibit different forms, e.g. certain adverbs (*here, soon*), particles (*already, too, only*) or prepositions (*on, after, without*), while the forms of expressions belonging to other categories may vary. English nouns have a singular and a plural form (*fridge, fridges*) as well as genitive forms of the singular and the plural (*fridge's, fridges'*). Adjectives have a positive, comparative and superlative form (*light, lighter, lightest* or *precise, more precise, most precise*) and an adverbial form (*lightly, precisely*). Verbs exhibit a fairly wide variety of forms which mark (among other things) grammatical **person** and **number** (*sings* vs *sing*), **tense** (*sings* vs *sang*) and **aspect** (*sings* vs *is singing*). Composite forms such as *have been singing* are also considered forms of the main verb *sing*. For each grammatical category, there are morphological rules for building the forms in the regular cases. But certain lexemes may be exceptional. Irregular verbs have special past tense and past participle forms (*sang, sung* instead of *singed*); some adjectives have special comparative, superlative and/or adverbial forms (*better, best, well* instead of *gooder, goodest, goodly*). A few nouns have non-standard plural forms (*child – children, mouse – mice, foot – feet, leaf – leaves, sheep – sheep*). Exceptional forms are also part of the definition of a lexeme. If a lexeme has different forms, one of them will be used as its **citation form** or **dictionary form**, i.e. the form in which it will be listed in a dictionary or cited when it is spoken about. For example, the non-genitive singular form of a noun is used as its citation form. Usually the citation form will be the morphologically simplest form of the lexeme.

Each grammatical form of a lexeme has a spoken form and an orthographic form (if there is a written standard for the language). Let us use the terms **sound form** and **spelling**, respectively. The sound form of the three grammatical forms *fridges, fridge's* and *fridges'* is the same, while their respective spellings differ. (With irregular nouns, these three forms may not coincide in their sound forms: cf. *children, child's, children's*).

To sum up, a lexeme is a linguistic item defined by the following specifications, which make up what is called the **lexical entry** for this item:

- its sound form and its spelling (for languages with a written standard);
- the grammatical category of the lexeme (noun, intransitive verb, adjective, etc.);
- its inherent grammatical properties (for some languages, e.g. gender);
- the set of grammatical forms it may take, in particular irregular forms;
- its lexical meaning.

These specifications apply to both simple and composite lexemes. Composite lexemes too, such as *throw in the towel* or *red light*, have a fixed sound form, spelling and lexical meaning. They belong to a grammatical category (intransitive verb for *throw in the towel* and noun for *red light*), they have inherent grammatical properties and the usual range of grammatical forms. For example, the grammatical forms of *throw in the towel* are those obtained by inserting the grammatical forms of the verb *throw*: *throws in the towel*, *threw in the towel*, etc.

In principle, each of the specifications of a lexeme is essential: if two linguistic items differ in one of these points, they are considered different lexemes. There are, however, exceptions. Some lexemes have orthographic variants, e.g. *rhyme/rime*, others may have different sound forms, e.g. *laboratory* may be stressed on either the first or the second syllable. The American and the British variants of English differ in spelling and sound form for many lexemes. As long as all the other properties of two orthographic or phonetic variants of a lexeme are identical, in particular their meanings, they will not be considered different lexemes but lexemes with a certain limited degree of variation.

That does not mean that minor differences do not count. They count in any event if they are connected with a difference in meaning. In German, the noun *Bank* has two meanings, ⟩bank⟨ as connected to money, and ⟩bench⟨. In the first case, its plural is *Banken*, in the second *Bänke*. Therefore, these are two lexemes. The word *Zeh* occurs in two gender variants, masculine *der Zeh* and feminine *die Zehe*. The first means ⟩toe⟨ as the part of the foot, the second one has a broader meaning, covering both ⟩toe⟨ and ⟩clove⟨ (of garlic). Since the two meanings are so closely related, one would hesitate to talk of two different lexemes here, but it would be possible. In general, one will assume two different lexemes if there is a difference in meaning accompanied by a difference in some other respect. If a form exhibits *minor* variation in only one point, we will be ready to assume only one lexeme. Since these criteria are all a matter of degree, there will be borderline cases hard to decide.

3.2 Homonymy, polysemy and vagueness

If one consults a more comprehensive monolingual dictionary one will hardly find a word with just one meaning given. If the definition of a lexeme is to reflect our intuitions about words and lexical meanings, this has to be taken into account. If one lexeme strictly had only one meaning, any variation in meaning would result in two different lexemes. In some cases, this is in accordance with our intuition. For example, *bank* as in *The Bank of England* and *bank* as in *the river bank* would be regarded as two different words which just happen to have the same sound form and spelling. But *body* when used to denote the whole physical structure of a human being or an animal, or just the trunk, or a corpse, or a group of people working or acting as a unit, would rather be considered one word with several meanings because we feel that, unlike with *bank*, the meanings of *body* are interrelated. In order to distinguish the two phenomena, the first is called homonymy, the second polysemy. Roughly, homonymy means lexemes with different meanings that happen to have the same sound form or spelling. Ideally, homonyms agree in all points that make up a lexeme except in meaning. In contrast, polysemy is a matter of one lexeme having several interrelated meanings, i.e. an instance of what was meant by 'minor variation' of lexical meaning. Hinging on the criterion as to whether or not different meanings are interrelated, the distinction between homonymy and polysemy is vague. It is best taken as characterizing two extremes on a scale. Both phenomena constitute **lexical ambiguity**: the same lexical *form* has different lexical *meanings$_e$*.

3.2.1 Homonymy

The adjective *light* can be used with two meanings. Let us talk of *light*$_{A1}$ if the adjective is taken as the opposite of *dark*, and of *light*$_{A2}$ if it is the opposite of *heavy* or *difficult*. However, *light*$_{A1}$ and *light*$_{A2}$ have not always had the same form; *light*$_{A1}$ derives from a historical source which in German developed into the present-day adjective *licht* (meaning, in one of its meaning variants, approximately the same as *light*$_{A1}$). Words with the same historical origin are called **cognates**. *Light*$_{A2}$ is a cognate of a different German word, the adjective *leicht* (⟩light, easy⟨). Due to their different origins, *light*$_{A1}$ and *light*$_{A2}$ are considered two different lexemes by most linguists. In general, different meanings are assigned to different lexemes if they have different historical sources. The idea is that, as long as their meanings remain distinct, different words do not develop into one, even if their sound forms and/or spellings happen to coincide for independent reasons.[7] In addition to *light*$_{A1}$ and *light*$_{A2}$ there is a noun *light*$_N$ which is related to *light*$_{A1}$ and means the kind of visible radiation as well as certain sorts of objects that emit light. A verb *light*$_V$ is also related to *light*$_N$ and *light*$_{A1}$.

The two adjectives *light*$_{A1}$ and *light*$_{A2}$ are an instance of what is called **total homonymy**: two lexemes that share all distinctive properties (grammatical category and grammatical properties, the set of grammatical forms, sound form and spelling) yet have unrelated different meanings. One would talk of **partial homonymy** if two lexemes with different unrelated meanings coincide in some but not all of their grammatical forms, e.g. the verbs *lie*$_1$ (*lay, lain*) and *lie*$_2$ (*lied, lied*). Partial homonyms can give rise to ambiguity in some contexts (*don't lie in bed!*) but can be distinguished in others (*he lay/lied in bed*).

Finally, homonymy can be related either to the sound forms of the lexemes or to their spellings: homonymy with respect to the written form is **homography**; if two lexemes with unrelated meanings have the same sound form, they constitute a case of **homophony**. The nouns *bow*$_1$ (rhyming with *low*; cf. *bow and arrow*; German cognate *Bogen*), *bow*$_2$ (rhyming with *how*; ⟩front of a ship⟨, German cognate *Bug*), *bow*₃ (like *how*; ⟩bending⟨; German cognate Ver-*beug*-ung) are all homographs, but only *bow*₂ and *bow*₃ are also homophones. Examples for words that are total homophones but not homographs would be the noun pairs *tail/tale*, *story/storey* or *cue/queue*. Partial homophones are numerous: *threw/through*, *write/right*, *there/their*, *whole/hole*, *to/two/too* and so on.

3.2.2 Polysemy

While homonymy is a rare and accidental phenomenon, polysemy is abundant. It is rather the rule than the exception. A lexeme constitutes a case of **polysemy** if it has two or more interrelated meanings, or better: **meaning variants**. Each of these meaning variants has to be learnt separately in order to be understood. The phenomenon of polysemy is independent of homonymy: of two homonyms, each can be polysemous (cf. *light*$_{A1}$ and *light*$_{A2}$). It results from a natural economic tendency of language. Rather than inventing new expressions for new objects, activities, experiences, etc. to be denoted, language communities usually opt for applying existing terms to new objects, terms hitherto used for similar things. Scientific terminology is one source contributing to polysemy on a greater scale. Some scientific terms are newly coined, but most of them will be derived from ordinary language use. Among the terms introduced here, *lexeme, homonymy, polysemy* are original scientific terms, while others, such as *meaning, reference* or *composition*, are ordinary expressions for which an additional technical meaning variant was introduced.

As an example let us consider the noun *light*: it means a certain sort of visible radiation, but also electric lamps, traffic lights or illuminated areas (cf. *light and shadow*). Clearly, these meanings are interrelated. Likewise, the different readings of *light*$_{A2}$ which correspond to the opposites *heavy* and *difficult*, are somehow interrelated although the relation is harder to define. Note that *heavy* itself, and with it its opposite *light*, is again polysemous (cf. *a heavy stone, heavy rain, a heavy meal*).

In principle, polysemy is a matter of single lexemes in single languages. To see the point, consider the colour adjectives in English. Many of them are polysemous, with meaning variants not primarily relating to colour properties. For instance, *green* may mean ⟩unripe⟨. This is motivated by the fact that the green colour of many fruits indicates that they are not yet ripe (the underlying process is called metonymy: green colour *stands for* something else, the degree of ripeness; see 3.4.4). From this, in turn, derives the meaning variant ⟩immature⟨ due to a metaphor that establishes a parallel between the development of personality and the process of ripening of fruits. This meaning variation is an accidental matter of English *green*. Due to the same motivations, it might, but need not, occur in other languages provided they have a word for the colour green. But there is no parallel for exactly this kind of variation in the case of the other colour words.

Although the colour of very many fruits is red when they are ripe, *red* cannot mean ⟩ripe⟨ or ⟩mature⟨. Likewise in German, *blau* (⟩blue⟨) also means ⟩drunken⟨, but English *blue* does not, nor does any other colour adjective in German or English mean ⟩sober⟨. Sometimes, words given as translation equivalents in different languages may have parallel meaning variants, but usually their variation will not match.

That polysemy is a matter of single lexemes does not mean that it is not governed by general principles. As we will see later, the relations between the interrelated meaning variants of polysemous lexemes exhibit clear patterns. The *kinds* of relations are, to a certain extent, predictable. But whether or not a certain lexeme in a certain language at a certain time will have a certain range of meanings is *not* predictable. Polysemy plays a major role in the historical development of word meanings because lexemes continually shift their meanings and develop new meaning variants.

3.2.3 Vagueness

Polysemy is not to be confused with flexibility of use. For very many lexemes, their proper application to a given case is a matter of degree. For example, whether or not we will refer to a child as a 'baby', depends on criteria such as the age of the child and its developmental stage. Both criteria are gradual. What one person considers a baby need not be considered so by another person. As a consequence, the denotation (2.2.2) of the word *baby* has flexible boundaries. This does not mean that the word *baby* has infinitely many meanings that differ in how the borderline is fixed between babies and ex-babies, as it were. Rather, the concept ⟩baby⟨ is in itself **vague**: it allows for adaptation to the given CoU. Vagueness can be observed with all concepts that depend on properties varying on a continuous scale. Colour terms like *red* have a vague meaning, because we conceive the range of colours as a continuum with fuzzy transitions. Whether something is 'big' or not, or 'good' or not is a matter of degree. In general, all gradable adjectives (i.e. adjectives with a comparative and superlative form) are vague.

Widespread vagueness in the lexicon should be considered another economic trait of language. For example, with the pair *tall/short*, language provides us with a rough distinction on the scale of body height. This is much more efficient for everyday communicative purposes than expressions with a more precise meaning, say, ⟩between 6 and 7 feet tall⟨. The issue of vagueness and the important role it plays will be taken up again in 9.5.

Vagueness may occur in combination with polysemy. For example, the meaning variants of $light_{A2}$ are a matter of different underlying scales (of weight, difficulty, etc.). These scales can be distinguished quite clearly. But for each scale, the meaning of *light* describes just a low degree on this scale, whence each meaning variant in itself is vague.

3.3 Synonymy

With the given background, the notion of **synonymy** can now be defined: two lexemes are synonymous if they have the same meaning. Synonymy in the strict sense, also called *total synonymy*, includes all meaning variants for two polysemous lexemes and it includes all meaning parts, i.e. descriptive, social and expressive meaning. While this condition is almost never fulfilled, there are many cases of *partial synonymy*. Two lexemes may have one meaning variant in common. For example, *spectacles* and *glasses* may both denote the same sort of objects that people wear on their noses to look through, but *glasses* may also just be the plural of *glass* in one of its other meanings. Similarly, *The United States* and *America* are used synonymously, but the latter may also be used for the whole continent consisting of North, Central and South America. Words with the same descriptive meaning but different social or expressive meanings (2.3, 2.4) may also be regarded partial synonyms.

More interesting, and more challenging than the question of synonymy, is the problem of semantic equivalence between expressions from different languages. This will be addressed in Chapter 8.

3.4 Sentence readings and meaning shifts

As stated in 1.2, the meaning of a sentence is derived in the process of composition and is thereby determined by its lexical components and its syntactic structure. Both can give rise to ambiguity of the sentence. If a sentence contains an ambiguous lexeme, the process of composition will yield as many meanings of the sentence as the ambiguous item has. If the sentence contains more than one ambiguous lexical item, the meanings will multiply. As we will see below, not all these meanings will reach the level of utterance meaning. But strictly speaking, all these are possible meanings$_e$.

3.4.1 Syntactic ambiguity

Independently of lexical ambiguities, the syntactic structure of a sentence may be ambiguous. Consider the following examples:

(1) a. *She watched the man with the binoculars.*
   b. *Flying planes can be dangerous.* (Chomsky)
   c. *John and Mary are married.*

In (1a) the PP *with the binoculars* can be related to the verb *watched* (meaning roughly the same as ⟩she watched the man *through* the binoculars⟨), or it can be taken as an attribute of the NP *the man* (⟩the man who had the binoculars⟨). In (1b), the phrase *flying planes* can be read as ⟩flying in planes⟨

and as ⟩planes that are flying⟨. (1c) can mean that John and Mary are married to each other or that they are both married, possibly to other people. Such sentences are syntactically ambiguous. Syntactic ambiguity usually results in semantic ambiguity, i.e. in different readings.

3.4.2 Interpretation in context

The process of composition yields one or more meanings$_e$ of the sentence. When it comes to interpreting words and sentences in their context, i.e. when one proceeds from the level of expression meaning to the level of utterance meaning (1.1), the meanings$_e$ of words and sentences may be modified. A sentence actually uttered in a CoU must fulfil certain requirements in order to qualify as a reasonable message. First, as a minimal requirement, it must not be self-contradictory, i.e. false in all possible CoUs, because in this case, it cannot be applied to any concrete situation whatsoever.[3] Second, it must in some way be relevant in the given CoU. (Both conditions can be captured in what will be called the Principle of Consistent Interpretation in 3.5.) Utterance meanings of a word or a sentence that pass these conditions are called possible **readings**.

Due to these additional constraints, the set of compositional meanings$_e$ of the sentence may undergo considerable changes. Three things can happen to a particular compositional meaning$_e$:

1 The meaning$_e$ may be taken over as it is and enriched with contextual information, e.g. the fixation of concrete referents.
2 The meaning$_e$ may be refuted and eliminated if it is contradictory or does not fit the CoU.
3 The meaning$_e$ may be modified by some kind of meaning shift in order to fit the CoU and subsequently be enriched with contextual information.

Option 2 may lead to a disambiguation of the sentence at utterance level, i.e. to a reduction of the number of possible readings. The meaning shifts involved in option 3 create new expression meanings and, out of them, utterance meanings. For example, when the sentence *I don't need your bicycle* in 1.1.2 was interpreted in the second scenario, *bicycle* was taken to refer to a playing card that carries the picture of a bicycle. This interpretation rests on a meaning shift of the word *bicycle*, by which its lexical meaning is replaced with a closely related new meaning$_e$. Thus for lexical items, the application of meaning shifts is another source of ambiguity, though one that only originates from interpretation in context.

3.4.3 Disambiguation and elimination

Let us first consider the case of disambiguation in context. The following sentences contain the ambiguous lexeme *letter* (⟩alphabetic character⟨ vs ⟩written message⟨):

(2) a. *Johnny wrote a <u>letter</u>.*
   b. *Johnny wrote a <u>letter</u> to Patty.*
   c. *Gamma is the third <u>letter</u> of the Greek alphabet.*

(2a) has two readings because the rest of the sentence, *Johnny wrote a* ____,
allows for both meanings of *letter*. (2b), however, has only one reading. The
addition of *to Patty* requires the message meaning of the word. Likewise in
(2c), the rest of the sentence would not make sense unless *letter* is understood as ⟩character⟨. Thus the immediate sentential environment of a word
may call for particular meaning variants and exclude others.

　　A sentence may also have no possible reading at all if its parts do not fit
together. Example (3) is self-contradictory and therefore disqualified at
utterance level. Due to its lexical meaning, the verb *shiver* requires a subject
referent that is animate and has a body. However, the lexical meaning of *age*
does not allow for this sort of referent:

(3)　*Johnny's age shivered.*

3.4.4. Metonymical shift

The following example is borrowed from Bierwisch (1983):

(4)　*James Joyce is difficult to understand.*

The sentence has at least four readings. If you relate the sentence to James
Joyce the writer, you may first of all take it as meaning that (i) the writings
of James Joyce are difficult to understand. But if you imagine a context
where the author is still alive, the sentence might as well mean that (ii) the
way he talks; (iii) the way he expresses himself; or (iv) the way he acts is
difficult to understand. In the first reading, the name *James Joyce* refers to
Joyce's work. In the other readings, it refers to the writer himself. Yet the
proper name *James Joyce* is not polysemous: we do not have to *learn* this
about the lexical meaning of this particular name. In principle, all names of
persons can be used for referring to their published work. The interpretation in context is due to a meaning shift generally available for all names of
people.

　　Similar shifts are very common. Consider the readings of *university* in the
following examples:

(5) a. *The university lies in the eastern part of the town.*
   b. *The university has closed down the faculty of agriculture.*
   c. *The university starts again on 15 April.*

The subject *the university* refers to the campus in (5a), to the institutional
body in (5b), and to the courses at the university in (5c). Again, this is not a

case of polysemy. The word *university* lends itself naturally to the meaning shifts that create these readings. We do not have to *know* each of them. Many other words with similar meanings exhibit the same kind of variation: *school, theatre, opera, parliament,* and so on. Also, the same kind of variation is paralleled in other languages. This kind of variation is not rooted in lexical ambiguity. Its source is more general.

If we take a closer look at the meaning shifts involved, we see that in each case the term *the university* refers to something that somehow *belongs* to a university. Let us assume that the word lexically denotes a certain kind of educational institution. Such an institution (unless it is a virtual university on the web) must be located somewhere, it must have an administration, and it must offer courses. It is in this sense that its campus, its committees and administration, and the courses offered belong to the university. Apparently, a term that denotes objects of a certain kind can also be used to refer to certain things that usually belong to such objects. The term, then, is felt to 'stand for' those things which belong to its referents proper: in (5), *the university* in this sense 'stands for' the campus, its administration and the courses. In (4), *James Joyce* stands for his work.[4] This use of terms is called **metonymy**: a term that primarily refers to objects of a certain kind is used to refer instead to things that belong to objects of this kind. The corresponding type of meaning shift will be referred to as **metonymical shift**.

The crucial condition of 'belonging to an object of this kind' can be made more precise if we use the notion of a concept. The word *university* is linked to a concept for universities as its lexical meaning. The concept specifies that a university is an educational institution with a location, teaching, teachers, students, an administration, and so on. A metonymical shift shifts the reference of the word from a standard referent, a university, to an essential element of the underlying concept.

3.4.5 Metaphorical shift

The four sentences in (6) are the opening lines of an article in an American news magazine (*Newsweek*, 19 October 1998, p. 30):

(6) a. *They were <u>China's cowboys</u>.*
  b. *The swaggering, fast-talking dealmakers <u>threw around</u> grand projects and big figures as if the money would never stop <u>flowing</u>.*
  c. *<u>Then the sheriff came to town</u>.*
  d. *Last week Beijing said it was shutting down one of the flashiest investment institutions* [name of the institution].

The sentences are about Chinese investment institutions and they are full of metaphorical language. Although there is a literal reading for the first sentence, it will not be taken in that sense. Rather, the next sentence tells us that (6a) refers to certain 'dealmakers'. We will therefore take the expression *China's cowboys* in a metaphorical sense: the persons referred to are not claimed to be cowboys, but to be in some way *like* cowboys. In this case, according to (6b), they resemble cowboys in that they are swaggering, fast-talking and throwing things around. The metaphor is further developed in (6c) with the appearance of the sheriff, another typical ingredient of a Wild West setting. Sentence (6d) explains who the 'sheriff' is: Beijing (the name of the Chinese capital metonymically stands for the Chinese government). This sentence takes us back from the metaphor to literal interpretations.

Let us define more explicitly what a metaphor is: concepts, notions, models, pictures from one domain, the source domain, are borrowed for the description of things in another domain, the target domain. In (6) the source domain is the Wild West and the target domain is the international invest-ment scene of China at the time when the article was published. To the majority of the magazine's readers, the source domain is better known than the target domain. Hence, concepts taken from the Wild West domain may help to describe to this particular readership what's going on in China. (A Wild West metaphor would probably be of less help to Chinese readers.) Every metaphor is the construction of a parallel: the dealmakers are likened to cowboys in certain respects, mainly their public behaviour, and the Chinese government takes the role of the sheriff in exerting its authority. In general, metaphorical language can be characterized as talking about things in the target domain in terms of corresponding things in the source domain.

A metaphor yields a new concept in the target domain, a concept that is similar to the original concept of the source domain in that it contains certain elements, although not all, of the source concept. Metonymy is quite different from metaphor. When we talk metonymically, we remain within the same domain. We borrow an element from the original concept, but the links to the other elements〉remain. *University* in the 〉campus〈 meaning remains immediately related to *university* in its 〉institution〈 meaning, James Joyce's work remains related to the person James Joyce. The relations between the general objects and the things, or aspects, belonging to it are only possible *within* one domain.

As with metonymical shifts, the meaning variation caused by metaphori-cal use is not a matter of lexical ambiguity. We would not say that, due to utterances like (6), the word *cowboy* is lexically ambiguous between 〉cowboy〈 and 〉someone who is not a cowboy but in certain respects like a cowboy〈. There are tens of thousands of words that can undergo **metaphorical shifts**. In addition, the metaphorical shifts occur in other languages in the same way.

3.4.6 Differentiation

The James Joyce example (4) is relevant in one more respect. The four readings mentioned differ in the way the verb *understand* is interpreted in context: it may relate to the author's work, to his articulation, his way of expressing himself and the way he behaves. Although in each case the 'understanding' is directed to different kinds of objects, it is reasonable to assume that the verb *understand* in all these cases just means ⟩understand⟨. If we attributed the different readings of *understand* to polysemy, we would end up in countless distinctions of lexical meaning variants of the majority of words. Note, for example, that understanding a sentence may relate to its articulation when uttered, its syntactic structure, its descriptive meaning or its utterance meaning. The different readings can be better explained if one assumes that *to understand* means to understand someone or something *in a certain respect* that is determined by the context.

The following examples (taken from Bierwisch, 1982: 11) can be explained in the same way:

(7) a. *John lost his friend in the overcrowded subway station.*
   b. *John lost his friend in a tragic car accident.*
   c. *John lost his friend, as he could never suppress making bad jokes about him.*

The common part *John lost his friend* has three different readings due to the respective sentence context/s. In (7a) *lose* means a loss of contact, in (7b) John's friend stops being his friend because the friend no longer exists, and in (7c) the friend is supposed to live on but stops entertaining a friendly relationship to John. In each case, the verb *lose* can be taken to mean something like ⟩stop having, due to some event⟨. What the context contributes to this is the meaning in which the ⟩having⟨ component is interpreted and the kind of event that causes the loss.

Types of shift	Lexical meaning		Shifted meaning	Process
metonymy	*the <u>university</u> starts in April*			building a new concept out of an element of the original concept
	⟩educational institution⟨	→	⟩courses at the university⟨	
metaphor	*they were China's <u>cowboys</u>*			building a new concept in the target domain by borrowing parts of the concept in the source domain
	⟩man who herds cattle⟨	→	⟩person behaving like a cowboy⟨	
differentiation	*James Joyce is hard to <u>understand</u>*			adding conditions to the original concept
	⟩perceive the meaning⟨	→	⟩interpret the text meaning⟨	

Table 3.1 Kinds of meaning shifts

The examples illustrate a third common kind of meaning shift. Bierwisch calls it conceptual differentiation. In this book, the simple term **differentiation** is preferred. It can be defined in general as a meaning shift which results in a special case of what the expression denotes in its lexical meaning. There are several more types of meaning shifts, but we will not go further into the matter. Table 3.1 displays the three types of shifts treated here.

3.5 The Principle of Consistent Interpretation

The driving force of the meaning modifications[5] due to interpretation in context is a principle according to which we try to make the parts of a sentence fit together and the whole sentence fit its context.

Principle of Consistent Interpretation
A complex expression is always interpreted in such a way that its parts fit together and that the whole fits the context.

This principle, if appropriately generalized, probably governs all interpretation whatsoever, because interpretation usually concerns a complex input and is always interpretation in some relevant context. As we have seen, its application to sentence interpretation at utterance level may lead to the elimination of meanings$_e$ as well as to the creation of new ones. The principle generally rules out self-contradictory readings: they are always due to parts within a sentence that do not fit together (recall (3)). It also rules out irrelevant readings: these do not fit the context of the whole.

We will now consider the examples discussed above once more, in a more systematic approach to the crucial notion of 'context'. As we will see, it is not identical with the notion of CoU (context of utterance) introduced in 1.1.2. More generally, it applies at several levels that are relevant for composition and the interpretation of the sentence as a whole.

The immediate context of a lexical item is first of all the syntactic phrase of which it is a part. For example, the NP *an old university* is the context of both the adjective *old* and the noun *university*. In order to make sense in a CoU, the noun *university* in this NP must refer to something that has age such that *old* can apply to it. This admits the ⟩institution⟨ reading and probably the ⟩campus⟨ reading of the word. To take the noun *university* in one of these readings means to fit it with the context provided by the whole NP.

The next important level of context of a lexical item is the **sentential context**, i.e. the rest of the sentence. In (2b), (2c) and (3), the sentential context eliminates certain meaning$_e$ variants. In other cases, the sentential context triggers meaning shifts in order to make all parts of the sentence fit together (and thereby fit their sentential context); see (5a, b, c) for metonymical shifts, (6b) for metaphorical shifts and (4) for differentiation.

Finally, the context of the whole sentence, the CoU, influences the interpretation of the sentence as an utterance. It partly determines which readings are possible. For example, it will hinge on the actual CoU of the James Joyce sentence whether we take it in one reading or the other. And it is due to the CoU (which includes the surrounding text) that (6a) and (6c) undergo their metaphorical shifts.

In 1.2.3 the process of composition was characterized as a bottom-up process, in which the meaning$_e$ of the whole is derived step by step from the meanings$_e$ of the elements (lexical items, grammatical forms and syntactic structure). In other words, the output of the process, the sentence meaning(s)$_e$, is determined by the input. When a sentence is interpreted in context, i.e. when its possible utterance meanings are determined, meaning shifts and meaning eliminations interfere with the process of composition. The interference constitutes a **top-down** element of the interpretation: the input may be re-interpreted in terms of appropriate outputs. Thus, to a certain extent the output determines the input. Consider, for example, the case of (5a), *The university lies in the eastern part of the town*: the interpretation of *the university* in its given context requires an output consistent with the context. In order to achieve this, the input *the university* is subjected to re-interpretation (institution → campus shift).

As we have seen, one effect of interpretation in context is the elimination of self-contradictory readings. It is important to realize that such readings are not eliminated by the process of semantic composition. They *must* not be, because otherwise self-contradictory sentences would not receive a meaning at all. Of course, they have a meaning: if they had not, we would not be able to qualify them as self-contradictory. Hence, semantic composition itself is blind to context requirements such as consistency.

3.6 Meaning shifts and polysemy

The kinds of meaning shifts to be observed during interpretation in context are also involved in polysemy. In very many cases of polysemy, meaning variants are interrelated by way of metonymy, metaphor or differentiation.

As to metonymy, recall the case of *green* with its secondary meaning ⟩unripe⟨. Here green colour is taken as metonymically standing for a certain stage of biological development. Other cases of lexicalized metonymy are the following:

(8) a. *The <u>asshole</u> did not even apologize.*   part for the whole, 'pars pro toto'
   b. *He talked to <u>celebrities</u>.*   property for a person with the property
   c. *His last <u>date</u> was in a bad temper.*   event for person involved
   d. *I wrote a <u>paper</u>.*   carrier for content
   e. *the <u>Green Berets</u>*   clothing for wearer

To parts of the body (8a) belong a person or animal. A property belongs to the one who has the property (8b): celebrities are persons who have the property of celebrity. To a date belongs the person one dates (8c). To a piece of paper with something written on it belongs what is written on it (8d). Pieces of clothing have their wearers; they are associated with the people wearing them (8e).

In (6b) the metaphorical use of the verb *flow* for money is so common that it can be considered a lexicalized meaning variant, in addition to the literal meaning of the flow of liquids. Other examples of lexemes with metaphorical meaning variants are terms like *mouse* for a computer mouse, *light*$_{A2}$ in *a light meal*, or the majority of idiomatic expressions like *throw in the towel, kick the bucket* or *make a mountain out of a molehill*. Most proverbs are metaphorical, e.g. *Birds of a feather flock together* or *A rolling stone gathers no moss*.

Differentiation too is a common source of polysemy: a lexeme may have a meaning variant that applies to a special case of what the basic meaning of the lexeme applies to. *Car* denotes some sort of vehicle in general, but nowadays preferably an automobile; *disc* may mean ⟩flat, thin, round object⟨ in general as well as ⟩magnetic disc⟨, ⟩compact disc⟨ or ⟩record⟨ in its differentiated meanings.

Checklist

lexeme
lexical meaning
grammatical category
grammatical forms
grammatical properties
sound form
spelling
citation form
idioms
ambiguity
homonymy
homography
homophony
polysemy
meaning variant
vagueness

synonymy
interpretation in context
readings
disambiguation
elimination of meanings
modification of meaning
meaning shift
metonymy
metaphor
source domain
target domain
differentiation
Principle of Consistent
  Interpretation
top-down
context

Exercises

1 Which properties determine a lexeme?
2 Find three composite lexemes (idioms) of each of the categories noun, intransitive verb and transitive verb.

3 What is the difference between homonymy and polysemy?
4 Discuss the ambiguity of the following words with the meanings indicated: do they constitute a case of polysemy or homonymy? Try to determine the historical sources.
   (a) *fraud* ⟩act of deceiving⟨ vs ⟩person who deceives⟨.
   (b) *calf* ⟩young of cattle⟨ vs ⟩fleshy back part of the leg below the knee⟨.
   (c) *sole* ⟩bottom surface of the foot⟨ vs ⟩flat fish⟨.
   (d) *point* ⟩sharp end of something (e.g. a knife)⟨ vs ⟩dot used in writing⟨.
   (e) *character* ⟩mental or moral qualities of a person⟨ vs ⟩letter⟨ (e.g. Chinese character).
   (f) *palm* ⟩inner surface of the hand⟨ vs ⟩palm tree⟨.
   (g) *ring* ⟩circular band of metal⟨ vs ⟩telephone call⟨.
5 What is the relation between the meaning of a word in its lexical meaning and the word in a metaphorical meaning? What is the relation between a word in its lexical meaning and in a metonymical meaning?
6 Identify the instances of metaphor and metonymy in the following passage (from the *Newsweek* article cited above):

   Sound like Asian contagion? So far, China has escaped economic disaster. But even in China, the mighty can fall. . . . Can China reform its financial system, but avoid the social unrest that has crippled the rest of Asia?

7 Find examples where two meanings of a polysemous lexeme are related by metaphor, metonymy or differentiation (three of each kind).
8 Discuss the meaning shifts underlying the use of *bean* for the head, *paw* for the hand, *snotnose* for a child.
9 Does the polysemy of so many words constitute an advantage or a disadvantage for communication?
10 Discuss the difference between polysemy and the variation of meaning due to metaphorical shift, metonymical shift or differentiation.
11 Discuss the ways in which the Principle of Consistent Interpretation affects the interpretation of a sentence in context.

Further reading

Tallerman (1998, Chapter 2) on lexemes, grammatical categories and their connection with syntax. Cruse (1986, Chapter 2 and Chapter 3) on lexemes and 'lexical units'. Lyons (1995, Chapter 2) and Lyons (1977, Chapter 1) on ambiguity.

Notes

[1] Only such complex lexical items are called idioms here that also can be taken in a non-idiomatic compositional meaning, e.g. *literally* ⟩throw in the towel⟨.

2   It has often been questioned if this historical criterion is really relevant. Average speakers do not know where the words they use come from. All that matters for them is some 'feeling' as to whether or not the two meanings have anything to do with each other. For instance, to many speakers of English the words *ear* for the body part and in *an ear of corn* appear to be the same word, although historically they are of different origins.

3   In 4.2 the term *self-contradictory* will be replaced by the technical term *logically false*.

4   Likewise, in the 'bicycle' example from Chapter 1, *the bicycle* stands for the card carrying the picture of a bicycle.

5   In recent semantic discussions, the term **coercion** has become familiar for the modification of meaning during the process of interpretation.

Meaning and logic

4

The logical approach to meaning is a first step into the investigation of meaning relations. Taking up the notions of truth and reference from Chapter 2, we will consider sentences from the perspective of their truth conditions. The logical view allows the introduction of basic concepts such as logical consequence (or entailment), logical equivalence and incompatibility. In the second part of the chapter these notions are applied to words.

4.1 Logical basics

4.1.1 Donald Duck and Aristotle

Let us start with the provocative (and highly important) question: 'Is Donald Duck a duck?' Suppose you are one of those who answer spontaneously: 'Why, of course!' In that case you would subscribe to the truth of (1):

(1)   *Donald Duck is a duck.*

Well, ducks are birds, and birds are animals. Would you also say that (2) is true?

(2)   *Donald Duck is a bird.*

And how about (3)?

(3)   *Donald Duck is an animal.*

It would not be surprising if you were less sure about the truth of (2) and would not subscribe to the truth of (3). But, if (1) is true, (2) is true; if (2) is true, so is (3). Hence, if (3) is false, there must be something wrong: (2) must be false as well and, consequently, (1) cannot be true either. That is logic: if Donald is a duck, then he is a bird. If he is not a bird, he cannot be a duck.

Well, then, let us take a second look at the original question. Why is it that we are inclined to say that Donald is a duck? Well, it is the fact that his name is Donald 'Duck' and that Donald *looks* like a duck, at least roughly, i.e. if we ignore his having arms with hands instead of a duck's wings. But names are just names, and beyond his looking like a duck there is little to be said in defence of Donald's duckness. Does he quack rather than talk? Does he swim or fly like a duck? Would we expect him to dive for food as ducks do? No. As far as we know, Donald Duck behaves, feels, and thinks in every respect like a human being. So, let us try this:

(4)   *Donald Duck is a human being.*

Have you ever seen a human being with a duck's body, with feathers, a beak and duck feet? Is he not much too short for an adult man? Could he run around without his pants all the time if he were not a duck? If we are serious about the initial question, we have to admit that (4) is not true either:

(5)   *Donald Duck is neither a duck nor a human being.*

But if we decide to take this stand, we are throwing out the baby with the bath water. According to (5), Donald could be anything *except* a duck or a human. This is certainly not what we want to say. If anything, Donald is a duck or a human. Somehow, he's both at the same time:

(6)   *Donald Duck is both a duck and a human being.*

He is a duck that behaves like a human, and he is a human being in a duck's guise. If we take (5) and (6) together, we get (7) and (8):

(7)   *Donald Duck is a duck and he isn't.*
(8)   *Donald Duck is a human being and he isn't.*

What does logic say about this? That is very clear: (6) contradicts (5), and (7) and (8), as they stand, are each self-contradictory. This cannot be: (6), (7) and (8) cannot be true. Therefore, something like Donald Duck cannot exist. The consequence is acceptable, in a sense. In a world where ducks are ducks and cannot be human, and vice versa (e.g. in what we consider the real world), we would not accept that something or someone like Donald really exists. We would not accept that (6), (7) and (8) are true of anything that really exists.

The underlying principle goes back as far as Aristotle. In his work *Metaphysics*, he formulated the following fundamental law of logic, and not only of logic, but of truth in general (Aristotle, *Metaphysics*, 1005b, p. 262):

Law of Contradiction
The same attribute cannot at the same time both belong and not belong to the same subject in the same respect.

What the principle says is simply this: a sentence, in a certain reading, cannot be true and false at the same time. (Aristotle assumes that, basically, every sentence says that some attribute (the predicate of the sentence) belongs to some subject.) Our reasoning about Donald Duck with the outcome of (5), (6), (7) and (8) violates this law. If (5) is true, (6) must be false, and vice versa. So, if (5) and (6) are both true, they must also be both false. (7) says that (1) is both true and false, and so does (8) for (4).

But, seriously, is not there something to be said in favour of the truth of (5), (6), (7) and (8)? Yes, there is. And if we take a closer look at Aristotle's law, we realize how our findings about Donald Duck can be reconciled with logic: we have to relate the categorization of poor Donald to different 'respects'. The apparent contradictions can be resolved if we replace (5), (6), (7) and (8) by the following:

(5′) *Donald Duck is neither a duck nor a human being in all respects.*
(6′) *Donald Duck is a duck in certain respects and a human being in others.*
(7′) *Donald Duck is a duck in certain respects, but he isn't in others.*
(8′) *Donald Duck is a human being in certain respects, but he isn't in others.*

Or more explicitly:

(5″) *Donald Duck doesn't behave like a duck and doesn't look like a human being.*
(6″) *Donald Duck looks like a duck but behaves like a human being.*
(7″) *Donald Duck looks like a duck but doesn't behave like one.*
(8″) *Donald Duck behaves like a human being but doesn't look like one.*

These sentences are no longer contradictory. They are, however, still not compatible with our experience of the real world. Hence, if we accept the truth of these sentences, we have to assume a different world for Donald Duck to exist in – and that, of course, is what we do.

As you might have noted, interpreting the original sentences (5) to (8) in the more explicit way of (5′) to (8′) or (5″) to (8″) is an instance of what we introduced in the last chapter as 'differentiation'. The expressions *be a duck* and *be a human being* are interpreted in a more specific reading than what they literally mean. The process is triggered by the need to make things fit into their context, i.e. by applying the Principle of Consistent Interpretation.

4.1.2 The Principle of Polarity

The basic notion of all logical considerations is **truth**. As was stated in 1.1.2 above, truth is not a property of sentences as such, although we mostly talk that way.[1] The question of the truth or falsity of a sentence arises only if the sentence is related to a certain CoU. Since the CoU may vary, sentences are true in some CoUs and false in others. Truth and falsity underlie the following fundamental principle:

Principle of Polarity
In a given CoU, with a given reading, a declarative sentence is either true or false.

This principle too goes back to Aristotle. It entails (for the notion of logical entailment see the next subsection) the Law of Contradiction since the formulation 'either true or false' is taken in the exclusive meaning of *either – or*: ⟩either true or false, but not both⟨. The ⟩but not both⟨ part is the Law of Contradiction. The Principle of Polarity adds to the Law of Contradiction the condition known as the **Law of the Excluded Middle** (Latin *Tertium non datur*, which means ⟩there is no third [possibility]⟨): there are only these two possibilities, truth or falsity, and no others, i.e. no in-between, no both-true-and-false, no neither-true-nor-false. Later in 9.5 we will see how this principle is reflected in the structure and use of natural language.

In order to have a convenient neutral term for being true or false, one speaks of the **truth value** of a sentence. A sentence has the truth value TRUE if it is true, it has the truth value FALSE if it is false. In general, the truth value of a sentence depends on certain conditions: is the situation expressed by the sentence in accordance with the facts in the given CoU or is it not? These conditions were introduced in 2.2.2 as the **truth conditions** of the sentence. The sentences in examples (9) and (10) have different truth conditions:

(9)   *The cat is in the garden.*
(10)   *There's milk on the floor.*

(9) is true if the cat is in the garden, and (10) is true if there's milk on the floor. In a given CoU, referring to a certain cat, a certain garden and a certain floor (i.e. the floor of a certain room), they may both be true, or both be false, or one may be true, and the other one false. Their truth conditions are, in principle, independent of each other.

4.1.3 Negation

Due to the Principle of Polarity, any declarative sentence, for example (11), is either true or false:

(11)   *John knows the solution.*

If I say *John knows the solution*, I make clear that I have made my choice between two possibilities: either John knows the solution or John does not know the solution. By asserting (11), I not only express that I think that John knows the solution, but also that I do not think that John does *not* know the solution. The utterance of any declarative sentence is understood as tacitly denying that its contrary is true. Thus, any statement that one can express in a language is in this sense polarized: it is the result of a decision between two, just two, opposite possibilities, yes or no, true or false. *Polarization*, as it were, pervades language totally.[2]

It is no surprise then that all languages have systematic means of expressing the polar contrary of a sentence. This is done by what is called **negation**. Negation reverses the truth value of a sentence; it makes a true sentence false and a false sentence true. In English, negation is usually formed by negating the finite verb of the sentence, using the auxiliary *do* if the verb is not an auxiliary itself.

(12) a. *John knows the solution.*   negation: *John doesn't know the solution.*
  b. *John will die.*   negation: *John will not die.*
  c. *John is clever.*   negation: *John isn't clever.*

In other cases, negation is formed by negating other parts of the sentence, for example so-called quantifiers such as *all*, *every*, *some*, *always* and the like, or by replacing them with appropriate negative expressions:

(13) a. *Mary is already here.*   negation: *Mary is not here yet.*
  b. *Everybody knows that.*   negation: *Not everybody knows that.*
  c. *She's always late.*   negation: *She's not always late.*
  d. *She sometimes apologizes.*   negation: *She never apologizes.*
  e. *Only John knows the reason.* negation: *Not only John knows the reason.*

For the present purposes, we need not be concerned with the exact rules and subtleties of negation in English. Let us simply define the **negation of a sentence** as follows

DEFINITION
  If A is a sentence that is not negated itself, then its **negation**
  (i) is true whenever A is false and false whenever A is true and
  (ii) is formed out of A by a standard grammatical procedure such as

- adding the auxiliary *do* to the verb phrase and *not* to the auxiliary (e.g. *did not know*);
- adding *not* to an auxiliary verb (e.g. *was not*);
- adding *not* to a quantifier expression (e.g. *not every*);
- substituting a positive expression by its negative counterpart (e.g. *some* by *no*).

There is only a handful of expressions that require negation by substitution: quantifier expressions containing *some* (*some – no, somewhere – nowhere*, etc.) and a couple of particles such as *already* and *still* (negation: *not yet* and *no more*). Negation by substitution is only relevant if regular syntactic negation with *not* is impossible. Usually, a (positive) sentence has exactly one negation, and this is what will be assumed throughout this chapter. For the sake of convenience **not-A** is used as an abbreviation of the negation of A.

4.2 Logical properties of sentences

Given the notion of truth conditions, a couple of basic logical properties of sentences can be defined. A 'normal' sentence will be true in some CoUs and false in others. This property is called **contingency**: a sentence (in a given reading) is **contingent** if it is neither necessarily true nor necessarily false. Thus, there are two kinds of sentences which are not contingent. The first kind is called logically true: a sentence (in a given reading) is **logically true** if it is true in all possible CoUs. Correspondingly, a sentence that is false in all possible CoUs is called **logically false**.[3] As is common practice in logics, '1' is used for TRUE and '0' for FALSE:

A contingent		A logically true		A logically false	
A		A		A	
1	possible	1		1	impossible
0	possible	0	impossible	0	

The sentences in (14) are logically true:

(14) a. *Either Donald Duck is a duck or he is not a duck.*
    b. *Every duck is a duck.*
    c. *Ducks are birds.*
    d. *Two times seven equals fourteen.*

(14a) is true in every CoU due to the Principle of Polarity. We might replace *Donald Duck* by any other subject and *is a duck* by any other predicate. It is the sentence pattern 'either x is p or x is not p' which makes the sentence true, independent of any contextual conditions. Likewise, (14b) is invariably true due to the structure of the sentence, and (14c) is true because the words *duck* and *bird* mean what they mean, i.e. due to the semantic facts of English. (14d) is a mathematical truth. *Two, seven* and *fourteen* when used as NPs like here always refer to the same abstract objects, the numbers 2, 7 and 14; their referents cannot vary with the choice of a CoU, nor can the outcome of multiplying 2 with 7. In philosophical terminology, sentences such as (14c) and (14d) are called *analytically true*, while the notion of logical truth (and falsity) is reserved for cases such as (14a) and (14b) which owe their truth (or falsity) to specific rules of logic. From a linguistic point of view, there is no essential difference between the type of truth represented by the four sentences: all four of them are true due to their structure and the meanings of the words they contain.

The following sentences are logically false:

(15) a. *Donald Duck is a duck and Donald Duck is not a duck.*
    b. *Donald Duck is neither a duck nor is he not a duck.*
    c. *Ducks are plants.*
    d. *Two times seven is twenty-seven.*

(15a) violates the Law of Contradiction; (15b) the Law of the Excluded Middle; (15c) violates the semantic rules of English and (15d) the rules of mathematics.[4]

The examples show that even logical truth and falsity rest on some basic assumptions:

- the Principle of Polarity;
- the semantics of the language.

These assumptions are absolutely indispensable. The Principle of Polarity is at the very heart of the notions of truth and falsity. The semantic rules of the language are necessary for being able to deal with questions of truth at all. If the sentences and the words they consist of did not have their proper meanings, there would be no point in asking any logical, or semantic, questions.

The logical properties of a sentence are connected to the information it may convey. Contingent sentences may be true or false. Thus, when they are actually used for assertions, they convey information about the situation referred to: it must be such that the situation expressed does in fact pertain. If John tells Mary *there is beer in the fridge,* she learns something about the situation referred to (provided John does not lie and Mary believes him). If John uttered a logically true sentence like *Ducks are birds,* Mary would not learn anything about the given situation. She would, at best, learn something about English. Similarly, she would ask herself what John wants to tell her by saying *Either Donald Duck is a duck or he is not a duck*. Taken as a *message*, as information about the world, it would be unin-formative. Only contingent sentences can convey information about the world.

4.3 Logical relations between sentences

The truth conditions of two sentences may be related to each other in various ways. The most important relation is logical entailment.[5]

4.3.1 Logical entailment

Recall our discussion above: necessarily, B in (16) is true, if A is true. This is an instance of entailment:

(16)   A. *Donald Duck is a duck.*
       B. *Donald Duck is a bird.*

The relation of logical entailment is defined by one crucial condition: it is impossible that B is false if A is true. (This is the case with A and B in (16): it is impossible that Donald is a duck (A true) and not a bird (B false). Hence, if he is a duck, he necessarily is a bird.

DEFINITION	A	B	
A logically entails B/B logically follows from A	1	1	
A ⇒ B	1	0	**impossible**
if and only if[6]:	0	1	
necessarily, if A is true, B is true.	0	0	

Two arbitrary sentences A and B may be independently true or false. This yields four possible combinations of truth values. Logical entailment rules out one of these four combinations, A-true-B-false. If A entails B, the truth values of A and B depend on each other in a particular way: B cannot be false if A is true, and A cannot be true if B is false. Thus, logical entailment results in a certain link between the truth conditions of the two sentences.

The definition of entailment does not tell us anything about the remaining three combinations of truth values. When we say that in (16) a entails b, we say so because of the general condition that ducks are birds. Remember that we found it difficult to decide whether Donald Duck is a duck or not. For the question whether A entails B this does not matter because logical entailment means that *if* A is true, *then* B must be true. If Donald is a duck, he *must* be a bird. But if he is not a duck, he still may be a bird or not. Donald might be a raven; then a is false and b is true. This is

B entails A

A	B	
1	1	
1	0	
0	1	impossible
0	0	

Table 4.1

A unilaterally entails B

A	B	
1	1	
1	0	impossible
0	1	possible
0	0	

Table 4.2

admissible. He might be a cow; then both a and b are false. This too is admissible. What is not admissible is his being a duck but not a bird. Let me give you three more examples of entailments.

(17) A *It's raining heavily.* ⇒ B *It's raining.*
(18) A *Ann is a sister of my mother.* ⇒ B *Ann is an aunt of mine.*
(19) A *Today is Monday.* ⇒ B *Today isn't Wednesday.*

If it is raining, but not heavily so, one can say (17B), but not (17A). Likewise, (18B) can be true without (18A) being true: Ann could as well be a sister of my father or the wife of an uncle of mine. That (19B) may be true and (19A) at the same time false, is immediately clear. In principle, the relation of entailment is asymmetric: A may entail B without B entailing A. (In general, a relation is symmetric if and only if *x is in the relation to y* entails *y is in the relation to x*, it is asymmetric if this does not hold.) Applying the definition of entailment to the case of B entailing A yields the picture in Table 4.1 (it rules out the combination B-true-A-false). Accordingly, B does *not* entail A iff B-true-A-false is possible.[6] If we add this condition to the condition for A entailing B, we obtain a table for A *unilaterally* entailing B (Table 4.2).

There is one way of reversing an entailment: if A entails B, then A is necessarily *false*, if B is *false*. Table 4.3 shows how the truth values of not-A and not-B co-vary with those of A and B. Ruling out the combination A-true-B-false is obviously the same as ruling out (not-B)-true-(not-A)-false.

A entails B = not-B entails not-A

A	B		not-B	not-A
1	1		0	0
1	0		1	0
0	1	impossible	0	1
0	0		1	1

Table 4.3

Hence, if Donald Duck is not a bird, he cannot be a duck; if it is not raining, it cannot be raining heavily, and so on. A $\Rightarrow$ B is equivalent to not-B $\Rightarrow$ not-A. For example, (16) yields:

(20) **not-B** *Donald Duck is not a bird.* $\Rightarrow$ **not-A** *Donald Duck is not a duck.*

Let us now take a look at a few examples which are *not* cases of logical entailment, although in each case sentence B would under normal circumstances be inferred from A. What matters, however, is whether the consequence is really necessary or whether it is based on some additional assumptions.

(21) A *Mary is John's mother.* $\not\Rightarrow$ B *Mary is the wife of John's father.*
(22) A *John said he is tired.* $\not\Rightarrow$ B *John is tired.*
(23) A *The beer is in the fridge.* $\not\Rightarrow$ B *The beer is cool.*

There are no *logical* reasons for drawing these conclusions. It is logically possible that parents are not married, that John was lying, or that the fridge does not work or the beer has not been in it long enough. In most cases we draw our conclusions on the basis of our world knowledge, i.e. of what we consider normal, plausible or probable. The notion of logical entailment does not capture all these regularities and connections. It just captures the really 'hard' cases of an *if-then* relation, those based on the Principle of Polarity and the semantic facts alone.

What does logical entailment mean for the meanings of A and B? If A and B are contingent and A unilaterally entails B, both sentences contain information about the same issue, but the information given by A is more specific than the information given by B. The (truth) conditions that B imposes on the situation are such that they are always fulfilled if A is true. Therefore, the truth conditions of B must be part of the truth conditions of A. In general, if no further logical relation holds between A and B, A will impose additional conditions on the situation referred to. In this sense, A contains more information, i.e. is more informative and more specific, than B. The situation expressed by A is a *special case* of the situation expressed by B. As we shall see in 4.3.5, this does not hold if A and/or B are not contingent.

One further property should be noted here: logical entailment is what is called a transitive relation. The general property of transitivity[7] is defined as follows: a relation R is transitive if and only if 'x is in relation R to y' and 'y is in relation R to z' entails 'x is in relation R to z'. Applied to entailment, this means that if A entails B and B entails C then A entails C. For example, *Donald is a duck* $\Rightarrow$ *Donald is a bird*; *Donald is a bird* $\Rightarrow$ *Donald is an animal*; hence *Donald is a duck* $\Rightarrow$ *Donald is an animal*. The property of transitivity immediately follows from the way entailment is defined. Suppose A $\Rightarrow$ B and B $\Rightarrow$ C; then if A is true, necessarily B is true; if B is true, necessarily C is true, hence: if A is true, necessarily C is true, i.e. A $\Rightarrow$ C.

4.3.2 Logical equivalence

The next relation to be introduced is immediately related to entailment:

DEFINITION	A	B	
A and B are logically equivalent,	1	1	
A ⇔ B	1	0	impossible
if and only if:	0	1	impossible
necessarily, A and B have equal truth values.	0	0	

Equivalence means having identical truth conditions. Like entailment, equivalence is a transitive relation, but unlike entailment it is a symmetric relation. Since the combinations A-true-B-false and A-false-B-true are both ruled out, the table combines the conditions for A ⇒ B and B ⇒ A: equivalence is **mutual entailment**. Thus, if A and B are contingent, A must contain all the information B contains and B must contain all the information A contains. In other words, the sentences must contain the *same* information. Let us consider a few examples:

(24) A *He is the father of my mother.* ⇔ B *He is my maternal grandfather.*
(25) A *Today is Monday.* ⇔ B *Yesterday was Sunday.*
(26) A *The bottle is half empty.* ⇔ B *The bottle is half full.*
(27) A *Everyone will lose.* ⇔ B *No-one will win.*

For (25), we have to assume that every Monday is necessarily preceded by a Sunday, an assumption that may be taken for granted for the point to be made here. The equivalence in (27) holds if we assume a reading of *lose* and *win* in which *lose* means ›not win‹. Given these assumptions, all four cases rest merely on the semantic facts of English. The equivalence in (24) is due to the synonymy of *maternal grandfather* and *father of the mother*.

4.3.3 Logical contrariety

The logical relations of contrariety and contradiction focus on falsity.

DEFINITION	A	B	
A is logically contrary to B /	1	1	impossible
A logically excludes B / B is incompatible with A	1	0	
if and only if:	0	1	
necessarily, if A is true, B is false.	0	0	

What follows from the defining condition is that the combination A-true-B-true is ruled out. It also follows that if B is true, A must be false. In other words: the relation is symmetric. We can thus talk of A and B being contraries, and could replace the defining condition by 'A and B cannot both be true'. Other common terms for contrariety are *logical exclusion* and *incompatibility*. Examples of incompatibility would be:

(28)   A *It's cold.*   B *It's hot.*
(29)   A *Today is Monday.*   B *Tomorrow is Wednesday.*
(30)   A *Ann is younger than Mary.*   B *Ann is older than Mary.*

Usually, two contrary sentences cannot both be true but they may both be false. It may be neither hot nor cold, it may be neither Monday nor the day before Wednesday, Ann may be of the same age as Mary. In other words, the *negations* of contraries are normally compatible, they may both be true.

There is a close connection between contrariety and entailment: A and B are logical contraries iff A entails not-B. Note that if A entails not-B, B also entails not-A: both relations rule out A-true-B-true. Applying this, for example, to the sentences in (28) we obtain that, equivalently to the incompatibility stated, we can state that *It's cold* entails *It's not hot*.

4.3.4 Logical contradiction

DEFINITION	A	B	
A and B are logical contradictories	1	1	impossible
if and only if:	1	0	
necessarily, A and B have opposite truth values.	0	1	
	0	0	impossible

Contradictories are necessarily contraries (but not vice versa). The definition of contradiction adds to the definition of contrariety the condition that A and B cannot both be false. If A and B are contradictories, in every CoU either A is true and B is false or B is true and A is false. Together, A and B represent a strict *either-or* alternative. The classical case of logical contradiction is formed by a sentence and its negation (31); (32) and (33) show, however, that there are other cases as well:

(31)   A *It's late.*   B *It's not late.*
(32)   A *Today is Saturday or Sunday.*   B *Today is Monday, Tuesday,*
                                                Wednesday, Thursday or Friday.
(33)   A *Everyone will win.*   B *Someone will lose.*

Although the B sentences in (32) and (33) are not negations (in the grammatical sense) of the A sentences, they are nevertheless logically equivalent to the respective negations, *today is neither Saturday nor Sunday* and *not everyone will win*. A sentence and its negation are per definition always logically contradictory.

Logical contradiction too is linked to the other relations. A and B are logical contradictories iff A is logically equivalent to not-B. In terms of

A	B	A $\Rightarrow$ B	A $\Leftrightarrow$ B	contraries	contradict
1	1			impossible	impossible
1	0	impossible	impossible		
0	1		impossible		
0	0				impossible

Table 4.4 Logical relations

entailment, contradiction can therefore be captured as follows: A and B are contradictories iff A entails not-B (ruling out A-true-B-true) and not-A entails B (ruling out A-false-B-false).

Table 4.4 displays the crucial conditions that define the four logical relations we introduced. Each 'impossible' entry corresponds to an entailment relation. Therefore all other relations can be defined in terms of entailment and negation:

(34) A and B are equivalent   *iff*   A entails B *and*
                                                 B entails A
      A and B are contraries   *iff*   A entails not-B
      A and B are contradictories   *iff*   A entails not-B *and*
                                                 not-A entails B

4.3.5 Logical relations involving logically true or false sentences

Assume we have two sentences A and B, and A is logically false. If we set up a table for the possible truth value combinations on the basis of this information alone, we receive entries 'impossible' in the first two rows, because A cannot be true, regardless of B (Table 4.5). Thus the table fulfils the crucial condition for A entailing B ('impossible' in row 2) and for A and B being contraries ('impossible' in row 1). Note that the choice of B does not play any role in this. Therefore, if A is logically false, it entails anything. This is harmless: the entailment will never become effective because A is never true. Another consequence of A being logically false is that A can never be

A logically false

A	B	
1	1	impossible
1	0	impossible
0	1	
0	0	

Table 4.5

B logically true

A	B	
1	1	
1	0	impossible
0	1	
0	0	impossible

Table 4.6

true together with any sentence B. Hence, logically false sentences are contrary to all other sentences. A similar picture arises if B is logically true (cf. Table 4.6). In this case too the entailment A $\Rightarrow$ B holds, regardless of A. Since B cannot be false, A-true-B-false is impossible. Applied to natural language sentences, we obtain, for example, the following entailments. In (35a), A is logically false, in (35b) B is logically true. *Mary is tired* is contingent. Putting (35a) and (35b) together, we obtain (35c) (because entailment is transitive):

(35) a. A *Ducks are dogs.* $\Rightarrow$ B *Mary is tired.*
    b. A *Mary is tired.* $\Rightarrow$ B *Ducks are birds.*
    c. A *Ducks are dogs.* $\Rightarrow$ B *Ducks are birds.*

You will probably find these results confusing and counterintuitive. The cases of entailment considered so far will have made you think that there must be some *reason* for A entailing B. There should be some *meaning connection* between the sentences. But what has Mary's being tired to do with ducks being birds or dogs or whatever? The answer is: nothing. Nonetheless, these are logical entailments. In the definitions of the logical relations it was never said that there must be a meaning connection between A and B. The crucial conditions are given in terms of impossible truth value combinations for A and B. If A-true-B-false is impossible for whatever reason, then A and B fulfil the conditions of entailment. And is not (35c) downright contradictory? Yes, A and B logically contradict each other, but the constellation nevertheless fulfils the condition that A-true-B-false is impossible. This illustrates a very important point, which we will say more about below: the logical relations are *not* meaning relations. They are relations between sentences in terms of their truth conditions but not in terms of their meanings. As the two examples show, logical relations may hold between sentences whose meanings bear no relationship whatsoever. Or (in the case of (35c)) they may hold *despite* the meaning relations between the two parts. As we will see, this does not mean that our intuitions about a connection between logical relations and meaning have to be thrown overboard altogether. If we exclude logically true or false sentences, a connection does exist. But for the moment, it is important to realize that logical relations do not warrant a meaning relation, let alone particular meaning relations. Table 4.7 shows the pictures resulting from A or B or both being non-contingent. Note that, in the particular cases assumed, all empty cells can be filled with 'possible' entries.

Table 4.7 contains results already mentioned: two logically true, or false, sentences are equivalent ('impossible' in rows 2 and 3 of cells 4 and 5); if one sentence is logically true and the other logically false, then they are contradictories ('impossible' in rows 1 and 4 of cells 3 and 6). But some results are counterintuitive in the way of the cases in (35). For example, due to 'impossible' in row 2 of these cases, we obtain entailments like the following:

1				2				3		
A contingent				A logically false				A logically false		
B logically true				B contingent				B logically true		

A	B			A	B			A	B	
1	1	possible		1	1	impossible		1	1	impossible
1	0	impossible		1	0	impossible		1	0	impossible
0	1	possible		0	1	possible		0	1	possible
0	0	impossible		0	0	possible		0	0	impossible

4				5				6		
A logically true				A logically false				A logically true		
B logically true				B logically false				B logically false		

A	B			A	B			A	B	
1	1	possible		1	1	impossible		1	1	impossible
1	0	impossible		1	0	impossible		1	0	possible
0	1	impossible		0	1	impossible		0	1	impossible
0	0	impossible		0	0	possible		0	0	impossible

Table 4.7 Logical relations resulting from logical truth or falsity

(36) case 3   A *2 plus 2 equals 3.*   ⇒   B *Ducks are birds.*
(37) case 4   A *2 plus 2 equals 4.*   ⇒   B *Ducks are birds.*
(38) case 5   A *2 plus 2 equals 3.*   ⇒   B *Ducks are dogs.*

Even more disturbing than these counterintuitive entailments are those cases where logical relations co-occur that one would normally consider incompatible: the cases 2, 3 and 5 all have 'impossible' entries in rows 1 *and* 2, which means that A entails B, but at the same time A and B are contraries.

All this, however, is perfectly in order. It does not mean that the logical relations are ill-defined. As we will see immediately, they do accord to our intuitions when they are applied to contingent sentences. What the 'pathological' cases (to use a term from mathematical jargon) show is that the concepts of entailment, equivalence, contrariety and contradiction lose their significance under special conditions.

4.3.6 Logical relations under the assumption of contingency

Let us now assume that A and B are both contingent. This has far-reaching consequences for the significance of the logical relations. First of all, we may insert the entry 'possible' into many cells of the defining tables. For example, the definition of entailment rules out A-true-B-false. If we also excluded A-true-B-true, the truth of A would be ruled out altogether and A would be logically false. Hence, the assumption that A is contingent allows us to fill

A	B	A $\Rightarrow$ B	A $\Leftrightarrow$ B	contraries	contradict
1	1	possible	possible	impossible	impossible
1	0	impossible	impossible	possible	possible
0	1		impossible	possible	possible
0	0	possible	possible		impossible

Table 4.8 Logical relations between contingent sentences

in 'possible' in row 1. Likewise, we can make the same entry in row 4: A-false-B-false must be possible because otherwise B would be logically false. Table 4.8 displays the resulting picture for the four relations. (You can easily figure out the other entries yourself.)

The restriction on contingent sentences renders the five relations much more specific. Compared to the original definitions in Table 4.4, the relations here all carry two 'possible' entries in addition to the defining 'impossible' entries, while the general definition of equivalence leaves open whether the cases A-true-B-true and A-false-B-false are possible or not. Fixing these issues makes equivalence between contingent sentences a more specific relation than equivalence in general. As a consequence, the more specific relations in Table 4.8 cannot co-occur freely. (Note that 'possible' and 'impossible' entries in the same row are incompatible, while 'impossible' and 'no entry' are compatible.) Entailment and equivalence cannot co-occur with contrariety and contradiction: for the former two relations, A and B can both be true, but not so for the latter two. Still, some cells remain open. But this is as it ought to be. If these cells too were filled with 'possible', all relations would be mutually exclusive. It would then no longer make sense to say, e.g. that if A and B are equivalent, then A entails B and B entails A.

Within the domain of contingent sentences a further logical relation can be introduced, the relation of non-relatedness, as it were. It is called **logical independence** and holds between two sentences if and only if all four truth value combinations are possible. This amounts to A entailing neither B nor not-B and B entailing neither A nor not-A.

When one tries to find examples for pairs of contingent sentences that are related by one of the logical relations (except independence), one will realize that, now indeed, this is only possible if the sentences bear some meaning connection. For non-contingent sentences to carry such a relation there must be some reason. For example, if two sentences have the same truth conditions and are hence logically equivalent, then they must have similar meanings, because it is the meanings that determine the truth conditions. It cannot be formally proved that a logical relation between contingent sentences is always due to some meaning connection. But the assumption is one of the most important working hypotheses for semantics. It can be formulated as follows:

> **Working hypothesis**
> If two contingent sentences exhibit the relation of entailment, equiva-
> lence, contrariety or contradiction, this is due to a particular way in
> which their meanings are related.

The restriction on contingent sentences does not impose any serious
limitation on the field of semantic research. Therefore, logical relationships
are very valuable instruments for the investigation of meaning relations not
only of sentences but also of words (to which we will turn in 4.5). However,
as we have seen in connection with non-contingent sentences, logical
relations do not in themselves constitute meaning relations – a point we
will return to in 4.6.

4.4 Sentential logic

Sentential logic[8] (SL, for short) is a simple formal system with rules for
combining sentences, usually simply represented by variables, by means of
certain basic connectives and interpreting the results in terms of truth and
falsity. Needless to say, the Principle of Polarity is assumed to hold: every
simple or complex SL sentence is either true or false. The only connectives
to be considered are those whose meaning can be exhaustively described in
terms of the truth values of the sentences they are applied to. (This rules out
connectives such as *because*, *before*, *but*, *nevertheless*, etc.) We will only
introduce two such connectives: $\neg$ for negation and $\wedge$ for ⟩and⟨. Usually,
more connectives are introduced but we will not need more than these two.

DEFINITION
Negation in SL
If A is an SL sentence, then $\neg$A is also one.
$\neg$A is true iff A is false.
Conjunction in SL
If A and B are SL sentences, then (A $\wedge$ B) is also one.
(A $\wedge$ B) is true iff A and B are both true.

The negation of A, $\neg$A, is read 'not A' (or, using the Latin word for *not*, 'non
A') and the conjunction of A and B, (A $\wedge$ B), is read 'A and B'. With these two
rules, we can form complex expressions such as:

(39) a. $\neg\neg$A
  b.   (A $\wedge$ B)
  c.   (A $\wedge$ $\neg$A)
  d. $\neg$(A $\wedge$ $\neg$B), etc.

It follows directly from the definitions above that certain complex sentences are logically false or logically true *due to their form*. For example, all sentences of the form $(A \wedge \neg A)$ are logically false: according to the definition of negation, A and $\neg A$ necessarily have different truth values; therefore they can never be both true, and so $(A \wedge \neg A)$ is necessarily false. Among the logically false sentences in (15), (15a) has this form. The other three cases call for different explanations.

4.5 Logical relations between words

The logical relations between sentences can easily be exploited to establish corresponding relations between lexemes and other expressions below sentence level. To be precise, this is possible for all predicate expressions (see Chapter 6); these include all nouns, verbs and adjectives, i.e. the major classes of content words. For establishing logical relations between two expressions, we insert them into an appropriate test sentence and check the resulting logical relations. Such test sentences are illustrated in Table 4.9. Since the words to be checked can apply to quite different sorts of things, it is convenient to use variables in the test sentences.[9]

	Test word	**Test sentence**
count noun	*car*	*x is a car*
mass noun	*mud*	*x is mud*
adjective	*dirty*	*x is dirty*
intransitive verb	*smell*	*x smells*
transitive verb	*sell*	*x sells y*

Table 4.9 Test sentences

Logical equivalence

Let us first consider the case of equivalence. Examples are hard to find, but here are two:

(40) A *x is a female adult*   ⇔   B *x is a woman*
(41) A *x costs a lot*   ⇔   B *x is expensive*

What follows from these equivalences for the meanings of the expressions? (40) means that whatever can be called a woman can be called a female adult and vice versa. More technically: the potential referents of *woman* and *female adult* are the same, i.e. the expressions have the same denotation.

Similarly, due to (41) *costs a lot* and *is expensive* are true of the subject referents under the same conditions. Rather than introducing a new term, we will extend the notion of logical equivalence to words and complex expressions such as *female adult* and *cost a lot*.[10] Two such expressions are logically equivalent iff they have the same denotation.

Logical subordination

Suppose the test sentences for two expressions result in entailment:

(42) a. A *x is a duck*   ⇒   B *x is a bird*
     b. A *x enlarges y*   ⇒   B *x changes y*

According to (42a), whatever can be called a duck can be called a bird. Put more technically, the denotation of *duck*, the more specific term, is included in the denotation of the more general term *bird*. Due to the second entailment, the denotation of *bend* is part of the denotation of *change*. Every act of bending something is an act of changing it.

The resulting relation between a general term and a specific term will be called **logical subordination** (*subordination* for short): an expression A is a subordinate of an expression B, iff the denotation of A is included in the denotation of B (Figure 4.1). If A is a subordinate of B, B is called a *superordinate* of A. In set-theoretical terms, A is a subordinate of B if and only if the denotation of A is a *subset* of the denotation of B. In the cognitive terms to be introduced in Chapter 9, the denotation of a subordinate term is a *subcategory* of the denotation of its superordinate terms.

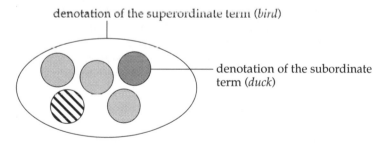

denotation of the superordinate term (*bird*)

denotation of the subordinate term (*duck*)

Figure 4.1 Denotations of *duck and bird*

Logical incompatibility

Usually, a superordinate expression does not have just one subordinate, but a set of co-subordinates. For example, all the other terms for types of birds, such as *owl, pigeon, penguin, sparrow, swan* are co-subordinates of *duck*. In addition, they are mutually exclusive: *x is a swan* logically excludes *x is an owl*, and so on for all other pairs. Two terms A and B will be called **logically incompatible** iff their denotations have no elements in common. The

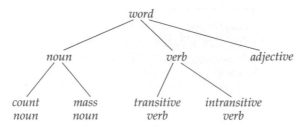

Figure 4.2 Hierarchy of word class terms

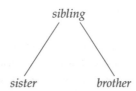

Figure 4.3 Hierarchy of sibling terms

denotation of *swan* could be represented by the hatched circle in Figure 4.1: an area included within the area for the denotation of *bird* and not overlapping with the area symbolizing the denotations of co-subordinates.

The representation of lexemes in hierarchy trees such as in Figures 4.2 and 4.3, a hierarchy for linguistic terms, is based on the two relations of subordination and incompatibility. Since trees are used for representing different relations and structures (e.g. syntactic trees for the syntactic structure), it is important to realize what the arrangement in a given kind of tree signifies. In trees that depict lexical hierarchies, the vertical lines express logical subordination. Co-subordinates are arranged at the same level and understood to be mutually incompatible.

The tree in Figure 4.2 is incomplete in several respects. Further subordinates of *word* could be added, e.g. *article* or *preposition*. We could also expand the tree by adding subordinates of *adjective*. Further subdivisions would be possible below the lowest level, distinguishing sorts of count nouns, intransitive verbs, etc. By contrast, the small tree in Figure 4.3 is, in a sense, complete. In English, there are only two specific terms for siblings: no further co-subordinates can be added to *sister* and *brother*. Also there are no English words for subordinates of *brother* and *sister*. (Other languages, e.g. Hungarian and Japanese, have different terms for elder and younger sisters and brothers.)

Logical complementarity

The subordinates in Figure 4.3 are not only incompatible but form an exhaustive alternative, a strict *either-or* constellation. The corresponding test sentences *x is a sister* and *x is a brother* are logical contradictories – provided we presuppose that x is a sibling. This logical relation is called

Corresponding sentence relation	Word relation	Example
equivalence	**equivalence**	*woman – female adult*
entailment	**subordination**	*bird – duck*
contrariety	**incompatibility**	*duck – swan*
contradiction	**complementarity**	*member – non-member*

Table 4.10 Logical relations between words

logical complementarity: two terms A and B are logically **complementary** iff their denotations have no elements in common and together exhaust the set of possible cases. The notion of complementarity is always relative to a given domain of relevant cases. Absolute complementarity does not occur in natural languages. Take any ordinary noun, for example, *banana*; try to imagine an absolute complementary, say, *non-banana*. The denotation of *non-banana* would have to exclude bananas, but include everything else that could be denoted by any noun whatsoever plus all those things for which we do not have any expressions at all. A word with such a meaning is hard to imagine. Good examples for complementarity are *member–non-member* (domain: persons), *girl–boy* (domain: children), *child–adult* (domain: persons), *indoors–outdoors* (domain: locations). A survey of the logical relations at word and sentence level is given in Table 4.10.

4.6 Logic and meaning

It will now be shown why logical relations are not to be confused with meaning relations such as synonymy and hyponymy (a term to be explained below).

4.6.1 The semantic status of logical equivalence

It is tempting to assume that logical equivalence means identity of meaning, and in fact this is often done in the literature.[11] On a closer look, however, this turns out to be wrong. All logical notions are based on truth conditions and denotations. The first point to be stated is that logical notions only concern descriptive meaning. Second, truth conditions and denotations do not even exhaust this part of the meaning.

Truth conditions and non-descriptive meaning

As to the first point, recall the criteria for correct use with respect to descriptive, social and expressive meaning that were stated in Table 2.5. If, for example, one describes the truth conditions of *this is a barbecue*, one thereby gives a description of the denotation of the word *barbecue*. This, in turn, says something about its descriptive meaning, which determines the denotation. In this sense, truth conditions bear on descriptive meaning. But they have nothing to do with social meaning and expressive meaning. For example, the German sentence and the English sentence in (43) differ in the meanings of the pronouns *Sie* and *you* (cf. 2.3.1; we take the rest of the sentences to be equivalent, in particular the verbs *verhaften* and *arrest*).

(43) a. *Ich werde Sie verhaften.*
　　b. *I will arrest you.*

The German pronoun of address *Sie* has the same descriptive meaning as *you*, but in addition a social meaning indicating a formal relationship between speaker and addressee(s). The difference, however, does not bear on the truth conditions. If the speaker of the German sentence used the informal pronoun of address instead, the resulting sentence would have exactly the same truth conditions, although it might be socially inappropriate. Similarly, expressions with the same descriptive but different expressive meanings do not differ in truth conditions. Opting, for example, for (44b) rather than (44a) is not a matter of the objectively given facts but of subjective preference.

(44) a. *John didn't take his car away.*
　　b. *John didn't take his fucking car away.*

Consequently, words and sentences may be logically equivalent, but differ in non-descriptive meaning. We will now see, that logical equivalence does not even mean equal descriptive meaning.

Logical equivalence and descriptive meaning

As we saw in 4.2, all logically true sentences have identical truth conditions. Hence they are all logically equivalent. Clearly, logically true sentences may differ in descriptive meaning (cf. the examples in (14)). The same, of course, holds for logically false sentences (see (15)). Thus non-contingent sentences provide a particularly drastic class of examples of logically equivalent sentences with different meanings. But even for contingent sentences, equivalence does not mean that they have the same descriptive meaning. To see the point, consider once more sentences (25)–(27), here repeated for convenience:

(25)　A *Today is Monday.*　　⇔　B *Yesterday was Sunday.*
(26)　A *The bottle is half empty.*　⇔　B *The bottle is half full.*
(27)　A *Everyone will lose.*　　⇔　B *No-one will win.*

Intuitively, in the three cases A and B do not have the same meaning, but somehow they amount to the same. They express the same condition in different ways. It is part of the meaning of (25A) that the sentence refers to the day that includes the moment of utterance, and part of the meaning of (25B) that it refers to the immediately preceding day. (26B) highlights what is in the bottle, and (26A) what is not. (27A) is about losing, (27B) about winning. What determines the situation expressed by a sentence, i.e. its proposition, are the elements of the situation and how they are interlinked. The situation expressed by (25A) contains the day of the utterance as an element and specifies it as a Monday. The situation expressed by (25B) is parallel, but different. More than simply defining truth conditions, a natural language sentence represents a certain way of describing a situation which then results in certain truth conditions. Whenever we speak, we make a choice among different ways of expressing ourselves, of putting things; we are not just encoding the facts we want to communicate. There is usually more than one way to depict certain facts.

Although less obvious, the analogue holds for lexemes. For example, in German the big toe is called either *großer Zeh* (›big toe‹) or *dicker Zeh* (›thick toe‹) or, by some people, *großer Onkel* (›big uncle‹). In Serbo-Croat the big toe is called *nožni prst*, ›foot thumb‹. These would all be terms with different descriptive meanings because they describe what they denote in different ways. More examples of logically equivalent expressions with different descriptive meanings can be easily found if one compares terms from different languages which have the same denotation. English has the peculiar term *fountain pen* for what in German is called *Füllfederhalter* (›fill feather holder‹, i.e. a ›feather holder‹ that can be filled) or just *Füller* (›filler‹, in the meaning of ›something one fills‹); in Japanese, the same item is called *mannenhitsu*, literally ›ten-thousand-years brush‹. For a bra, German has the term *Büstenhalter*, ›bust holder‹; the French equivalent *soutien-gorge* literally means ›throat(!) support‹, while Spanish women wear a ›subjugator‹ (*sujetador*) or ›support‹ (*sostén*) and speakers of the New Guinea creole language Tok Pisin put on a ›prison of the breasts‹ (*kalabus bilong susu*). Different languages may adopt different naming strategies for the same categories of things. An interesting field is terms for technical items. The English term *power button* (e.g. of an amplifier) rests on the concept ›button‹, which is borrowed from the domain of clothing, and connects it in an unspecific way with the concept ›power‹, again a metaphor. The equivalent French term is *interrupteur d'alimentation*, literally ›interrupter of supply‹; the object is primarily named after its function of interrupting the current – a somewhat arbitrary choice, since the power button can also be used for switching the device on; the second part *d'alimentation* specifies what is interrupted, namely the ›alimentation‹, a metaphorical term for power supply, originally meaning ›feeding‹, ›nourishing‹. German has yet a different solution for naming that part: *Netzschalter*, ›net switcher‹, where ›Netz‹ is the mains.

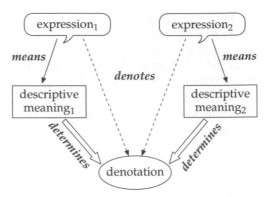

Figure 4.4 Logically equivalent expressions with different descriptive meanings

Thus, let us fix the following important point:

> Logical equivalence is not a sufficient criterion for having the same meaning.

In other words: logically equivalent expressions are not necessarily synonymous (3.3). Equivalence is not even sufficient for descriptive synonymy. The converse is, of course, true: since the descriptive meaning determines truth conditions and denotations, two expressions with the same descriptive meaning necessarily are logically equivalent. Employing the semiotic triangle in a somewhat distorted form, Figure 4.4 displays a configuration of two equivalent expressions with different descriptive meanings.

4.6.2 The semantic status of logical entailment

The fact that the denotation of a logical subordinate is a subset of the denotation of the superordinate may be due to a reverse relation between the descriptive *meanings* of the two terms. Let us roughly consider the descriptive meaning as a set of conditions that a potential referent must fulfil. Then a 'duck' must fulfil all conditions a 'bird' must fulfil plus those particular conditions that distinguish ducks from other sorts of birds. The descriptive meaning of *duck* in this sense contains [all the conditions which make up] the descriptive meaning of the superordinate term *bird*. This is what we intuitively mean when we say that the term *duck* is 'more specific' than the term *bird*. Generally, A ⇒ B may be due to the fact that the meaning of A fully contains the meaning of B. This is the case, for example, for the sentences in (45): A has the same meaning as B except for the addition that the beer is cool.

(45) A *There's cool beer in the fridge.*
      B *There's beer in the fridge.*

However, since entailment is only a matter of truth conditions, there need not be such a close connection between sentences or other expressions related by entailment. (46) is a simple example of two sentences A and B where A entails B, but the meaning of B is not contained in the meaning of A:

(46) A *Today is Sunday.*
      B *Tomorrow is not Friday.*

The analogue holds for logical subordination between words. Consider, for example, the expressions *son of x's mother-in-law* and *x's husband*. One's husband is necessarily a son of one's mother-in-law. Hence, *x's husband* is a subordinate of *son of x's mother-in-law*. But while the meaning of *x's husband*, i.e. the definition of the potential referent, is something like ⟩man x is married to⟨, the meaning of *son of x's mother-in-law* is ⟩male child of the mother of the person x is married to⟨. The latter contains the mother-in-law as an element of the definition, but this element is not part of the definition of *husband*. Therefore, the meaning of the superordinate is not part of the meaning of the subordinate.

Some authors use the term *hyponymy* for logical subordination.[12] In this volume, *hyponymy* will be reserved for the meaning relation that holds between A and B if the meaning of A is fully contained in the meaning of B. The notion will be formally introduced in the next chapter. The point to be stated here, in analogy to the relationship between logical equivalence and identity of meaning, is thus:

> Logical entailment and subordination do not necessarily mean that the meaning of one expression is included in the meaning of the other.

Analogues hold for the other relations, logical incompatibility and complementarity. For example, as we could see in connection with (32) and (33), A and B can be logical contradictories without one being the negation of the other (cf. the definition of negation on pp. 61–2).

4.6.3 Logic and semantics

The discussion has shown that logical properties and relations do not directly concern meaning. Rather, they concern denotations and truth conditions, an aspect of linguistic expressions which is *determined* by meaning, more precisely by descriptive meaning. A logical approach to meaning is therefore limited as follows:

- It does not capture those parts of meaning that do not contribute to the determination of truth and reference. Expressions with the same descriptive meaning but different social or expressive meanings cannot be distinguished by logical methods.
- It does not capture descriptive meaning itself, but only some effects of it.
- It does not capture differences between the descriptive meanings of expressions with identical truth conditions or denotations. In particular, it fails to yield any insights into the meanings of non-contingent sentences.

If the limitations of the logical approach, and the nature of the results it is able to produce, are carefully kept in mind, it is, however, a powerful instrument for the semanticist. Due to the fact that truth conditions and reference are determined by descriptive meaning, the logical approach can produce the following kinds of results:

- If two expressions are not logically equivalent, their meanings are different.
- If an expression A does not entail an expression B, the meaning of B is not part of the meaning of A.
- If one of the logical relations holds between two expressions, their descriptive meanings must be closely related.

The logical approach therefore provides us with simple instruments to test expressions for their meaning relations with others. This makes logical relations very important data for semantic analysis. If two expressions are equivalent, or if one entails, or excludes, the other, this is a fact which semantic analysis has to account for.

Checklist

Law of Contradiction	logical entailment
Law of the Excluded Middle	logical equivalence
Principle of Polarity	logical contradictories
truth	logical contraries
truth conditions	logical independence
truth value	logical equivalence
negation	subordinate
contingent	superordinate
logically true	complementarity
logically false	logical incompatibility

Exercises

1   For the following sentences, which one is the proper negation, A or B? Check the truth conditions of A and B: which one is necessarily true if the positive sentence is false?

(a) *It's always raining here.*   A *It's never raining here.*
   B *It's not always raining here.*
(b) *All the kids are sick.*   A *All the kids are not sick.*
   B *Not all the kids are sick.*
(c) *Somebody helped me.*   A *Nobody helped me.*
   B *Somebody did not help me.*
(d) *She's still here.*   A *She's not yet here.*
   B *She isn't here anymore.*

2   Which of the following statements are true, which ones are false?
   (a) If A is logically true, then not-A is logically false.
   (b) If A is contingent, then not-A is either logically true or logically false.
   (c) A and not-A are always logically contrary.
   (d) If A entails not-B, then B entails not-A.
   (e) It is logically impossible that A entails not-A.
3   Define logical equivalence, logical contrariety and logical contradiction in terms of logical entailment.
4   Check the following pairs of sentences A and B: which truth-value combinations are possible? Do they represent cases of logical entailment, equivalence, contrariety, contradiction or none of these relations?
   (a) A *John sold the book to Mary.*   B *Mary bought the book.*
   (b) A *I turned the light off.*   B *It's dark now.*
   (c) A *Many liked the show.*   B *Nobody liked the show.*
   (d) A *Some of the kids are sick.*   B *Some of the kids are not sick.*
   (e) A *Only 50 per cent of the people here have a job.*
   B *Fifty per cent of the people here don't have a job.*
5   Which logical relation applies to the following pairs of words?
   (a) *vehicle, bus*   (b) *bus, train*
   (c) *married, unmarried*   (d) *pleasant, unpleasant*
   (e) *buy, sell*   (f) *above, below*
6   Which possible parts of meaning are not captured by the logical method and why are they not?
7   Discuss the limits of the logical method for the investigation of descriptive meaning.
8   Discuss the ways in which the logical method is useful for the investigation of word meaning.

Further reading

Cruse (1986, Chapter 4) for logical relations between words. Partee et al. (1993, Chapter 6) for definitions of the logical properties and relations with respect to logic.

Notes

1   When we talk of sentences in this chapter, it is tacitly understood that we talk of *declarative* sentences. The question of truth or falsity does not immediately apply to interrogative sentences (questions), imperative sentences (commands) or other non-declarative sentence types.

2   This trait of human language will play an important part in the discussion of prototype theory in 9.5.

3   In other terminologies, logically true sentences are called *tautologies* (*tautological*) or *analytical* and logically false sentences *contradictions* (*contradictory*). Informally logically false sentences were referred to as 'self-contradictory' above.

4   As we have seen in 4.1.1, sentences such as (15a) and (15b) are readily reinterpreted as to make *some* sense. But this does not keep such sentences from being logically false in their literal reading.

5   An alternative term is *logical consequence*.

6   *If and only if*, sometimes abbreviated *iff*, connects two conditions that are equivalent. *If and only if* constructions are the proper form of precise definitions.

7   There is no connection between the notion of a 'transitive relation' and the syntactic notion of a 'transitive verb'.

8   Sentential logic is also called *propositional logic* and *statement logic*. We prefer the term *sentential logic*, because the units of the system are sentences, rather than statements or propositions. It is sentences which are connected by connectives, and it is sentences for which the logical notions are defined.

9   In English, count nouns and mass nouns differ as follows: count nouns usually allow both singular and plural forms, they require an article when they are in the singular; mass nouns allow only for the singular (when a mass noun is used in the plural, its meaning is shifted as to yield a count noun reading), they can be used as 'bare mass nouns' without an article.

10   Some authors consider logical equivalence a variant of synonymy, for example Cruse (1986, p. 88), who uses the term *cognitive synonymy* for the same relation. Synonymy and equivalence must, however, be distinguished, a point we will come back to in 4.6.1.

11   For example in Lyons (1995, p. 63).

12   For example, Lyons (1977), Cruse (1986).

Meaning relations

5

It is very difficult to describe the meanings of lexemes or sentences explicitly. In fact, semanticists do not even agree as to what kind of entities meanings are. (The 'mentalist' point of view presented here, which regards meanings as concepts, is the prevalent view but not uncontroversial.) It is, however, relatively easy to establish meaning *relations* between sentences or expressions. One influential position, the structuralist position, holds that the description of meaning is exhausted by the description of meaning relations (7.1.1). We do not share this view. This notwithstanding, meaning relations are most important semantic data.

5.1 Hyponymy

5.1.1 The meaning relation

Hyponymy proper can be defined as follows: an expression A is a **hyponym** of an expression B iff the meaning of B is part of the meaning of A and A is a subordinate of B. In addition to the meaning of B, the meaning of A must contain further specifications, rendering the meaning of A, the hyponym, more specific than the meaning of B. If A is a hyponym of B, B is called a **hyperonym** of A.[1] Hyponymy is a relation between words that results from a relation between their meanings and leads to a relation between their denotations: the meaning of the hyponym contains the meaning of the hyponym, and the denotation of the hyponym is a subcategory of the denotation of the hyperonym. The relations are shown in Figure 5.1 which integrates the semiotic triangles for a hyponym/hyperonym pair.

Examples of hyponymy are numerous. One group consists of pairs of subordinates and superordinates in hierarchies like the ones in Figures 4.2 and 4.3. Another group of cases is constituted by pairs of simple lexemes and compounds containing the simple lexeme as their second part, such as

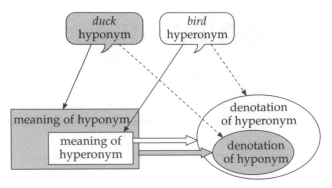

Figure 5.1 Hyponymy

sentence meaning (hyponym)–*meaning* (hyperonym), *river boat–boat*, etc. It must be cautioned, however, that not all compounds are hyponyms of the corresponding simple words: a dragonfly or a barfly is not a fly, a cauliflower is not a flower. Pairs of hyponyms beyond any doubt are expressions resulting from simple syntactic combinations such as adding an adjective to a noun or an adverb to a verb: for example *green cap* and *cap*, *tall girl* and *girl*, *walk slowly* and *walk*, etc.[2]

5.1.2 Regular compounds

One of the major mechanisms of word formation, i.e. the part of grammar that rules the formation of new words out of the ones available in the lexicon, is (morphological) composition.[3] It allows, among others, the formation of compound nouns out of two nouns. For regular compounds, there is a corresponding semantic rule which can be described as follows: a regular compound has two parts, the first is called the **modifier**, the second the **head**; the modifier adds a specification to the meaning of the head noun. For example, in *apple juice*, the modifier *apple* adds the specification ›produced from apples‹ to the concept ›juice‹. Similarly, *park bench* means ›bench in a park‹, *headache pill* ›pill for treating headache‹, *company flat* ›flat provided by a company‹, *flower shop* ›shop where flowers are sold‹ and so on. In any case, the meaning of the head noun is fully contained in the meaning of a regular compound and the compound is a logical subordinate of the head. Hence the compound is a hyponym of the head noun.

The meaning of the modifier is also bound into the meaning of the compound, but not in the same way as the meaning of the head. Therefore the resulting meaning relation between the compound and the modifier is not hyponymy (apple juice is not an apple, a flower shop not a flower, etc.). Rather, the meaning relation is a special relation to be defined in terms of what the referents of modifier and compound have to do with each other. The meaning relation between *flower* and *flower shop* is: referents of the first

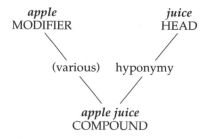

Figure 5.2 Meaning relations between a regular compound and its parts

are sold in referents of the second. Special though this meaning relation is, it provides a basis for a general pattern of composition (cf. analogous compounds such as *stationary shop, ticket counter, hot dog stand*). The other examples mentioned, *park bench, company flat* and *apple juice* represent other patterns. Figure 5.2 displays the meaning relations between a regular compound and its parts.

5.2 Oppositions

If people are asked to specify the opposites of words like *old, buy* and *aunt*, they will answer spontaneously. The answers will vary, however, because words may have different kinds of opposites. The intuitive notion of opposites covers a range of different meaning relations. In this section, we will take a closer look at them. The technical term for such relations is **oppositions**.

This is what people answer if they are asked to give the opposites of *old, buy* and *aunt*:

(1) *old*:   (i) *new*   (ii) *young*
    buy: (i) *sell*   (ii) *steal, borrow, rent*
    aunt: (i) *uncle*   (ii) *nephew, niece*

The two opposites of *old* reveal that *old* is polysemous. *Old* as an opposite of *young* relates to age, primarily of living creatures. But the two opposites can also be used for inanimate entities that are metaphorically conceived as subject to developments such as growth, ripening and ageing (cf. *a young nation, an old wine, a young language*). In such cases, *young* and *old* denote early and late stages of development, respectively. However, *old* can also be used for cars, books, buildings, words. *Old* then means that the respective object has been in use for a long time (probably resulting in wear and tear, in becoming out of date, etc.); *new* is the opposite of this meaning variant. As to their relation to *old*, both opposites are of the same kind: *old* denotes one extreme on a scale, while *young* and *new* denote the other extreme. The difference between *new* and *young* and the two corresponding meanings of *old* concerns the underlying scale.

What counts as the opposite of *buy* is less clear. If we take a look at the second set of verbs (*steal, borrow, rent*), we realize that all these verbs denote alternative ways of acquiring things. *Borrow* and *rent* contrast with *buy* in that the transfer of possession is (meant to be) temporary. This meaning element is absent in case of *buy* and *steal*. *Buy* and *rent* involve a compensation with money, *steal* and *borrow* do not. The three opposites under (ii) are of the same kind: they are alternatives in certain respects, but they do not denote the other extreme on a scale.

The opposite *sell*, however, is of a different kind. There are two ways of viewing the relation between *buy* and *sell*. First, any event of buying is at the same time an event of selling: if x buys something from y, then y sells that thing to x. To conceive of an event as an instance of selling rather than buying is just a converse way of conceptualizing this transfer: an object z changes from the possession of y into the possession of x, while x pays y an equivalent amount of money in exchange for z. *Buy* describes the event as an action on the part of the new possessor x, *sell* describes it as an action on the part of the original possessor y. They express the same with reversed roles. Alternatively, we can compare x buying something with x selling it. Then, *buy* and *sell* are opposed in the sense that *buy* means x's moving into the possession of the object and *sell* x's moving out of it. Viewed in this way, the two verbs express opposite directions of a certain kind of change, metaphorically conceived of as a movement of the subject referent.

Whenever we think of oppositions in the intuitive sense, we try to find something in common to the meanings of the two expressions and a crucial point in which their meanings differ. In the case of the opposition *aunt/uncle*, the point in common is the kind of kinship relation: being a sibling of a parent, the spouse of a sibling of a parent or some other relative one generation back but not in direct line. What differs is the sex of the relative. If we consider the pairs *aunt/nephew* and *aunt/niece*, we encounter the same kind of relation as between *buy* and *sell* under the first, reversed-roles, perspective: if x is an aunt of y, then y is a nephew or niece of x. The kinship link between x and y is the same, but *aunt* refers to one side of the link and *nephew/niece* to the other. The relation is not strictly reversed, since the terms *aunt*, *nephew* and *niece* also contain a specification of sex. We cannot say that if x is an aunt of y, then y is a nephew of x, because y could also be a niece of x. Nor can we say that if x is a nephew of y, then y is an aunt of x, because y could also be an uncle.

5.2.1 Antonyms

Two expressions are called **antonyms** iff they denote two opposite extremes out of a range of possibilities. The prototypical examples are pairs of adjectives such as *old/young*, *old/new*, *big/small*, *thick/thin*, *good/bad*,

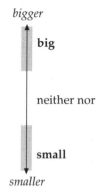

Figure 5.3 Antonymy of *big* and *small*

light/dark, difficult/easy. Their meanings can be illustrated by means of a scale of age, size, diameter, quality, brightness, difficulty, etc. which is open on both sides. One might object that scales such as the scale of size are not open at the lower end, i.e. that zero size delimits the scale at its bottom. However, in our imagination, things can be smaller and smaller; for every small thing there can be something smaller. There is no smallest size and hence no lower bound of the scale of size. The scale of size asymptotically approaches zero size, but does not include it. (Note that we cannot say something is 'small' if it has no size at all.) One of the adjectives denotes the upper section, the other one the lower section of the scale. There is a neutral middle interval where neither expression applies. Every value on the scale that lies above the neutral interval counts as, for example, 'big', every value below the neutral interval counts as the opposite, e.g. 'small' (cf. Figure 5.3).

Antonyms are logical contraries but not contradictories (4.3): the negation of one term is not equivalent to the opposite term. For example, *not big* does not mean the same as *small*, something may be 'not big and not small'. *X is small* entails *x is not big*, and *x is big* entails *x is not small*, but *x is not small* does not entail *x is big*. Words for the neutral case are rare and rather artificial recent inventions (*middle-aged, medium-sized*). Normally, the neutral case can only be expressed by such cumbersome expressions as *neither difficult nor easy*. Antonymous adjectives of the type illustrated in Figure 5.3 are called scalar adjectives. They are 'gradable' and therefore allow for the full range of adjectival forms and constructions: comparative (*bigger than*), superlative (*biggest*), equative (*as big as*), or modifications such as *very big*.

In very many cases, the antonym of an adjective is formed by prefixing *un-* or its Latin-origin equivalent *in-/im-/ir-/il-*: *pleasant/unpleasant, likely/unlikely, adequate/inadequate, probable/improbable, rational/irrational, logical/illogical*. In each case, the unprefixed adjective is felt to be positive, not in the sense of an expressive meaning part, but as intuitively denoting the section at the upper end of the scale, while the prefixed opposite is the negative counterpart at the lower end of the scale. We shall see below that pairs of this form (A vs *un*-A, etc.) are not necessarily antonyms. The prefixation also occurs with pairs of expressions that form a different type of opposition.

Antonymy is not restricted to adjectives. There are antonymous pairs of nouns such as *war/peace*, *love/hate* and some antonymous pairs of verbs: *love/hate*, or *encourage/discourage*. The pair *all/nothing* is antonymous as are pairs of adverbs such as *always/never*, *often/seldom*, *everywhere/nowhere*.

5.2.2 Directional opposites

Pairs such as *in front of/behind*, *left/right*, *above/below* have much in common with antonyms. For each such pair there is a point of reference from which one looks in opposite directions on a certain axis. Imagine yourself standing in a normal upright position, your head not turned or bent. Then the direction in which you look is what is denoted by *in front of (you)* while *behind (you)* denotes the opposite direction. The two directions are distinguished in several ways: the body has a front, which includes the face, the breast, etc., and it has a back; when one walks in the usual way, one walks into the direction that is *in front of* one. Thus, the body defines an axis in space, the front–back axis, or primary horizontal axis. Another axis defined by the body is the vertical head–feet axis. The extension of the direction from the body centre to the head defines the direction *above*, the opposite direction is denoted by *below*. Finally, the body with its two eyes, two ears, two arms, two legs and its general lateral symmetry defines another horizontal axis, the left–right axis. The three axes and how they relate to the corresponding expressions are depicted in Figure 5.4.

The type of opposition represented by *in front of/behind* is called **directional** opposition. Directional opposites are related to opposite

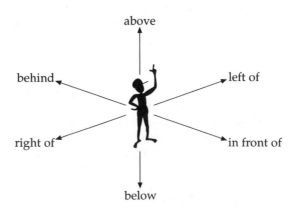

Figure 5.4 Directions

directions on a common axis. Further examples that involve the vertical axis are: *top/bottom, high/low, up/down, upstairs/downstairs, uphill/downhill, rise/fall, ascend/descend* and many more. Examples related to the primary horizontal axis are *forwards/backwards, advance/retreat*.

A similar axis is the time axis. We talk about things happening 'before' vs 'after' a certain time, or 'later' vs 'earlier'. Thus, pairs such as *before/after, past/future, since/until, yesterday/tomorrow, last/next, precede/follow* are directional opposites related to the time axis. A further case is provided by the verb tenses past and future: the past tense locates the situation expressed before the 'now' of the utterance, the future tense locates it after 'now'.

Also related to time are pairs of directional opposites like *tie/untie, pack/unpack, wrap/unwrap, dress/undress, put on/put off, get on/get off, switch on/switch off, embark/disembark, charge/discharge, enter/leave, begin/stop, start/finish, fall asleep/wake up, appear/disappear, open/close,* and many more. One member denotes the coming about, or bringing about, of a certain state, while the other member denotes a process or action by which the state is ended. Among the examples discussed earlier, the pair *buy/sell* in its second interpretation is of this type.

5.2.3 Complementaries

The type of opposition represented by *aunt/uncle, buy/rent* or *buy/steal* is known as complementary opposition. Complementary opposites are logically complementary (4.5): the negation of one term is equivalent to the other term, e.g. *not even* (of numbers) means the same as *odd*. Each expression denotes one out of the only two possibilities in some domain of cases. In this domain, complementary opposites represent an either-or alternative. Complementary adjectives are not gradable, they do not permit the comparative, superlative, equative form or modification with *very*, etc. (They are, however, sometimes used as though they were gradable: cf. *Mary is more married than John is*. What happens here is a meaning shift from the original meaning to a gradable meaning, triggered by the use of the comparative form.[4]) Examples are *female/male* (as a specification of sex), *even/odd* (of numbers), *possible/impossible, free/occupied*. As some of the examples show, prefixation with *un-* or *in-* is also used for the formation of complementary opposites.

Complementarity more typically occurs with nouns, e.g. pairs of terms for persons of opposite sex, or pairs such as *member/non-member, official/non-official*. The meanings of two complementaries are identical except for one crucial feature in which they differ (cf. the examples *aunt/uncle* or *buy/rent*).

5.2.4 Heteronyms

So-called heteronymy involves more than two expressions. A typical example is the set of terms for the days of the week, the set of basic colour terms (8.4) or terms for kinds of animals, plants, vehicles, etc. A set of heteronymous terms jointly covers a wider range of possibilities. Logically, two heteronyms are contraries: if x is Sunday, it cannot be Monday; if x is a dog, it cannot be a duck, etc. But unlike antonymy, heteronymy is not related to scales; heteronyms are not opposite extremes, but just members of a set of different expressions which often have a common hyperonym. There are large fields of heteronymous terms, such as the sets of co-subordinates in larger hierarchies: terms for plants, flowers, animals, birds, breeds of dogs, kinds of clothing, drinking vessels, food, vehicles, etc. Co-hyponyms occurring at the same level in a natural lexicalized hierarchy always form a set of heteronyms. Apart from nouns, there are many fields of heteronymous verbs, such as the different verbs of motion (*walk, run, fly, swim*), and verbs denoting human activities such as *eat, work, sleep, dance*, etc.

5.2.5 Converses

The pairs *buy/sell* in the first analysis and *aunt/niece-nephew* represent what are called converses. This kind of relation is restricted to expressions whose meanings involve two or more elements. Such terms express a relation in the widest sense, e.g. an action involving two participants, a comparison, or a kinship relation. **Converses** are defined as follows: two expressions are converses of each other if and only if they express the same relation with reversed roles. Examples are *above/below, before/after, borrow/lend, wife/husband*, as well as some of the technical terms introduced here: *entail/follow from, hyponym/hyperonym*. These pairs of expressions give rise to the following logical equivalences:

(2) *above/below*:   *x is above y*   ⇔   *y is below x*
    before/after: *x is before y*   ⇔   *y is after x*
    borrow/lend: *x borrows z from y*   ⇔   *y lends z to x*
    wife/husband: *x is the wife of y*   ⇔   *y is the husband of x*[5]
    entail/follow from: *x entails y*   ⇔   *y follows from x*
    hyponym/hyperonym: *x is a hyponym of y*   ⇔   *y is a hyperonym of x*

Converses differ from other types of opposites in that they do not correspond to a uniform logical relation. The pairs *above/below, before/after, borrow/lend, hyponym/hyperonym* are contraries (for example, *x is above y* logically excludes *x is below y*). *Wife* and *husband* constitute complementaries. *Entail* and *follow from* are logically independent because if A entails B it may or may not be the case that A also follows from B (i.e. B also entails A). Some expressions could even be considered their own converses, namely all terms which express symmetric relations, like *different from, sibling of, married to*. X is different from (a sibling of, or married to) y if and only if y is different from (a sibling of, or married to) x. To the extent that the term *opposition* is reserved for expressions with different meanings, converseness is restricted to expressions that denote asymmetric relations.

One major group of converses is provided by the comparative forms of antonymous adjectives:

(3) *thicker/thinner*:   *x is thicker than y ⟺ y is thinner than x*

For transitive verbs, passive constructions provide a general means of conversion:

(4) *watch/be watched by*:   *x watches y*   ⟺ *y is watched by x*

Related to the passive conversion is a productive pattern for pairs of converse nouns in English: noun derivations from verbs with the suffixes *-er* and *-ee*. For example, x is an employ*ee* of y iff y is the employ*er* of x.

As some of the examples may have shown, one and the same pair of expressions can constitute opposites of more than one type. *Buy/sell* can be considered converses as well as directional opposites. Many directional opposites, e.g. spatial prepositions such as *above/below, to the right of/to the left of*, etc. are at the same time converses.

Examples	Type	Characterization	Logical relation
big/small *war/peace* *to love/to hate*	**antonyms**	opposite extremes on a scale	contraries
above/below *before/after* *lock/unlock*	**directional opposites**	opposite directions on an axis	contraries
even/odd *girl/boy* *voter/non-voter*	**complementaries**	either-or alternatives within a given domain	complementaries
Monday/ Tuesday/. . . *red/green/ blue . . .*	**heteronyms**	more than two alternatives within a given domain	contraries
buy/sell *wife/husband* *bigger/smaller* *employer/ employee*	**converses**	the same with reversed roles (relations only)	(various logical relations)

Table 5.1 Types of oppositions

5.3 Lexical fields

5.3.1 The notion of a lexical field

Most lexical items form groups with other lexemes. Antonyms belong together as opposites, as do pairs of words such as *father* and *mother* or *adult* and *child*, or sets of words such as the terms for the days of the week, for colours, for numbers, for pieces of furniture or other kinds of things within one superordinate category.

Semantic theories of different orientations, in particular structuralist approaches (see Chapter 7), have tried to capture this phenomenon by the notion of a **lexical field**. The literature offers very different definitions. Here, the following informal characterization will be adopted. A lexical field is a group of lexemes that fulfils the following conditions:

- the lexemes are of the same word class;
- their meanings have something in common;
- they are interrelated by precisely definable meaning relations;
- the group is complete in terms of the relevant meaning relations.

5.3.2 Small fields

Some fields are quite small. For example, each pair of antonyms, such as *thick* and *thin* forms a lexical field of two members. The meanings of the two antonyms have in common that both relate to an end section of the same scale, they are related by antonymy, and the group is complete since there are no other adjectives that share this meaning part. Polysemous words with two different antonyms, such as *old* with its antonyms *new* and *young*, belong to two different fields, $old_1/young$ and old_2/new. Strictly speaking, it is not words that belong to lexical fields but words-with-a-certain-meaning.

Complementary expressions such as *girl* and *boy* also form a field of two, viz. the field of terms for children specified for sex. If we add the sex-neutral expression *child* (in its non-relational meaning ⟩non-adult⟨, not in its relational meaning ⟩offspring of⟨) to this field, we obtain the field of general terms for children. This field is structured by two different meaning relations: hyponymy between *child* and *boy*/*girl* and opposition in terms of sex between *girl* and *boy*. There are other lexical fields of three elements with the same structure, e.g. *adult*/*woman*/*man* or *horse*/*mare*/*stallion*. We can unite the field of general terms for children with the field for general terms for adults. The resulting six expressions form a field of six words linked by the additional meaning relation of opposition in terms of age that relates the members of the pairs *child*/*adult*, *girl*/*woman* and *boy*/*man*. The result is shown in Figure 5.5. Different meaning relations are symbolized by different kinds of arrows.

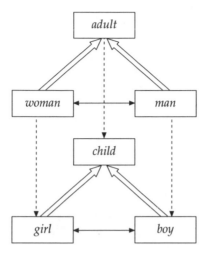

Figure 5.5 The lexical field of general person terms

The meaning relations that constitute a lexical field may be rather particular (e.g. the sex and age oppositions). The six prepositional expressions in Figure 5.4, *above, below, in front of, behind, right of, left of,* form a field of three opposite pairs relating to three axes in space that are orthogonal to each other. The names for the seven days of the week are not merely heteronyms but are interrelated by a cyclic order *Sunday* → *Monday* → *Tuesday* → *Wednesday* → *Thursday* → *Friday* → *Saturday* → *Sunday* → . . . The relation of one name to the others in terms of this cycle is part of its meaning. This is the reason why sentences such as (5) are logically true.

(5) *If today is Monday, tomorrow is Tuesday.*

5.3.3 Taxonomies

Terms for animals, plants, food or artefacts such as furniture, vehicles, clothes, musical instruments, etc. form lexical fields of considerable size. Their underlying structure is a hierarchy with two or more levels: a topmost hyperonym like *vehicle*, a level of general terms such as *car, bicycle, boat, aeroplane* and further levels of more specific kinds of cars, bicycles, boats, aeroplanes, etc. Such systems represent a special type of hierarchies, called **taxonomies**: subordinates in taxonomies (sometimes called taxonyms) are not just arbitrary subordinates but hyponyms that denote *sub-kinds*. The hierarchy of word class terms in Figure 4.2 is a taxonomy: nouns, verbs and adjectives are kinds of words, count nouns and mass nouns are kinds of nouns, etc. The hierarchy of the three sibling terms *sibling, sister* and *brother* in Figure 4.3, however, is not a taxonomy: brothers and sisters are not *kinds* of siblings. Referents of co-hyponyms in taxonomies differ in many

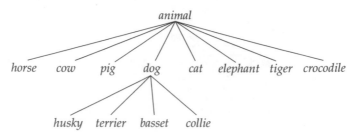

Figure 5.6 An incomplete taxonomy of animal terms

properties. Referents of co-hyponyms of small, often binary, hierarchies such as *sibling/sister/brother* differ only in one property, e.g. in sex. Figure 5.6 contains a section of the animal taxonomy. We will come back to taxonomies and their properties in 9.3.

5.3.4 Meronymies

Many objects in the world are conceived as a whole consisting of different parts. And correspondingly, our concepts for complex objects contain these parts as elements. One of the best examples of a complex object is the human body with its various parts, their subparts, and so on. 'Parts are not only sections of the body but defined in terms of specific functions. The head is the part of the body that carries the most important sense organs, i.e. eyes, ears, nose and tongue; it contains the brain, etc. The face forms the front side of the head; it contains the eyes, the nose and the mouth; it serves facial expression. Within the face, the mouth is used for eating, drinking, speaking, breathing, biting, kissing, smiling, etc., the tongue serves for articulation, tasting, licking, swallowing and other purposes.

A small section of the system of body-part terms in English is given in Figure 5.7. A system of this type is not to be confused with a hierarchy based on hyponymy. The vertical lines stand for the part–whole relation. In terms of potential referents, it means for example that a potential referent of *face* is part of a potential referent of *head*.

The technical term for the constituting meaning relation is **meronymy** (from ancient Greek *meron* ⟩part⟨; the term *partonomy* is also used), a system based on meronymies is called a mereological system, or mereology. If A is a **meronym** of B, then B is a **holonym** of A (from ancient Greek *holos* ⟩whole⟨). Meronymies involving nouns can be spelt out with the help of sentences of the form 'an A has a B', e.g. *a head has a face, a face has a mouth, a mouth has a tongue, a tongue has a tip*, etc. This is, however, not a reliable test for meronymy. Every person has a mother, a weight, an age, and so on, but these are not parts of the person.

There is a further important difference between lexical hierarchies and meronymic systems: unlike hyponymy and subordination, meronymy is

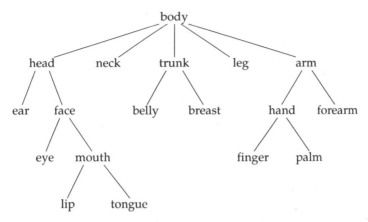

Figure 5.7 An incomplete meronymy of body part terms

not generally a transitive relation. Although in Figure 5.7 the term *eye* is linked to *face* and *face* is linked to *head*, this does not result in the same kind of link between *eye* and *head*. If 'part' is taken in the sense of constitutive part, i.e. something that essentially contributes to making up the whole, then an eye is not a part of the head, as the tongue is not a part of the face, or the face a part of the whole human body.

So much on meaning relations may suffice for the chapters to come. Meaning relations will play a prominent role in Chapter 7 on meaning components.

Checklist

hyponymy
   hyperonym
   regular compounds
oppositions
antonymy
scalar adjectives
directional opposition
complementaries

converses
heteronymy
lexical field
taxonomy
meronymy
   holonym
   part–whole relation

Exercises

1   What are meaning relations? How do they differ from logical relations?
2   If A is a hyponym of B, what does this mean for the way in which (a) the meanings, and (b) the denotations, of A and B are related to each other?
3   Explain the difference between hyponymy and meronymy.

4   Which special feature distinguishes taxonomies from arbitrary hierarchies based on hyponymy?
5   Determine the meaning relations that hold between the following pairs of words; it may be necessary to distinguish different meaning variants:
   (a) *table, bed*   (b) *get on, get off* (a train, etc.)
   (c) *top-down, bottom-up*   (d) *before, after*
   (e) *same, different*   (f)   *more, less*
6   The adjective *little* has several antonyms. Try to determine the pairs of opposites and the meaning *little* has in each case.

Further reading

Cruse (1986) on what is there called 'sense relations'. Foley (1997, Chapter 6) on kinship terms from an anthropological perspective (lexical fields of kinship terms were extensively studied in anthropological linguistics.)

Notes

[1]   Hyponymy is often not distinguished from logical subordination. This is the result of a tendency to restrict semantics to the investigation of descriptive meaning and this, in turn, to the logical aspects of meaning. See the discussion in 4.6, in particular 4.6.2.

[2]   But even here exceptions occur: an 'alleged thief' is not necessarily a thief, a 'former butcher' not necessarily a 'butcher'.

[3]   Not to be confused with semantic composition.

[4]   Thus meaning shifts (3.4) can even be triggered by the exceptional use of certain grammatical forms.

[5]   The equivalence only holds if it is assumed that spouses are of opposite sex.

[6]   The word *body* is ambiguous in that it can denote either the trunk or the trunk plus the head and the limbs; *body* is used in the latter meaning here.

Predication

6

We have so far considered the meanings of single words, either in isolation (Chapters 2 and 3) or in relation to other words of the same kind (Chapters 4 and 5). We will now have a look at the way in which different kinds of words interact to form meaningful phrases and sentences, addressing in more detail the mechanism of composition (1.2). We will see that a phrase or a sentence is by no means a simple sequence of words, one added to the other like beads on a string. Rather, sentences have a sophisticated structure in which each part plays its own role and interacts with the others in its own way. The focus will be on the central semantic property of verbs, nouns and adjectives: their providing predications about one or more of the potential referents of the sentence. An example in 6.1 will take us into the matter. After the introduction of the basic concepts in 6.2, we will take a look at the way in which the major types of verbs, nouns and adjectives participate in predication (6.3 and 6.4). After a very brief introduction of predicate logic notation in 6.5, the second half of the chapter will be concerned with general issues of predication. The notion of *semantic roles* is introduced in 6.6. It plays an important role in understanding the grammar of verbs. In 6.7, the discussion turns to preconditions of predication, so-called selectional restrictions, and their importance for sentence interpretation.

6.1 Predications contained in a sentence

Let us take a look at the following example, a simple English sentence, and try to determine the proposition it expresses.

(1) *Johnny sent an application to a dubious company.*

The first word, *Johnny*, represents a special kind of noun, a proper name. Like pronouns (*she, I, who, something*) proper names form complete NPs.

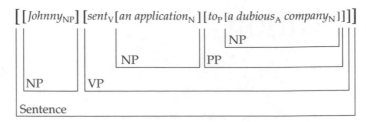

Figure 6.1 Grammatical structure of sentence (1)

The VP contains a finite verb, i.e. a verb which carries tense and, in English, 'agrees' (see 6.6) with the subject of the sentence. Here the subject is the NP *Johnny* and verb tense is simple past. The indefinite article *a(n)* and the noun *application* form another NP, the so-called direct object of the verb. The last three words, *a dubious company* form a third NP, in this case also containing an adjective between article and noun. This NP is part of a PP (prepositional phrase) headed by the preposition *to*. The PP is the so-called indirect object of the verb. The total VP consists of the finite verb, the direct object NP and the indirect object PP. In Figure 6.1 the sentence is analysed into its syntactic components.

Let us assume a CoU in which (1) is true. Then the three NPs each provide a description of one referent. The subject NP describes its referent as an entity called *Johnny*, the direct object NP characterizes its referent as an 'application' and the indirect object NP provides the information that its referent is a dubious company. Let us call the three referents r_j, r_a and r_c, respectively. The verb contributes the information that they participate in an event of sending, r_j being the sender, r_c the recipient and r_a the object sent. Thus the meaning of the sentence constitutes complex information about these three referents. If an expression provides information about a referent, it is said to make a 'predication', or to 'predicate', about it. In Table 6.1, it is sorted out which words contribute which predications about which

Word	Predication
Johnny	r_j is Johnny
sent	r_j sent r_a to r_c r_a was sent to r_c by r_j r_c was sent r_a by r_j
application	r_a is an application
dubious	r_c is dubious
company	r_c is a company

Table 6.1 Predications contributed by the words in (1)

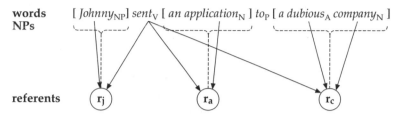

words
NPs   [*Johnny*ₙₚ] *sent*ᵥ [*an application*ₙ] *to*ₚ [*a dubious*ₐ *company*ₙ]

referents   rⱼ   rₐ   r𝒸

Figure 6.2 Predication structure of sentence (1)

referents. For the time being, we disregard the event referent of the verb (but see 6.3.2). The indefinite article and the preposition *to* are omitted from the list because they do not contribute predications.

The simple analysis shows two interesting things. First, while the nouns and the adjective relate to only one of the referents, namely the referent of the NP they belong to, the verb relates to all three referents. Second, different words in the sentence contribute predications about the same referents. Figure 6.2 depicts these relations. A broken line connects each NP to its referent, arrows point from the single words to those referents they provide information about. Figure 6.2 illustrates the central role of the verb: by predicating about all three referents, the verb ties the whole sentence together. The three NPs, in contrast, independently supply information about one referent each.

6.2 Predicates and arguments

The meanings of the predicating words in the sentence are concepts that concern one or more entities: ⟩application⟨, ⟩dubious⟨ and ⟩company⟨ concern one entity each, the event concept ⟩send⟨ concerns three. Such concepts are called **predicates**, the entities they concern are their **arguments**. Predicates are 'applied' to their arguments: for example in (1), ⟩dubious⟨ is applied to r_c and ⟩send⟨ is applied to r_j, r_a and r_c. Predicates with one argument are called one-place predicates, predicates with two arguments two-place predicates, and so on. If a predicate is applied to an appropriate set of arguments, it yields a truth value and it will be said to be true or false of its arguments. For example, if we assume a CoU where (1) is true, all the predicates are true of their arguments. But in a different CoU the predicates might yield the truth value FALSE. For example, the predicate ⟩company⟨ would be false if John sent an application to the army instead (unless the army is considered a company). Predicates define conditions on their arguments which they must fulfil for the predication to be true. You can think of a predicate as a proposition (2.2.1) with an empty slot for each argument. The truth value of the proposition depends on which arguments are filled into the empty slots.

Expressions with a predicate as meaning are called **predicate terms**. (In the literature, you will often find the term *predicate* used indiscriminately for predicate terms as well as their meanings.) Predicate terms can be verbs, nouns, adjectives or adverbs (like *rapidly*). Whether or not proper names like *Johnny* constitute predicate terms is a controversial issue. Many semanticists hold that they are just names, i.e. direct expressions for their referents. Alternatively, such nouns can be considered predicate terms that express the property of 'being called (Johnny, etc.)'. Both positions have their merits. The first position will be adopted here, but the second in Chapter 10.

Argument *terms* specify the arguments of a predicate term. But there is not always a separate term for each argument of each predicate in a sentence. In (1) the predicate expressed by *sent* has three arguments, and for each of them there is an NP that specifies it. Thus the predicate term *sent* is syntactically connected to three argument terms. The nouns in the sentence, however, simply predicate about their referents. As predicate terms they are not connected to separate argument terms. In what follows, the term **complement** will be used for all argument terms that form a separate syntactic constituent with its own referent.[1] If the argument of a predicate term is at the same time its referent, it will be called a **referential argument**. Some arguments are neither referential nor specified by a complement, e.g. the arguments of adjectives within an NP. For example, the argument of *dubious* in (1) is neither specified by a separate NP, nor is it the referent of the adjective (adjectives in general do not refer), but the referent of the whole NP *a dubious company*.

With respect to predication, special terms have been introduced for all parts of the semiotic triangle: *predicate term* for the expression part, *predicate* for the meaning part and *argument(s)* for the potential referent part. The links between expression and referent and between meaning and referent were also relabelled. The result is shown in Figure 6.3.

6.3 Verbs

Verbs are combined with a separate argument term for each of their arguments, except for the event argument to be introduced and discussed

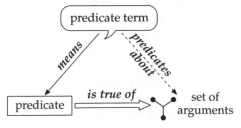

Figure 6.3 The semiotic triangle for predication

in 6.3.2. The event argument is not counted when we classify a verb as one-place, two-place, etc. The discussion will be confined to the most frequent types of verbs. If verbs, nouns and adjectives are categorized as one-, two- or three-place predicate terms, this is based on the number of arguments in standard constructions. Obviously, it is almost always possible to add further optional argument specifications to a given predicational construction. It would make little sense to try to count all *possible* arguments that might be specified for a given argument term. The issue of how many arguments a given lexical item has is, however, not trivial and will be taken up again at the end of this section.

6.3.1 Major types of verbs

Intransitive verbs

Intransitive verbs are one-place predicate terms. The only argument is specified with an NP which, in English, is always the <u>subject</u> of the sentence.

(2) a. *The cat is **sleeping**.*
   b. *The snow has **melted**.*
   c. *The door **opened**.*
   d. *The author of the love letter did not **succeed**.*

Transitive verbs

Transitive verbs are two-place predicate terms with two argument terms, the <u>subject</u> and the <u>direct object</u> of the sentence.

(3) a. *The cat is **eating** the dog's food.*
   b. *He **wants** your help.*
   c. *The dog cannot **open** the door.*
   d. *Thirty-one students **filled in** the questionnaire.*

Note that in (3d) the words *in the questionnaire* do not form a PP. *In* is part of the particle verb *fill in*, rather than a preposition. You will have noticed that the verb *open* appears as an intransitive verb in (2c) and as a transitive verb in (3c).

Ditransitive verbs

Ditransitive (or bi-transitive) verbs have three argument terms. For one group, the third argument term is an <u>'indirect object'</u>. In standard English word order, an indirect object is either placed before the direct object or it is marked with *to* and placed after it.

(4) a. *He'll* **give** *my sister* *the keys*.   *He'll* **give** *the keys* *to my sister*.
   b. *I* **showed** *them* *the photograph*.   *I* **showed** *the photograph* *to them*.

Other syntactic categories of complements

It should be mentioned that verb complements are not confined to NPs. Many verbs have prepositional complements with a lexically fixed preposition, cf. *depend on, refer to, differ from*, etc. Other verbs, e.g. verbs of motion like *go* or *put*, can be combined with a wide range of PPs. Some verbs take *that*-clauses as complements (*know, believe, assume, say*), infinitives (*try/manage/begin to*) or gerunds (*start/stop/keep –ing*), to mention only the most common types.

Alternative grammatical means of specifying arguments

There are other ways of specifying arguments of verbs than combining the verb with a complement. For example, English imperative sentences usually have no subject. The corresponding argument is then construed as the addressee(s). The imperative sentence in (5a) expresses the same proposition as the corresponding declarative sentence (5b). *Put* is a three-place verb with a direct and a prepositional object.

(5) a. **Put** *the keys* *on the window-sill*.
   b. *You* **put** *the keys* *on the window-sill*.

In languages such as Spanish or Italian, the grammatical person and number are reflected in verb inflection. The subject itself can be omitted in suitable CoUs and the resulting sentences are equivalent[2] to sentences with the corresponding personal pronouns in subject position.

(6) (Spanish)
   a. *habl-o*   *árabe*   ⇔   *yo*   *hablo árabe*
       speak-1s Arabic   I   speak-1s Arabic
   b. *habl-as* *árabe*   ⇔   *tú*   *hablas árabe*
       speak-2s Arabic   you   speak-2s Arabic

6.3.2 Referential verb arguments

Nowadays it is widely assumed that verbs also predicate about a referential argument for the event described, in addition to the arguments hitherto mentioned. (This view was adopted in 2.2.1.) There are good reasons for assuming a referential argument for verbs. First, the event argument can be considered as serving as the argument of the tense element of the verb meaning, which reasonably constitutes a predication of its own. For example, in (1) the past tense form *sent* of the verb expresses that the event of sending happened before the time of utterance. Second, the referential verb argument can be considered the argument of certain adverbs, e.g. *carefully* in *John closed the envelope carefully*. Third, there are many nouns derived from verbs that denote an event of the kind the verb expresses, e.g. the simple *-ing* derivation in (7).

(7) *Johnny's sending an application to the company did not succeed.*

If we assume that the verb *send* has an event argument, then the meaning of the noun *sending* can be straightforwardly derived. By the derivation the referential argument of the verb becomes the referential argument of the noun. The subject (agent) argument of the verb appears as a relational argument of the noun in the typical possessive construction (see 6.4.1). Specifications of the remaining arguments are the same for the noun as for the verb.

6.3.3 Deciding on the number of arguments

The question as to how many arguments a predicate term involves is often difficult to decide. Let us mention just two aspects of the problem. Very many verbs appear in more than one construction with a different number or a different quality of argument terms. One sort of variation can be dealt with in a relatively straightforward way: the occurrence of the same form in different grammatical categories, e.g. the above-mentioned form *to open* with an intransitive and a transitive use. These must be considered to be two different verbs as they belong to different word classes (intransitive vs transitive verbs). Intransitive *open* predicates of its subject argument a certain change of state. Transitive *open* predicates of its subject argument an action which leads to a corresponding change of state of the direct object argument. Thus intransitive and transitive *open* express different predications about their respective subject arguments. Their meanings are clearly different.

The second type of variation is more difficult to handle. A verb like *eat* can be used in a wide range of constructions including the types instantiated by the following examples:

(8) a. *Fred* is *eating* spaghetti.
   b. *Fred* is *eating* spaghetti *with a plastic fork.*
   c. *Fred* is *eating* spaghetti *with a plastic fork from a big bowl.*
   d. *Fred* is *eating* *with a plastic fork from a big bowl.*
   e. *Fred* is *eating* *from a big bowl.*
   f. *Fred* is *eating.*

In all these constructions, unlike in the case of intransitive and transitive *open*, the verb *eat* predicates the same of its subject argument. In view of (8f) one might feel that all complements except the subject are optional. But the direct object argument is different. The concept ⟩eat⟨ necessarily involves a second argument. Eating cannot be defined without relating to something that is eaten. Therefore that argument is understood to be involved in the situation described, even if it is not specified. *Fred is eating* is interpreted as *Fred is eating <u>something</u>*. This is why we feel that the direct object is omitted in (8d, e, f). This does not hold for all the other arguments that can be added: *Fred is eating* is not necessarily interpreted as *Fred is eating with something* or *Fred is eating from something*. Neither something eaten from nor something eaten with constitutes a necessary component of an eating event. Accordingly, specifications of such arguments are not syntactically missing if they are absent. Thus the basic number of arguments for ⟩eat⟨ is two, and *eat* is a transitive verb, although its direct object can be omitted. It must be added that not all transitive verbs allow the omission of the direct object. Along with many others one such verb is *eat*'s close relative *devour*.

6.4 Nouns and adjectives

6.4.1 Major types of nouns

One-place nouns

The majority of nouns constitute one-place predicate terms. Unlike verbs, one-place nouns are not combined with a separate argument term. They are primarily used as the head of referring NPs that function, for example, as a verb complement (but see 6.4.3 for the 'predicative' use.)

(9) *The **dog** managed to open the **door**.*

In (9) the argument of the one-place noun *dog* is the referent of the subject NP *the dog*, and analogously for the noun *door*. Both nouns have a referential argument.

Relational nouns

Some nouns constitute two-place predicate terms. These are called relational nouns. One group is kinship terms, e.g. *uncle* and *sister* in (10).

(10) *My **uncle** is going to marry Molly's **sister**.*

The two NPs *my uncle* and *Molly's sister* each have a referent: the speaker's uncle and Molly's sister, respectively. These are the referential arguments of the relational nouns *uncle* and *sister*. In addition to the referential argument, each noun has an argument for the one the referent is a relative of. In the terminology of kinship relations, this is called the *propositus*. In the case of *Molly's sister*, the propositus is Molly. It is specified by the NP *Molly's*, which is linked to the noun *sister* by means of the possessive *'s*. In the case of *my uncle*, the propositus argument is the speaker, specified by the possessive

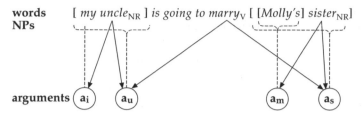

Figure 6.4 Predication structure of sentence (10)

pronoun *my*. Thus both NPs refer to an additional argument, the speaker and Molly, respectively.

In addition to the relational nouns, (10) contains the two-place verb *marry*. Thus the proposition expressed comprises three two-place predications: that someone is an uncle of the speaker's, that this someone is going to marry someone else, and that this other person is a sister of Molly's. An analysis in the style of Figure 6.2 may help to illustrate how the predicates are related to their arguments. In Figure 6.4 the subscript 'NR' is short for 'relational noun'. The four arguments a_i, a_u, a_m and a_s are short for the speaker, the speaker's uncle, Molly and her sister.

The relational argument of two-place nouns is usually specified with a possessive construction. There are three common alternatives. In the simplest one, a possessive pronoun precedes the relational noun (*my* uncle). Alternatively, a full NP with a possessive *'s* can be placed before the noun (*the children's* uncle). Finally, a 'possessor' can be specified by an *of*-PP following the noun (*an uncle of my mother*). Possessive arguments of nouns are generally not syntactically obligatory. They are counted as arguments proper because the meaning of the respective nouns cannot be defined other than in terms of two arguments.

There are many more relational nouns: words like *friend, neighbour, rival, boss*, abstract nouns like *name (of), height (of), occupation (of)* or linguistic notions such as *meaning (of), pronunciation (of), subject (of), argument (of)*. In some cases, relational arguments are specified by non-possessive PPs, cf. *ticket to, attack on, discontent with, equivalence to*.

6.4.2 Major types of adjectives

One-place adjectives

Most adjectives are one-place predicate terms when used in their basic form, the positive, as opposed to the comparative form. Adjectives are used in two ways. In the attributive use, the adjective, within an NP, precedes the head noun, e.g. *a dubious company, a red balloon, the stupid driver*. As we have seen, the argument of the adjective then is the referential argument of the noun. Therefore the argument of a one-place adjective is neither a referential argument of the adjective nor is it specified by a separate argument term. It is, as it were, parasitic.

It should be mentioned that not all combinations of an adjective and a noun function this way. For example, in the NP *the alleged murderer*, the adjective cannot be interpreted as providing an independent predication about the referent of the NP: an 'alleged' murderer is not someone who is (a) alleged and (b) a murderer. Rather, in such cases the adjective modifies the predication expressed by the noun. While the noun *murderer* predicates of its argument that he or she is a murderer, the combination *alleged murderer* predicates that the argument is alleged to be a murderer. Other adjectives functioning that way are *former*, *future* or *potential*.

The second way of using adjectives is the **predicative** use. In the most common predicative construction in English, the adjective is combined with the so-called copula verb *be*, or a similar verb such as *become*, to form the VP of the sentence.

(11) *John is **silly***.

Not incidentally, adjectives like *alleged* and *former*, which do not express an independent predication, cannot be used in this way.

Two-place adjectives

Some adjectives, e.g. *other than*, *different from*, *similar to*, *fond of*, *satisfied with*, *keen on*, have a second argument. It is invariably specified by a PP complement, i.e. by a separate argument term. With respect to their first argument, these adjectives behave like one-place adjectives. Combined with the PP complement they can only be used in predicative constructions such as a copula sentence or the relative clause construction in (12b) (which constitutes a second variant of predicative use). In attributive use as in (12c), adjectives with complements are ungrammatical.

(12) a. <u>My uncle</u> is very **fond** <u>of Molly's sister</u>.
   b. *She wore a sweater **similar** <u>to yours</u>*.
   c. **She wore a **similar** <u>to yours</u> sweater*.

A special case of two-place adjectives are one-place adjectives in their **comparative** form. The comparative adds a further argument to the adjective, an entity the first argument is compared to. Thus *big* is one-place, and *bigger* is two-place. The second argument is specified by a *than*-PP, i.e. a complement proper. If the comparative is formed of a two-place adjective, the result is a three-place predicate term (cf. (13c)).

(13) a. <u>Her hair</u> was **oilier** <u>than Julio's</u>.
   b. *I hardly can imagine <u>a book</u> **more boring** <u>than this one</u>*.
   c. *Actually, <u>my uncle</u> is **more fond** <u>of Molly</u> <u>than of her sister</u>*.

6.4.3 Arguments of nouns and adjectives in predicative use

Not only adjectives but also NPs, and therefore nouns, can be used predicatively. Predicative NPs do not refer.

(14) a.   *John is a **teacher**.*
  b.   *John is **silly**.*

Both sentences have only one referent, that of the subject NP *John*. Syntactically the subject NP is a complement of the copula. Semantically it is passed on, as it were, to the predicate terms that form the VP with the copula, i.e. to the noun phrase *a teacher* or the adjective *silly*. Thus predicative NPs and adjectives are parasitic, for their first argument, on the copula. Further complements of nouns are specified in the same way as in their referential use. The predicative use does not affect the syntactic structure of the NP.

(15) a.   *This is my **uncle**.*
  b.   *This is a **ticket** to Novgorod.*

In languages like Russian which lack a copula, the subject can be considered a complement. The equivalents of (14a, b) would simply be (16a) and (16b):

(16) a.   *John **učitel'*** ('John teacher')
  b.   *John **durak*** ('John silly')

Table 6.2 displays the main types of predicate terms and the way in which their arguments are specified in the sentence. Predicative uses are not

Type		First argument	Further arguments
verb intransitive	*the bell **rang***	complement	—
verb transitive	*she **opened** the door*	complement	complement
noun 1-place	*the **postman***	referential	—
noun relational	*asking her **name***	referential	possessor
	*a **letter** from Johnny*	referential	complement
adjective 1-place	*a **pink** envelope*	parasitic	—
adjective compar.	***thicker** than the last one*	parasitic	complement
adjective 2-place	***full** of promises*	parasitic	complement

Table 6.2 Types of predicate terms and how their arguments are specified

included. Verbs, nouns and adjectives differ in the way their first argument is integrated into the sentence structure, but they are similar in that further arguments take the form of separate argument terms, usually NPs or PPs. For the second argument of relational nouns there is a special group of (possessive) constructions.

Before the topic of predication is continued, a brief section about predicate logic is inserted. Ultimately derived from the predicational structure of natural language (i.e. ancient Greek), more than 2000 years ago by Aristotle, it is a formal system widely used in semantics for the analysis and representation of sentence meaning.

6.5 Predicate logic notation

In so-called predicate logic (PL), a simple notation has been developed for predication. The basic expressions of predicate logic are one-place, two-place, etc. predicate terms, on the one hand, and so-called individual terms, on the other. Individual terms serve as argument terms and are interpreted as referring to 'individuals', where these are whatever may serve as an argument of one of the predicates. There are two sorts of individual terms, individual constants and individual variables. Roughly speaking, individual constants can be thought of as proper names and individual variables as something like third person personal pronouns, i.e. expressions that refer to some particular individual given in the CoU. For the current purposes, we define a predicate logic language with the following basic expressions (again, referential verb arguments are disregarded).

one-place predicate terms	**cat, application, dubious, company, sleep**[3]
two place predicate terms	**marry, sister, uncle**
three place predicate terms	**send_to**
individual constants	**j** [for Johnny], **m** [for Molly], **i** [for the speaker]
individual variables	x, y, z

The predicate terms, more precisely *predicate constants*, are combined with argument terms in a uniform way. In the most common notation, predicate terms are followed by the appropriate number of individual terms enclosed in parentheses and separated by commas. The following would be simple PL formulae with the meanings indicated.

(17) a. **application**(x)   x is an application
   b. **uncle**(j, m)   Johnny is an uncle of Molly
   c. **send_to**(j, x, y)   Johnny sends x to y

The notation of predicate logic reflects the view that predicates are incomplete propositions with empty slots for arguments. This is why the logical properties and relations, originally defined for sentences, can be applied to predicate expressions (4.5). When combined with the appropriate number of argument terms, a predicate term yields a **formula** which is either true or false and hence a sentence in the sense of sentential logic (4.4). Formulae can be combined with sentential connectives such as negation and conjunction. This allows us to analyse the predicational part of a natural language sentence by 'translating' it into a predicate logic formula. The single predications are connected by a truth-conditional conjunction. In the following examples, referents not specified by a proper name are represented by variables. Tense, aspect (e.g. the progressive form of the verb) and articles are neglected.

(18) a. *The cat is sleeping.*
      $cat(x) \land sleep(x)$[4]
   b. *Johnny sent an application to a dubious company.*
      $send\_to(j, x, y) \land application(x) \land dubious(y) \land company(y)$
   c. *My uncle is going to marry Molly's sister.*
      $uncle(x, i) \land sister(y, m) \land marry(x, y)$

The method makes transparent which predications a sentence contains, to which arguments they are applied and how the different predications interact by sharing arguments. In Chapter 10, predicate logic will be treated in more depth and detail and the method of semantic analysis by translation into a formal language will be of central concern.

6.6 Thematic roles

The different arguments of a verb predicate are referred to as its **roles**, or **participants**. A transitive verb has two roles, for example, the eater and the thing eaten, the opener and the opened, the helper and the helped, etc. Grammar consistently distinguishes the different roles of a more-place verb. When the verb *eat* is used in its active mode, the eater is always specified by the subject of the verb *eat* and the thing eaten by its direct object. (The analogue holds for more-place nouns and adjectives.) An important question then is whether there is *cross-verb* consistency in the way the roles of verbs are marked. Is there something common to the role of the eater and the role of the helper that is responsible for their appearing as the subject of the sentence? Is there something in common to all subjects, or to all direct or indirect objects? Can the roles that are encoded in tens of thousands of verbs be consistently categorized into a small number of abstract roles? Are these abstract roles universally applicable to all roles of all verbs in all languages? Semanticists and syntacticians have tried to answer these questions positively. There is a good chance of succeeding, but things are not straight and simple. A first look at the data clearly shows that the subject does not always denote the same role. Consider, for example, intransitive and transitive *open* in the following sentences:

(19) a.   *The door$_O$ opens.*
    b.   *This key$_I$ opens the door$_O$.*
    c.   *The child$_A$ opened the door$_O$.*
    d.   *The child$_A$ opened the door$_O$ with her own key$_I$.*

While these sentences represent different concepts of opening, it is intuitively clear that they all fit into one scheme with three roles, (i) an animate agent A opening something; (ii) an object O that becomes open; (iii) an instrument I used to open O. In (19a), the subject specifies O, in (19b) I and in (19c) and (19d) A. Conversely, O is specified by the subject in (19a) but by the direct object in (19b)–(19d). The instrument I appears as the subject in (19b) and as a prepositional adjunct in (19d). The patterns do, however, exhibit certain regularities: if A is specified, it appears as the subject. O is always specified in the object position as long as it is not the only argument term.

Since the first attempts, back in the 1960s, at establishing a set of universal roles, many theories have been developed in different theoretical frameworks. It is now common practice to speak of **thematic roles** (θ-roles, theta-roles, with the Greek letter θ 'theta' for <u>th</u>ematic) or **semantic roles**. Some draw a distinction between thematic roles and semantic roles, but the difference need not concern us here. The inventory of thematic roles differs from theory to theory, but the roles in Table 6.3 are uncontroversial.[5]

General thematic roles are useful in several respects. For example, they help to account for the meaning relations holding between the three different verbs *open* used in (19a), (19b) and (19c, d), respectively. For predicate terms, a description of their arguments in terms of roles, their so-called **argument structure** constitutes an important part of their distinctive properties. Thematic roles also allow a proper description of phenomena like passive, which change the argument structure of a verb in a specific way.

The mechanism by which a language distinguishes the different arguments of predicate terms is called **linking**. We will not go into this complex matter here. As far as English is concerned, some simple linking rules can be stated that were already indicated in connection with (19): an agent role always appears in subject position, a theme can only be the subject if no agent is present. These rules hold for active sentences. In passive sentences, themes and other roles can be made the subject of the sentence. The agent complement is deleted, but it can be specified by an additional *by*-PP.

(20)   *The door* (theme) *was opened* (passive) [*by the dog* (agent)].

Role	Description	Examples
agent	performs the action expressed by the verb	_Johnny_ wrote a love letter _the cat_ has eaten the egg _she_ gave me the keys _you_ put the keys on the desk _my uncle_ marries Molly
theme/ patient	undergoes the action/change/event expressed by the verb	Johnny wrote _a love letter_ the cat has eaten _the egg_ she gave me _the keys_ you put _the keys_ on the desk my uncle marries _Molly_ _the door_ opened _the snow_ is melting
experiencer	experiences a perception, feeling or other state	_I_ heard him the outburst surprised _her_
instrument	an instrument, or a cause, by which the event comes about	_this key_ opens the door he opened the door _with a key_ she was shaking _with fear_
locative	a location	the keys are _on the desk_
goal	goal of a movement	put the keys _on the desk_
path	path of movement	she rode _through the desert_

Table 6.3 Thematic roles

The subject and the direct object in English sentences differ in three ways, which illustrate three general linking strategies to be observed in the languages of the world.

- **Word order**. The subject NP precedes the finite verb, the direct object follows it.
- **Case**. The subject is in nominative case, the object in objective case. In English, though, the difference shows up only with some pronouns (_I, he, she, we, they_ vs _me, him, her, us, them_ and _who_ vs _whom_).
- **Agreement**. The form of the verb varies with the grammatical properties of the subject, in the case of English with the grammatical person (1st, 2nd and 3rd) and number (singular or plural). Agreement shows up in the 3rd person singular -_s_ of full verbs in the present tense (_he/she/it speaks_ vs _I/you/we/they speak_) and in the forms of the verbs _be_ and _have_ (_I am, you are, she is; I was, we were; have_ vs _has_).

6.7 Selectional restrictions

A predicate term cannot be combined with *arbitrary* complements. In addition to the requirements of grammar, argument terms underlie semantic restrictions due to logical conditions imposed on possible arguments terms. The discussion will be restricted to verbs, but the same applies to adjectives and nouns.

6.7.1 Selectional restrictions of verbs

Two somewhat strange examples may illustrate what kinds of conditions are involved.

(21) a.   *The cook has murdered an eggplant.*
    b.   *The potatoes are frying the cook.*

If taken literally, the two sentences describe impossible situations. The verb *murder* requires a living being as its theme/patient argument, usually a human being. Only a minority of speakers of English would use the verb *murder* also for the killing of animals, probably none would use it for plants or even fruits. Likewise, the verb *fry* requires an agent argument capable of acting. It need not be a person – one could imagine an animal putting, and keeping, something on a hot stone in order to get it fried. But potatoes cannot fill this role. There are fewer problems with the theme argument of (21b). Although highly unlikely, the theme of a frying event can be a person: people are friable. But the theme role too underlies logical restrictions. For example, words, numbers, properties or addresses cannot be fried.

    The logical conditions on arguments are called **selectional restrictions** (also *selection restrictions*). The notion is motivated by the idea that a predicate term selects, and thereby restricts, the range of possible arguments. Let us assume, for example, that the verb *vaccinate* requires a human being as its agent. Then, in appropriate CoUs, the following sentences comply with the selectional restrictions:

(22) a.   *The doctor himself vaccinates John.*
    b.   *The next one vaccinates John.*

The choice of the subject term in (22a) guarantees that the selectional restrictions are fulfilled: doctors are persons. It is, however, not necessary that the noun in the complement NP entails *human being*. The selectional restrictions only require that the *referent* of the complement is a person. The potential referents of the subject NP *the next one* in (22b) are by no means necessarily persons: the NP can refer to almost anything, because the pronoun *one* can replace an arbitrary count noun. But if the subject refers to a person in the given CoU, (22b) is semantically correct.

To work out the selectional restrictions of a particular predicate term can be a very difficult task. Take, for example, the theme argument of the transitive verb *open*. What kinds of things can be opened? We can open a door, e.g. by sliding it open, and thereby create an opening in the wall that can be passed through. We can open a room by opening a door to the room. We can open our mouth. We can open our eyes. Or our arms. Or a fist. We can open a bottle or a tube by removing or opening its lid. We can open an envelope by slitting it open, or a letter by unfolding it, or a book. We can open a bank account, or a business. We can open a ceremony. We can open a computer file. We can open perspectives. These are not only different kinds of objects, but in addition *open* in almost each case means something slightly different. If I open a door or a lid, the argument that is 'opened' is moved, or removed, in order to create an opening in the enclosure of a spatial region (e.g. a room or the interior of a bottle). If I open a bag, or an envelope, the theme argument is the enclosure and the result of the act is an aperture in the enclosure. If I open a room, a trunk, a garden, a shop, a box, or my mouth, I refer to an object which *has* an enclosure in which then an aperture is brought about. So, actually, there are two or three different roles involved in these kinds of opening events: (i) a spatial region (e.g. a room) which is rendered accessible; (ii) its enclosure; and (iii) possibly, a (re)movable part of the enclosure that provides, or blocks, access to the region. Each of these roles goes with its own selectional restrictions. In the variants *open a fist*, *open a book*, *open the arms*, *open the wings* (of a bird), the theme arguments play yet a different role and the verb is used to express a different kind of process similar to spreading or unfolding. In the variant represented by *open a ceremony*, the selectional restrictions of the theme argument require an event or a procedure. Opening it, we start the ceremony and thereby 'enter' a certain sequence of events. Yet another selectional restriction governs the use of *open* in *I opened the style file*, or *you must open a bank account* or *she opened a computer business*.

It would be wrong to conclude that the selectional restrictions for the theme argument of transitive *open* are so general that they cover almost anything. Rather, the verb is multiply polysemous. In each of its meaning variants, the verb expresses a different process with respect to its theme argument and imposes different selectional restrictions. If we take these restrictions seriously, we will be able to explain how the meaning variants are related, e.g. the readings of *open* in *open one's eyes* and *open one's eyelids*. (By the way, this is a nice example of two expressions with the same truth conditions but different meanings, recall 4.6.1.)

One important point to be observed with selectional restrictions is that they apply not only when the predication is true of its arguments. Consider the three sentences in (23):

(23) a. *The dog opened it.*
    b. *The dog didn't open it.*
    c. *Did the dog open it?*

According to (23a), the predicate ⟩open⟨ is true of the dog and the referent of *it*, according to (23b), it is false, according to (23c) it may be true or false. Invariably, however, the referent of *it* must fulfil the selectional restrictions of (at least one meaning variant of) *open* for its theme argument. Thus the selectional restrictions of predicate terms apply whenever the predicate term is *used*, not only when it is true of its arguments. The logical conditions captured by the selectional restrictions are prior to the question of truth or falsity. They must be fulfilled in order to be able to decide whether in the given CoU the predicate is true or false of its arguments.[6]

6.7.2 The process of fusion

The combination of a predicate term with a complement results in two sources of information about the argument. First, the complement provides an explicit specification of it. Second, the predicate contributes implicitly the selectional restrictions for the argument. These two pieces of information are conjoined when the meaning of the sentence is composed. We can think of the process as a logical conjunction (i.e. combination by *and*) of the two pieces of information. Let us call the process **fusion**, borrowing a term from Jackendoff (1990). It is illustrated in Figure 6.5. Fusion may have different results:

1 If the selectional restrictions are less specific than the argument specification, then the total description is identical to the argument specification.
2 If the selectional restrictions are more specific than the argument specification, then the total description is identical to the selectional restrictions.
3 If the selectional restrictions and the argument specification are incompatible, the total description is contradictory, i.e. inapplicable to any concrete situation.

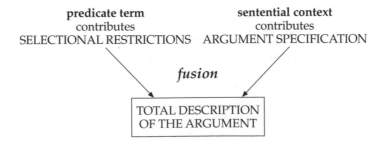

Figure 6.5 The mechanism of argument description

Example (22a), *the doctor himself vaccinates John*, illustrates case 1: the selectional restrictions add nothing to the total description, because they are already part of the argument specification. In (22b), *the next one vaccinates John*, the selectional restrictions substantially contribute to the total description, making it more specific. (21a, b) constitute examples where fusion leads to contradiction. The example shows that the selectional restrictions of a predicate term for its arguments are part of its meaning, since they contribute independently to the proposition of the sentence.

When composition is subjected to the Principle of Consistent Interpretation (3.5) which governs interpretation in context, contradictory results are generally ruled out. Thus, sentences such as (21a, b) will end up with no consistent reading at all (this is why they qualified as examples above). In other cases, the elimination of contradictory fusion will lead to disambiguation. Consider, for example, (24), assuming for the sake of the argument that the verb *drink* imposes the selectional restriction 'liquid' on its theme argument:

(24)   *She drank the coffee.*

The object NP *the coffee*, taken for itself, does not necessarily denote a liquid. 'Coffee' can also be coffee powder, coffee beans or coffee plants. In (24), the selectional restriction 'liquid' rules out all but the drink variant of the meaning of *coffee*. The result is a disambiguation of the noun *coffee*.

Conversely, we can observe disambiguation of the verb:

(25) a.   *She corrected her uncle.*
     b.   *She corrected the error in the style sheet.*

In (25a) the specification of the theme/instrument argument requires a meaning variant of the verb in which it can be applied to persons, ruling out a reading such as the one required in (25b).

6.7.3 Selectional restrictions and meaning shifts

If fusion leads to contradiction, it may be possible to obtain an admissible reading by means of a meaning shift. Let us first consider an instance of metonymy:

(26)   *Moscow declares the Chechen rebels defeated.*

The verb *declare* requires a human being or organization as its agent argument, but the given specification *Moscow* is the name of a geographic entity. In order to avoid a contradiction, we will change the meaning of *Moscow* by a metonymical shift (location → institution located there) in order to meet the selectional restrictions of the verb. Note how the selectional restrictions serve as a guide that indicates the direction of the meaning shift.

In the case of metaphorical shifts, it is often the predicate term whose meaning is shifted, as in (27). The literal meaning of the verb *evaporate* requires some kind of physical substance. The subject, however, refers to a certain mental state. To remedy the conflict, the verb meaning is shifted to the more general meaning ⟩vanish completely⟨ with selectional restrictions that allow for this kind of argument.

(27)   *His courage evaporated.*

The processes of metaphor and metonymy regularly affect selectional restrictions. If an argument term undergoes a metonymical shift, the resulting referent usually is of a different logical sort, cf. 'university' as a location vs 'university' as an institution vs 'university' as the university personnel. Likewise, metaphorical interpretation of an argument causes a shift into a different conceptual domain, usually also of a different logical sort, e.g. when 'money' is conceived of as a liquid that may 'flow'. If a predicate is interpreted metaphorically, as e.g. *evaporate* in (27), the selectional restrictions change too, as to match with the sort of objects that make up the target domain.

6.7.4 Semantic irregularity

The massive occurrence of meaning shifts in the interpretation of actual sentences blurs a question that is central to semantic analysis, the question of semantic irregularity. The notion of selectional restrictions provides us with one clear type of cases: if a specification of an argument term in the sentence is logically incompatible with the selectional restrictions, then the construction is semantically irregular. Simple as this seems to be, we have seen that semantic regularity is a question of the readings assumed for the predicate term and its argument specifications. For instance, sentence (21a) above, *the cook has murdered an eggplant* is semantically irregular only if we assume the lexical meanings of *murder* and *eggplant*. It becomes regular, i.e. interpretable, if we allow an appropriate meaning shift of either the verb or the direct object. (Possible interpretations are left up to your imagination.) It therefore makes more sense to avoid the simple notion of semantic acceptability and to replace it by a description of the conditions under which it is possible to make sense of a complex expression. We may then distinguish between degrees of acceptability, such as (i) interpretable on the basis of the lexical meanings of all components; (ii) interpretable by means of common types of meaning shifts; and (iii) interpretable only by means of uncommon types of meaning shifts. Probably, a fourth category, 'interpretable by no means at all', does not exist.

6.8 Summary

This chapter focused on predication, the semantic function of the main word classes, verbs, nouns and adjectives. Built into a sentence, each of these 'content words' adds a predication to the total proposition, about one or more referents. The three major word classes differ in how their arguments are specified (Table 6.2). Verb arguments, except for the event argument, are specified by complements, i.e. separate syntactic constituents with a referent of their own. One-place nouns are mainly used as referring expressions that predicate their referents. One-place adjectives are parasitic for their argument. One of the most important insights concerning sentence meaning is the fact that the predications contained in a sentence are inter-connected by argument sharing. If you take a look back at the examples, in particular the analyses in Figure 6.2 and Figure 6.4, you will see that the network of predications includes all referents of the sentences. It is this network structure that makes a sentence a coherent semantic unit. The verb has the key role in this structure. It occupies the centre of the network like a spider in its web holding all the threads. This role of the verb corresponds to the fact that most verbs are two- or more-place predicates.

Since the meaning of a sentence is a network of predications about its referents (including reference time and event referents), the sentence as a whole can be considered one complex predicate expression about the situation referred to. For example, sentence (1) renders a complex predication about a situation: an event e takes place, at some time t; e is an event in the past (cf. past tense); it is an event of sending that involves three referents r_j, r_a and r_c, with r_j the agent, r_a the theme and r_c the goal of sending; r_j is a certain 'Johnny', r_a is an application, and r_c is a company and dubious. This is what the sentence, due to the sophisticated grammar of English, is able to express in not more than nine words. Slightly accommodating Figure 6.3 for the application to sentences, we obtain the picture in Figure 6.6 for the sentence as a complex predication about the situation referred to.

The study of predication also sheds light on the mechanism of composi-tion. First, composition is for the most part a matter of integrating all the

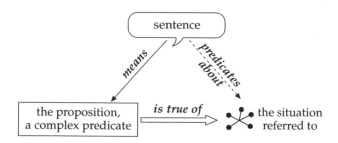

Figure 6.6 The sentence as a complex predication

predications contained in the word meanings into an overall structure. Second, we have seen how predicate terms and complements interact in the process of fusion in providing the total description of the argument.

This concludes the first part of the book, in which central semantic phenomena and concepts were introduced and interconnected. Part II will outline three major theoretical approaches. Chapters 7, 8 and 9 again will focus on word meaning, but what was said about predication will serve as background relevant in several respects. The topic of composition is taken up again in Chapter 10 on formal semantics.

Checklist

predicate
  one-place, etc.
predicate term
argument
argument term
argument specification
complement
referential argument
argument sharing
verbs
  intransitive verbs
  transitive verbs
  ditransitive verbs
  subject
  direct object
  indirect object
  referential argument
nouns
  one-place nouns
  relational nouns
  possessive construction
  predicative use
adjectives
  one-place adjectives

two-place adjectives
  comparative
  attributive use
  predicative use
predicate logic
thematic roles
participants
  agent
  theme, patient
  experiencer
  instrument
  locative, goal, path
linking
  case
  agreement
  word order
selectional restrictions
fusion
elimination of meanings
meaning shifts
metaphor
metonymy
semantic irregularity

Exercises

1 What is the difference between a predicate and a predicate term, between an argument and an argument term? Discuss the four notions and explain how they are connected.

2 Discuss the ways in which arguments are specified in the sentence for different types of predicate terms.

3   Give an analysis in the style of Figure 6.4 of the following two
    sentences.
    (a) *The woman took her frightened daughter to the dentist.*
    (b) *The customers eat potato chips with wooden toothpicks.*
4   Express the predications contained in the two sentences in predicate
    logic formulae like those in (18).
5   Determine the thematic roles of the verb arguments in the two
    sentences.
6   The following examples illustrate three types of predicative NP
    constructions. Discuss the ways in which the NP *a born loser* gets its
    argument in each type of construction.
    (a) *Peter is a born loser.*
    (b) *She called him a born loser.*
    (c) *Peter, a born loser, managed to be fired within three hours.*
7   Try to describe the correspondences between the two uses of the verbs
    drop, break and *load* in terms of thematic roles:
    (a) *She dropped her bag on the floor.* vs *The bag dropped onto the floor.*
    (b) *She broke the bottle.* (active)   vs *The bottle was broken.* (passive)
    (c) *She loaded the truck with bricks.* vs *She loaded bricks onto the truck.*
8   Try to formulate the selectional restrictions (consult a dictionary for
    possible polysemy):
    (a) of the verb *write* for its direct object argument;
    (b) of the adjective *expensive* for its only argument.
9   Explain in terms of selectional restrictions how the metonymical
    readings of the following sentences come about:
    (a) *The university lies in the eastern part of the town.*
    (b) *The university has closed down the faculty of agriculture.*
    (c) *The university starts again on 15 April.*

Further reading

Givón (1993, Chapter 3) for an extensive discussion of verb types and
    thematic roles. Tallerman (1998, Chapter 6) on the basic facts of linking
    and Chapter 7 on passive and causative constructions. Radford (1988,
    Chapter 4) on complements and adjuncts, Chapter 7 on thematic roles
    and selectional restrictions. Palmer (1994) on thematic roles and
    grammatical relations across languages. Saeed (1997, Chapter 6) on
    thematic roles.

Notes

[1] In syntactic approaches, a distinction is drawn between obligatory and optional
    argument terms. Only the former are called *complements*, the latter *adjuncts*. A
    general definition of the distinction is notoriously difficult and depends on the

theory adopted. We will not tackle the problem and use the term *complement* in a wide sense that also includes optional argument specifications.

2   Because the pronoun is usually omitted, its use results in some sort of emphasis on it. In this sense, the pronoun, if present, is not redundant.

3   It is common practice to use bold type for predicate and individual constants that correspond to natural language words.

4   A formula such as '**sleep**(**cat**)' would violate the rules of PL syntax, because the predicate term **cat** is not allowed to be used as an individual term in the argument position of **sleep**.

5   Often thematic roles are written with small capitals (THEME, etc.). In this book small capitals are reserved for category names (see Chapter 9).

6   Therefore selectional restrictions constitute so-called **presuppositions**. See also Chapter 9, note 6.

Part II

THEORETICAL APPROACHES

In Part I, we took our first steps into the field of semantic analysis and theorizing. A scientific notion of meaning was introduced that is more precise than the colloquial sense of the word and helps to distinguish the phenomena relevant for semantics from those belonging to other areas of science (Chapter 1). Different parts of meaning were distinguished, the most prominent part being descriptive meaning (Chapter 2). The consideration of ambiguities and meaning modifications (Chapter 3) paved the way for the investigation of lexical meaning. We dealt with different kinds of semantic relations: the logical relations based on truth conditions and reference (Chapter 4) and the meaning relations introduced in Chapter 5. In Chapter 6 we considered lexical units from the perspective of predication, thereby forming a picture of sentence meaning.

In the second part, three major theoretical approaches to meaning are introduced. Structuralism (Chapter 7) is the oldest one. The theory focuses on meaning relations and is the framework in which the first theory of semantic decomposition was developed, i.e. a theory of explaining lexical meanings in terms of meaning components. This theory, known as feature semantics, still enjoys considerable popularity. It is introduced in Chapter 7 on decomposition, together with other approaches that are far superior. In Chapter 8 we will take a look at language comparison and the question of semantic universals. The famous investigations of Berlin and Kay on colour term systems will lead us to the question of categorization: how are meanings related to their denotations, or conversely, how are denotations represented in our minds by the corresponding concepts? How is our semantic knowledge related to our knowledge about the world we live in? These questions are the focus of Chapter 9 on cognitive semantics. Chapter 10 will turn again to sentence meaning and the mechanism of composition. The major approach in this field is formal semantics, a theory that is based on truth and reference and formal logic.

The three theoretical orientations, structuralism, cognitive semantics and formal semantics, are not so much rival approaches, but are to a certain extent complementary. Structuralism focuses on meaning relations, cognitive semantics on the relation between meaning and denotation and formal semantics on the relation between expression and denotation. Some day, we may hope, there will be a theory that will comprise all these aspects in one approach; but up to now, no such theory exists.

Meaning
components

7

While the assessment of semantic phenomena forms a very important step of developing a semantic theory, theorizing itself only starts when one tries to *explain* the phenomena. For example, the senses of *uncle* and *aunt* are related in the same way as those of *sister* and *brother*, and *Violetta is an aunt of Christopher* logically entails *Christopher is a nephew of Violetta* (provided *Christopher* refers to a male person and *Violetta* to a female one). But how can this be derived from the meanings of the relevant terms? Likewise, verbs carry selectional restrictions for their arguments (6.7). How can this be accounted for in a principled way? There are many different semantic theories. Each one defines the notion of meaning differently and uses different means for the representation of meanings, some formal, some informal. Almost all of them, however, share a basic strategy of explaining the semantic data, a strategy that ties in with our intuitive notion of meaning: they assume that the meanings of most words are complex, composed of more general components. The meaning of a lexical item is analysed by identifying its **components** and the way in which they are combined. In a sense, the process of semantic analysis is the converse of the process of composition by which we determine the meaning of a complex expression on the basis of its components and its structure. Therefore analysis into meaning components is called **decomposition**. A decompositional theory allows the pursuit of the following objectives:

M **Meaning.** Providing models for word meanings.
What kind of entities are lexical meanings? What is their structure? How are meanings to be represented?

B **Basic meanings.** Reducing the vast variety of lexical meanings to a limited number of basic meanings.
Are there lexical items which are semantically basic? How can the meanings of non-basic items be built up from more basic ones?

P   **Precision.** Providing a means of representation that allows a precise interpretation of lexical items.

R   **Meaning relations.** Explaining meaning relations within and across lexical fields.

C   **Composition.** Explaining the compositional properties of lexical items.
With which kinds of expressions can the item be combined? How does its meaning interact with the meanings of the expressions it is combined with?

Selectional restrictions represent one kind of phenomena relevant for the last point.

A more ambitious decompositional semantic theory would further strive to develop an analytical apparatus that can be used for different languages. With such an apparatus it is possible to compare the meanings of expressions from different languages.

L   **Language comparison.** Determining the semantic relations between expressions of different languages.
Are there expressions with the same meaning in other languages? If not, how are the meanings of similar expressions related to each other?

For example, English and Japanese terms for 'brother' can be described as in Table 7.1 (the propositus is the possessor argument of the term (6.4.1), i.e. the person whose relative the term refers to.) Japanese distinguishes between elder and younger siblings. Furthermore, there are pairs of formal and informal terms with the same descriptive meaning. If the relative is treated as superior, the formal terms (*onîsan* and *otôtosan*) are used. Obviously none of the four Japanese terms is equivalent to the English word *brother*; they all relate to *brother*-like hyponyms.

	Meaning component specifying the referent's			Social meaning
	.. kinship relation to propositus	.. sex	.. age relation to propositus	
E *brother*	⟩sibling⟨	⟩male⟨	—	—
J *ani*	⟩sibling⟨	⟩male⟨	⟩elder⟨	informal
J *onîsan*	⟩sibling⟨	⟩male⟨	⟩elder⟨	formal
J *otôto*	⟩sibling⟨	⟩male⟨	⟩younger⟨	informal
J *otôtosan*	⟩sibling⟨	⟩male⟨	⟩younger⟨	formal

Table 7.1 Meaning components of English and Japanese terms for 'brother'

Four different approaches to decomposition will be introduced. Each of them adopts a different conception of meaning with its own merits and shortcomings. The first one to be introduced is the structuralist approach, now almost a century old, which has exerted an enormous influence on the development of modern linguistics and will therefore be treated in greater detail and without restriction to semantics.

7.1 The structuralist approach

7.1.1 Language as a system of signs

The one who is generally credited with the approach known as **structuralism** is the Swiss linguist Ferdinand de Saussure (1857–1913). The outlines of his approach appeared in 1916 under the title *Cours de linguistique générale* ('Course of general linguistics'), a compilation of material from lectures Saussure held around the year 1910.

To Saussure, a language is an abstract complex system of relations and rules that underlies all regularities to be observed in actual language use. The system is formed by signs which are related in multiple ways. A **sign**, e.g. a word, consists of two parts. One part is its sound form. The other part is its meaning. The association between form and meaning of a sign is fixed by conventions of language use. The association is *arbitrary*, i.e. a word could as well have a different meaning, and the meaning could be associated with a different expression – provided the conventions of the language were different. Saussure emphasizes that the sign and its parts are real entities in the minds of the speakers, mental or cognitive entities in modern terminology.

What distinguishes the structuralist approach is the method of analysis and the resulting concept of linguistic signs. Saussure argues that language is to be studied exclusively 'from within'. The language system is a very complex structure formed by units at different levels: single sounds, syllables, words, syntactic phrases, sentences. Each unit is related to the smaller units it consists of and to the larger units it is a part of, and also to all sorts of other units which are similar in some respect or other. A sign constitutes a sign only as part of a system – only insofar as it is related to, and different from, the other signs of the language. This holds for both the form and the meaning of a sign. Form and meaning are only defined 'negatively', i.e. by differing in specific ways from the other signs. They have no positively defined 'substance'. Neither the form nor the meaning of a sign could exist independently of the language system it belongs to.

Let me illustrate these abstract considerations with a concrete example. The French word *rouge*, standard pronunciation [ʁuʒ],[1] means ⟩red⟨. Its sound form is a string of three sound units (**phonemes**), /r/, /u/ and /ʒ/, for which there are certain conventions of articulation. Each of the phonemes allows for considerable phonetic variation; /r/, for example is usually pronounced [ʁ]; but it can also be pronounced as in Italian (rolled [r]) or even as the [x] in German *Buch*. As long as it can be distinguished from the other sounds of French, in particular /l/, its actual articulation may vary. Japanese /r/ can even be pronounced [l] because Japanese does not have two phonemes /l/ and /r/ but just one of this type (so-called liquids). Thus, Saussure argues, a sound unit of the system is not primarily defined by its articulation or acoustic quality but by its relation to the other sound units.

The other component of the sign, the meaning of French *rouge*, is similar to the meaning of English *red* or German *rot* (but see the next chapter for other languages). The exact range of colours that the word denotes depends on which other colour terms compete with *rouge*: *orange* (⟩orange⟨), *rose* (⟩pink⟨), *violet* (⟩purple⟨) and *brun* (⟩brown⟨). If, for example, French lacked a term for purple, the respective range of colours would be divided between the words for red, brown and blue, resulting in an extension of the range of *rouge*. A sign, according to structuralism, *is constituted by* being different from the other signs of the system. Its form and its meaning are the sum of their differences and relations to the other forms and meanings of the system.

The structuralist notion of meaning is thus radically relational. Strictly speaking, it implies that we cannot determine the meaning of a lexeme independently, but only its relations to the meanings of other lexemes. This notion of meaning is not commonly accepted. While it has been adopted by some semanticists (e.g. in Cruse, 1986), alternative theories have been developed, in particular cognitive semantics (Chapter 9). The cognitive approach does view the meaning of a lexeme as something that can in principle be investigated and described independently. According to this theory, meanings are considered integral parts not of a system of linguistic meanings but of our overall cognitive system, which can be studied by the methods of cognitive psychology.

In terms of the semiotic triangle structuralism focuses exclusively on the left side of the schema (Figure 7.1). Semantics is not a matter of reference

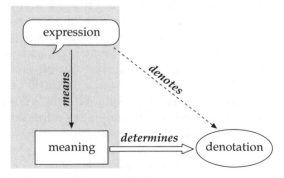

Figure 7.1 The focus of structuralist semantics

and denotation. Rather, it concerns the sign, i.e. a pair of form and meaning, and how it is related to other signs.

7.1.2 Syntagmatic and paradigmatic relations

All linguistic units – sounds, syllables, words, phrases, sentences – can be combined into more complex units. In the original terminology of structuralism, such a complex is called a **syntagm** (from ancient Greek *syntagma*, ⟩compound⟨. A syllable is a syntagm of phonemes, a word taken as a sound unit is a syntagm of syllables; as a semantic unit, a word may be a syntagm of morphemes (e.g., *un-natur-al*, see 7.2.1); a syntactic phrase like the NP *a lucky decision* is a syntagm of words, a sentence is a syntagm of phrases. For each kind of syntagm there are specific formation rules and within each syntagm the **constituents** are related to each other in specific ways. The general term for the relations within a syntagm is **syntagmatic relations**. The syntagmatic relations that a given unit bears to other constituents are determined by its combinatorial properties. For example, an English NP may take the form article+noun but not noun+ article. Thus English articles have the combinatorial property of preceding the noun in an NP. Let us consider the syllable /set/ as an example (Figure 7.2). The syllable is a syntagm of three phonemes /s/, /e/ and /t/, that occupy the three basic positions of a syllable, commonly called onset, nucleus and coda. The syntagmatic relations are first of all those of order: the onset precedes the nucleus and the nucleus precedes the coda. In addition, nucleus and coda form a unit within the syllable, the so-called rhyme. Therefore the relation that holds between nucleus and coda is closer than, and different from, the relation between nucleus and onset.

For each position we can determine which units can occur in this position. The set of all alternatives is called a **paradigm**[2] (from ancient Greek *paradeigma*, ⟩something shown side by side⟨. The onset position of the syllable /set/ can be filled by certain, but not all consonant phonemes (for example /ŋ/, the last sound of *sing* is not possible here) and by certain consonant clusters such as /fr/, which we will disregard here. The nucleus position defines a paradigm that consists of all vowel and diphthong phonemes. The coda paradigm consists of all consonant phonemes that can occur in syllable-final position (excluding, for example, /h/, /y/ and /w/).

onset		nucleus		coda	
/b/	bet	/i/	sit	/k/	sec-tion
/p/	pet	/æ/	sat	/p/	sep-tet
/s/ /e/ /t/	set	/s/ /e/ /t/	set	/s/ /e/ /t/	set
/m/	met	/u:/	soot	/n/	cen-tury
/w/	wet	/aɪ/	cite	/l/	cell
. . .	. . .	. . .	. . .	. . . . . .	

Figure 7.2 Three paradigms defined by the syntagm /set/

Structuralist concept	Definition
syntagm	complex unit
syntagmatic relations	relations between the constituents of a syntagm
combinatorial properties syntagmatic properties	properties of a unit that determine its syntagmatic relations: how it can be combined with other units
paradigm	set of all elements that can fill a certain position in a syntagm
paradigmatic relations	relations between the elements of a paradigm
contrastive properties paradigmatic properties	distinctive properties of the elements of a paradigm

Table 7.2 Basic structuralist concepts

The units within a paradigm exhibit relations of difference and similarity. These are called **paradigmatic relations**. For example, the opposition voiced vs voiceless distinguishes /b/ and /p/ within the onset paradigm. Let us call the corresponding properties of the units, e.g. voice (being voiced), their **contrastive** properties.

Table 7.2 displays the basic structuralist concepts. They allow the definition of basic notions such as *syntactic category* (a paradigm of syntactic units), *word class* or *grammatical category* (a paradigm of lexical units, 3.1) or *lexeme* (a unit with certain paradigmatic and syntagmatic properties).

7.2 Applying the structuralist approach to meaning

7.2.1 Semantic units: morphemes and lexemes

When applying the approach to meaning, one has to determine what the semantic units of a language are, and describe them in terms of their combinatorial and contrastive properties. Words may share meaningful parts with other lexemes. Therefore, words (or lexemes) are not the smallest semantic units of a language. Consider, for example:

(1) a.   *meaningful, beautiful, harmful, successful, useful, sorrowful*
  b.   *ugliness, cleverness, baldness, usefulness, carelessness, laziness, fitness*
  c.   *clearing, hearing, cleaning, thinking, meeting, brainstorming*

The meanings of these and many other words can be derived from the meaning of the first part and the meaning of the suffix (ending): *-ful, -ness*,

-*ing*. The suffix -*ful* can be attached to a large number of nouns and yields an adjective that, very roughly, means ⟩having much of N⟨ or ⟩being full of N⟨. Thus, the suffix -*ful* has a meaning of its own. Likewise, the meanings of the other two suffixes can roughly be defined as ⟩the property of being A⟨ for -*ness* attached to an adjective A, and ⟩situation where someone V-s (something)⟨ for words of the form V-*ing*. It should be noted, though, that along with these examples where the meaning can be straightforwardly decomposed into the meaning of the suffix and the meaning of the first part, there are quite a number of lexemes that contain such a suffix without allowing for straightforward decomposition. For example, *meaning* does not mean a situation where somebody means something, *wilderness* does not denote the property of being wilder and *lawful* does not mean ⟩full of law⟨.

The two components of *cleaning*, the verb *clean* and the suffix -*ing*, cannot be further divided into meaningful parts. Such minimal semantic units are called **morphemes**.[3] *Clean* can be used as a word on its own. It therefore constitutes what is called a **free** morpheme. The suffix -*ing* is a **bound** morpheme as it can only occur as a part of a word. The bound morphemes in (1) serve the derivation of words from others. A second class of bound morphemes, the **grammatical** morphemes, is used to build the different grammatical forms of words. Among the comparatively few examples in English are the third person singular present tense ending (*eat-s*), the noun plural ending (*horse-s*), the possessive ending (*king-'s*), the past tense ending (*wash-ed*), the comparative ending (*high-er*) and the ending -*ing* used to form the progressive form of verbs (*be wash-ing*), the present participle (*the ring-ing bell*) and the gerund (*I hate iron-ing*).

7.2.2 Paradigmatic and syntagmatic semantic relations

When meaning relations were discussed in Chapter 5, we assumed that the related items were of the same word class. Word classes are essentially paradigms. Hence, meaning relations such as the oppositions, hyponymy, meronymy and the more specific relations structuring certain lexical fields (5.3) are paradigmatic relations. For example, all terms for the days of the week can be inserted into the empty position of the syntagm *today is ___*. Within the resulting paradigm, we can assess the meaning relations between the terms.

Syntagmatic meaning relations hold between the constituents of a syntagm. They consist of the way in which the meanings of the constituents are combined to yield the meaning of the whole syntagm. Let us consider two simple examples. In (2) a transitive verb is combined with a subject NP and an object NP to form a sentence:

(2) *Mary seized the bottle.*

The syntagmatic meaning relation that holds between the subject NP and the verb is that of the NP specifying the verb's agent. The object NP is related to the verb as its theme specification. The semantic relations of the NPs to the verb are indicated by their syntactic position (6.6).

(3) *the red balloon*

The combination *red balloon* in (3) describes the potential referent of the NP as a red balloon. Both the adjective and the noun are one-place predicates of the potential referent (6.2.4). Thus the syntagmatic meaning relation between adjective and noun is one of sharing their argument.

Predicate terms carry selectional restrictions. These conditions constrain the choice of expressions that can be combined with the predicate terms (6.7). Thus they constitute syntagmatic, or combinatorial, semantic properties of verbs, adjectives and nouns. In addition to selectional restrictions, which impose logical conditions on argument specifications, lexemes may have combinatorial properties that restrict their usage further. For example, German has different systems of terms for animals and people. Where people 'essen' (eat), animals 'fressen', drinking of people is 'trinken', of animals 'saufen'. People have a 'Mund' (mouth), but animals a 'Maul', 'Schnauze', etc.[4] Such distinctions give rise to language-specific combinatorial meaning properties.

7.3 Semantic features

7.3.1 Binary semantic features

One of the areas where the structuralist approach proved particularly fruitful was phonology. As early as in the 1920s and 1930s the Prague School of structuralism developed a phonological theory where the phonemes were described by sets of distinctive binary **features** corresponding, for example, to the mode and place of articulation.[5] The use of features not only allowed the explanation of contrastive and combinatorial properties of the phonemes within one language. Features could also be established across languages, enabling a comparison of the sound systems of different languages. Because of its great success, the feature approach was adopted in other areas of linguistics, including semantics.

In the variety of approaches subsumed under the label of **feature semantics**, semantic features are used as meaning components. For instance, the lexemes in (4a) would receive a common semantic feature [FEMALE], those in (4b) receive the feature [MALE], while neither feature is assigned to the expressions in (4c) (it is common practice to write features within square brackets and with small capital letters):

(4) a. *girl*   *woman*   *sister*   *wife*   *queen*   [FEMALE]
   b. *boy*   *man*   *brother* *husband*   *king*   [MALE]
   c. *child*   *person* *sibling* *spouse*   *monarch*   (sex not specified)

The features [FEMALE] and [MALE] are not just different but complementary. We can therefore replace them with one *binary* feature, either [FEMALE] or [MALE], that assumes the value + or the value –. For the sake of brevity and male chauvinism, the [MALE] variant is chosen.[6] The general feature [MALE] is written [±MALE] or just [MALE], the fact that the feature has the value + or – is indicated by [+MALE] and [–MALE], respectively. The term *feature* is used for both features without a value ([MALE]) and features with a value ([–MALE]).

The words in (4) share the property of denoting persons. This can be captured by another feature [+HUMAN] that distinguishes them from the terms in (5). (We assume the primary animal readings of the terms.)

(5) a. *mare bitch cow ewe*   [–HUMAN]   [–MALE]
   b. *stallion cock tomcat bull* [–HUMAN]   [+MALE]
   c. *horse pig sheep fish*   [–HUMAN]

With [HUMAN], [MALE] and an additional feature [ADULT], the meanings of the six general person terms (5.3.2) can be described as in Table 7.3. The right side is a so-called feature matrix.

A feature with the value + or – constitutes a one-place **predicate** about the potential referent of the lexeme. For example, if a noun carries the feature [+ADULT], its referents have to fulfil the condition of being adult; if it carries the feature [–ADULT], they have to be not adult; if it has neither feature, no condition with respect to being adult is imposed on its referents. Thus, in feature semantics word meanings are considered combinations of a number of one-place predications. For example, according to the analysis

	Features and their values			[HUMAN]	[ADULT]	[MALE]
child	[+HUMAN]	[–ADULT]		+	–	
girl	[+HUMAN]	[–ADULT]	[–MALE]	+	–	–
boy	[+HUMAN]	[–ADULT]	[+MALE]	+	–	+
adult	[+HUMAN]	[+ADULT]		+	+	
woman	[+HUMAN]	[+ADULT]	[–MALE]	+	+	–
man	[+HUMAN]	[+ADULT]	[+MALE]	+	+	+

Table 7.3 Features and a feature matrix for the six general person terms

in Table 7.3, the meaning of the word *boy* is ⟩human and not adult and male⟨.

7.3.2 Application to paradigmatic relations

Binary features are directly related to certain logical relations and the corresponding meaning relations. Two expressions with opposite values for some feature [α] are logically incompatible, e.g. *boy* and *mare*, regardless of the rest of their meanings. If their meanings differ *only* in the value of one feature (*boy* vs *girl*), they are complementary opposites as the rest of their meaning defines a semantic domain within which they are contradictory. Hyponymy holds if two expressions have the same meaning except for an additional feature [+α] or [−α] for one of them (e.g. *child* and *boy*) (see Table 7.4). As will be argued later, hyponymy (of this type) and complementary opposition are the only meaning relations that can be captured with binary features.

Meaning of A		Meaning of B	Logical relation	Meaning relation
X and [+α] *boy*	**vs**	Y and [−α] *mare*	incompatibility	*(undetermined)*
X and [+α] *boy*	**vs**	X and [−α] *girl*	incompatibility	complementary opposition
X and [+α] X and [−α] *girl, boy*	**vs**	X *child*	subordination	hyponymy

Table 7.4 Binary features and logical relations

7.3.3 Application to combinatorial meaning properties

Features can be used to formulate selectional restrictions. For example, if a verb (e.g. *vaccinate*) carries the selectional restriction ⟩human⟨ for its subject referent, the restriction can be described by the feature [+HUMAN]. It must, however, be carefully observed what this is a feature of: it is a feature of a complement argument of the verb, not a feature of the verb itself. If it were the latter, it would have to relate to the referent of the verb, i.e. the event expressed (6.2.5). But the event, e.g. of vaccinating, is not a human being, rather the agent is that performs the action. Conditions on complements of the verb can, in fact, be captured by a decompositional analysis of verb meanings, as we shall see in 7.4, but not with the binary feature approach.

7.3.4 Ideal properties of semantic features

So far only single features have been extracted from the meanings of lexemes. The natural next step in feature analysis is the attempt to decompose lexical meanings completely into binary features. The result for a particular lexeme would be a finite list of features that captures all relevant properties of its referents and differs from the feature list of any other non-synonymous lexeme in at least one feature. This, however, has proved very difficult. It is by no means obvious how, for example, the set of co-hyponyms of large taxonomies such as the animal or plant taxonomy should be distinguished systematically by binary features.

Formally, a trivial feature analysis is always possible. We could, for example, distinguish the animal terms *bear, pig, rabbit, tiger, donkey, kangaroo*, etc. by simply introducing as many binary features [±BEAR], [±PIG], [±RABBIT], etc. and assigning to each animal term a positive value for its 'own' feature and a negative value for each other feature. *Tiger* would be [−BEAR], [−PIG], [−RABBIT], [+TIGER], [−DONKEY] and [−...] for all the other features (the result is shown in Figure 7.3). This approach would capture in an extremely plain way one major aspect of the structuralist notion of meaning: that the meaning of a unit is the sum of its differences to the meanings of the other units of the system. Clearly, such an 'analysis' would not explain anything beyond the mere incompatibility of the different animal terms (and this only if we tacitly assume that the features themselves are mutually incompatible, i.e. if we already presuppose what should be explained). The main point of decomposition is, of course, the *reduction* of meaning to more basic and ultimately minimal components. At least we would expect all the expressions in Figure 7.3 to carry a common feature [+ANIMAL]. The use of this feature would then lead to the employment of features less specific

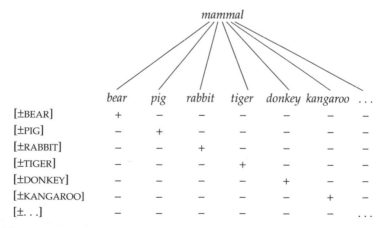

Figure 7.3 A trivial feature matrix for co-hyponyms in the animal taxonomy

than [TIGER], etc. This leads us to a first important postulate for any feature approach, and in fact for any decompositional theory:

> Features should be **primitive**, i.e. not further analysable.

The 1:1 analysis into as many features as there are expressions to be distinguished suffers from a further principal drawback: the features are very special. For example, the feature [±PIG] would only be of use when it takes the value +, i.e. with terms for more specific kinds of pigs or for male, female or baby pigs. The feature value [–PIG], though a necessary component of the meanings of all other animal terms contributes almost no information (I do not know much about the meaning of *rat* if I know that rats are [–PIG]). A feature system should provide distinctions that can be used more widely, e.g. [±DOMESTIC]. Features must not be *ad hoc*, i.e. created just in order to provide a solution to a particular problem, while disregarding more general aspects.

> Features should be **general**.

Of course, generality is a matter of degree. But what is certainly ruled out are features that are distinctive for a handful of lexemes only.

If we try to find more general features that allow us to structure the taxonomy of animals, we will soon fall back upon our knowledge from biology lessons, trying to apply the criteria of scientific classification such as the distinction between rodents and other orders. But, as will be argued more thoroughly in 9.5, a distinction must be drawn between semantic knowledge, i.e. the knowledge of meanings, and world knowledge, i.e. knowledge about the entities we have words for. Semantic analysis has to be based on *linguistic* data, namely, the meaning relations observable within the language system. After all, we are not doing the work of biologists etc., but of linguists.

> Features should be **linguistically motivated**.

What would constitute relevant *linguistic* data, apart from the hyponymy relations between the levels of the taxonomy? There are several kinds of relevant phenomena:

Selectional restrictions of verbs. There are, for example, specific verbs for the sounds certain animals produce: e.g. *miaow, bark, chirp, neigh* or for modes of running such as *gallop, trot,* etc. The selectional restrictions of such verbs give rise to corresponding features in the meanings of animal terms.

Verbs with implicit arguments. The German verb *reiten* (a cognate of the English verb *ride*), is interpreted as ⟩to ride a horse⟨ if the respective argument is not explicitly specified otherwise. Similarly, there might be adjectives which are only used when referring to properties or conditions of certain kinds of animals.

Lexicalizations of distinctions within certain kinds or groups. For some kinds of animals there are general terms along with terms for the sexes (*horse* vs *mare, stallion*) or their young (*kitten, chicken, puppy, calf, lamb, cub, foal,* etc.). There are specific terms for horses of certain colours, e.g. *sorrel* for a horse of a light reddish-brown colour. The more specific terms (*mare, foal, sorrel*) require features that they share with the more general terms (*horse*). In other cases, the same word may be used to form expressions for the males or females of different kinds of animals, e.g. *hen* and *cock* for most kinds of birds. The terms for these animals too must share a feature.

Mereological relations. There are cases of different terms for the same body part, for instance *snout, muzzle, trunk* or *beak* for mouth and nose. Thus, animal terms can be grouped together according to the expressions used for their body parts: terms for animals with a snout, animals with a beak, etc. We also may distinguish terms for animals with special body parts, e.g. with 'claws', 'hoofs', 'fins', 'feathers', 'scales', with 'fur' or a 'shell', or with a 'tail', a 'mane', an 'udder', and so on. Although features like these border closely on extralinguistic scientific characterizations, they nevertheless are linguistic features. We cannot explain the meaning of *fin, feather, udder,* etc. without relating the meaning of the words to the meanings of the words *fish, bird, cow,* etc. or hyperonyms of them. Note that such a criterion is different from saying that, for example, seagulls can be distinguished from other kinds of birds by the fact that their eggs are a certain colour: there is no lexical relation between the word *seagull* and the respective colour word.

Metonymical relations. Similar to mereological relations are relations between, for example, terms for animals and terms for the flesh of the animals when used as food (*pig–pork, cow/bull/ox–beef, sheep–mutton*) or between terms for animals and terms for their eggs (*fish–roe, frog–spawn*). These relations are metonymical: the referent of one expression is conceptually linked to the referent of the other.

In general, there is a meaning connection between lexical items whenever it is possible to form analytical sentences (4.1.4), so-called **meaning postulates**, that express the relation.

(6) a. *a mare is a female horse*
   b. *a kitten is a baby cat*
   c. *pork is meat from pigs*
   d. *roe is the eggs of fish*
   e. *birds have feathers*
   f. *birds have a beak as their mouth*

Although such linguistic data will take us a bit further along the way to an exhaustive analysis, it is by no means clear whether it is possible to find a set of appropriate features to distinguish the great number of animal terms or other large taxonomies. In fact, it is commonly accepted that for many lexemes an exhaustive analysis into binary features that are at the same time primitive, general and linguistically motivated, is impossible. Such features are called **classemes**, or **markers**. It is markers which allow an explanation of the combinatorial properties as well as the more general contrastive properties. Markers may also play a role in grammar. For example the feature [±HUMAN] is responsible for the choice of the pronouns *who* vs *what*, or [±MALE] for the choice between *he* and *she*. Markers also fulfil a further important condition, related to the aim of language comparison:

> Features should be **universal**.

Indeed, features such as [±MALE], [±HUMAN], [±ANIMATE], etc. play an important role in the structure of the lexica of very many languages.

For most lexemes, however, there will remain a residue of meaning that cannot be captured by markers. For such cases, the notions of **semes** and **distinguishers** were introduced. Semes serve for specific, more or less unique, distinctions within particular lexical fields. For example, in the lexical field of the verbs *buy, rent, take, borrow*, etc. one can use the semes [±PERMANENT] or [±FOR MONEY]. Semes are primitive and linguistically motivated, but they are neither general nor, in most cases, expected to be universal. Distinguishers are used for whole meaning residues. If the meaning of *mare* were analysed just into the two features [−MALE] [+HORSE], [−MALE] would be a marker and [+HORSE] a distinguisher. Distinguishers are neither primitive nor general; they are improbable candidates for universality, but they may be linguistically motivated.

7.3.5 Evaluation of the binary feature approach

While the analysis of lexical meanings into a set of binary features can be used for explaining some semantic data, the limitations of the binary feature approach (BFA) are in fact severe.

> BFA is only applicable to a limited range of lexemes.

Apart from the problem of unanalysable meaning residues, there appear to be quite a few lexical categories whose meanings cannot be reasonably reduced to a set of binary features. Verbs in general seem less appropriate for this approach. Certain traits of verb meanings can be captured by binary features. For example, the fact that *buy* means an exchange of goods for money can be covered by a feature [+MONEY]. But the essential part of its meaning, common to *buy, rent, take, steal*, etc., namely a predication that involves two or more arguments, is impossible to represent by means of binary features that constitute one-place predicates.

These observations lead us to the next important point:

> Most kinds of meaning relations cannot be accounted for by BFA.

As we saw in 7.3.2, the BFA captures incompatibility, complementary opposition and certain cases of hyponymy, probably not including larger taxonomies. It cannot capture conversion (*parent–child*) or other types of oppositions, including antonymy, since the type of logical relations holding between such opposites is different from the logical relations that can result from combining binary features. Apart from that, all kinds of more specific relations within lexical fields present insurmountable difficulties: mereological relations, cyclic orders as in the field of *Monday, Tuesday*, etc., the meaning relations between modifier and compound, or those among number terms: it is impossible to capture the meaning relations between *three, seven, twenty, hundred* and *three hundred and twenty-seven* by means of binary features. This insufficiency is due to the most severe drawback of BFA:

> There is only one type of possible meaning components and only one way of combining components into complex meanings.

As stated above, binary features are essentially one-place predicates about the referent of the lexeme. For example, the decomposition of the meaning of *woman* into the three features [+HUMAN], [−MALE], [+ADULT] is equivalent to the following PL definition (cf. 6.5):

(7)   x is a *woman*   = $\text{human}(x) \wedge \neg\text{male}(x) \wedge \text{adult}(x)$

In the same way, every representation by binary features is equivalent to a finite conjunction of as many one-place predicates (negated, if the feature value is −), all with the same argument which represents the potential referent of the term. This leads us to the next severe restriction.

> In BFA it is impossible to impose conditions on other elements than the potential referent.

As we have seen, certain phenomena such as selectional restrictions require the possibility of imposing conditions on complement arguments of predicate terms. Similarly, we might, for example, want to distinguish terms for items of clothing with respect to the sex of the wearer, or terms for body parts of either female or male persons. But it would be inappropriate to assign a feature [−MALE] or [+MALE] to the words *bikini* or *prostate*: it is not the bikini or the prostate that is female or male, but the persons for whom bikinis are designed or who have this type of organ.

To sum up, BFA is much too simple an approach to be able to meet the complexities of semantic phenomena in natural languages. The use of binary features may be appropriate when dealing with the small and limited areas of phonology or syntax, where only a comparatively small set of units or categories has to be distinguished and analysed with respect to their relations within the system. However, the lexicon of a language is of a complexity incommensurable to that of the sound system or system of word classes or forms. It forms a large part of our utterly complex cognitive system. It should, however, be emphasized that the failure of BFA in semantics does not mean that the structuralist approach as such has failed. Its strong emphasis on linguistic data and the systematic relations within languages helped linguistics to develop its theoretical methods of today. The basic notions and methods of structuralism are compatible with semantic theories quite different from BFA.

7.4 Semantic formulae

One phenomenon that gave rise to the development of alternative decompositional approaches is the existence of systematic meaning relations between verbs, or between verbs and adjectives, as given in (8):

(8) | stative | inchoative | causative |
|---|---|---|
| x is **open** | x **opens** | y **opens** x |
| x is **hard** | x **hardens** | y **hardens** x |
| x is **dead** | x **dies** | y **kills** x |
| x **has** y | x **gets** y | z **gives** y to x |

The 'stative' verbs and adjectives in the first column denote a certain state of x. The 'inchoative'[7] verbs in the second column express the coming about of this state of x. The third column consists of 'causative' verbs, used to express that someone (or something), y, brings the state of x about. While the stative and inchoative expressions have the same number of arguments, the causative verbs have an additional agent argument, the 'causer'. There are hundreds of such triplets in English, and in addition many pairs of verbs, or pairs of an adjective and a verb, which would fill two of the three places in a column with the third term lacking in the lexicon, for example, *wet/–/wet, –/lie down/lay down*. In some cases the expressions that enter this scheme have the same form (but note that they represent different lexemes as each belongs to a different grammatical category), as in the case of *open/open/open* and *harden/harden*. In others, the terms are related in form: *hard/harden*, and historically also *dead/die*. But the forms of the terms may as well be morphologically unrelated (*small/–/reduce*). There is a systematic meaning relation between the three members of each triplet. It can be captured by logical entailments, such as:

(9) a. *y hardens x* ⇒ *x hardens* and *x hardens* ⇒ *x will be hard*
   b. *z gives y to x* ⇒ *x gets y* and *x gets y* ⇒ *x will have y*

Clearly, a BFA approach is not able to explain these phenomena. One could, for example, assign a common feature [+OPEN] to the three terms in the first group in (8), and distinguish the three elements by two additional features, say [–CHANGE] for the adjective and [+CHANGE] for the two verbs and [+CAUSE] for distinguishing the third item from the other two. This would help to keep the three elements of a group apart and mark the terms of different groups in the same row as terms with common semantic characteristics, but it would not allow the explanation of the exact meaning relations.

7.4.1 Dowty's decompositional semantics

A classical, though not the earliest, decompositional approach to this phenomenon is Dowty (1979), a theory developed in the framework of Montague Grammar, which will be introduced in Chapter 10. Dowty analyses the adjective $open_A$ as a stative expression not further decomposed into meaning components. Using the notation of predicate logic, he represents the meaning of *x is open* by a simple formula in which the state term **open** is used as a one-place predicate constant:

(10) a. *x is open$_A$*:   **open**(x)

The meaning of the intransitive verb $open_{IV}$ is then represented by means of an operator BECOME which can be applied to any stative formula:

(10) b.   *x opens*$_{IV}$:   BECOME(**open**(x))

The component BECOME is used to express a change from a situation where the stative formula is false to a situation where it is true. If 'BECOME(**open**(x))' is true at a certain time t, then '**open**(x)' is false before t and true afterwards. It thus follows from the meaning representations of *open*$_A$ and *open*$_{IV}$ that *x opens*$_{IV}$ entails *x will be open*$_A$.

For the causative verb *open*$_{TV}$, Dowty employs an operator CAUSE which takes two argument terms, a simple individual term for the causer, and a formula for the event caused. The meaning of *y opens*$_{TV}$ *x* is represented as in (10c) and interpreted as ›y causes x to become open‹. Hence, *y opens*$_{TV}$ *x* logically entails *x opens*$_{IV}$.

(10) c.   *y opens*$_{TV}$ *x*:   CAUSE(y, BECOME(**open**(x)))[8]

Crucially, the meaning of *open*$_{TV}$ does not simply contain the three meaning components CAUSE, BECOME and **open** in the way the meaning of *woman* is thought to contain the three meaning components [+HUMAN], [−MALE] and [+ADULT] in BFA (three one-place predicates linked by conjunction). Rather, the three components combine with each other in a specific way. The component CAUSE is a two-place predicate; its first argument is the agent argument of the verb, its second argument is BECOME(**open**(x)), a complex containing the two meaning components BECOME and **open**. BECOME is used as a one-place predicate with a (stative) situation argument. This argument, in turn, consists of the one-place predicate **open** applied to the theme argument of the original verb.

An analogous analysis can be given for the other groups in (8). For example:

(11) a.   *x has y*:   **have**(x,y)
   b.   *x gets y*:   BECOME(**have**(x,y))
   c.   *z gives y to x*:   CAUSE(z, BECOME(**have**(x,y)))

The explanatory potential of the approach is obvious. There are hundreds if not thousands of inchoative and causative verbs whose meanings can be decomposed in this way. The decomposition completely uncovers the meaning relations that hold within and across the groups. This particular analysis is less concerned with the question of whether meaning components such as **open** or **have** are primitives. It might well be the case that some of them can be further decomposed, but this would not reduce the explanatory power of this kind of approach.

7.4.2 Jackendoff's Conceptual Semantics

Jackendoff's Conceptual Semantics[9] is another theory that deals with semantic phenomena concerning verbs. The foundations of his theory are quite different from Dowty's. Unlike Dowty, Jackendoff assumes that meanings are concepts represented in our mind. To him, basic semantic components are at the same time conceptual components out of which the human mind is capable of composing all kinds of concepts it operates with. The way in which meanings are decomposed in Jackendoff's approach is, however, similar to Dowty's. We cannot go deeper into the foundations of his theory nor enter into the details of his semantic representations, but will confine the discussion to a few examples that give an idea of one more way in which meanings can be decomposed.

With tense neglected, the sentence *John went home* would be analysed as (12a):

(12) a. *John went home:* $[_{Event}$ GO($[_{Thing}$ JOHN], $[_{Path}$ TO($[_{Place}$ HOME])])]

This looks more complicated than it actually is. Let us first omit the square brackets together with their subscripts. We then obtain a structure of the same kind as those used by Dowty:

(12) b. *John went home:*   GO(JOHN, TO(HOME))

GO is a primitive concept, and meaning component, for a movement of an object along a path. Correspondingly, the concept GO has an object argument and a path argument. In (12) the primitive concept JOHN fills the first argument position. The second position is occupied by TO(HOME), a specification of the path in terms of its goal. The one-place operator TO is another primitive concept, which takes a (concept for a) place as its argument, in this case HOME, and yields a concept for a path to this place. If we now return to the more complex notation in (12a), we see that each pair of square brackets [ ] encloses one concept; the subscript at the left bracket assigns the concept to one of a few basic categories: Event, Thing (including persons), Path and Place, others being Action, State, Time, Amount or Property. From (12a) we can abstract a semantic representation of the verb *go* by omitting the arguments of the GO concept and replacing them by empty slots.

(12) c.   *go:* $[_{Event}$ GO($[_{Thing}$ __], $[_{Path}$ __])]

It could be argued that (12) does not really constitute an instance of decomposition since the meaning of *go* is essentially represented by a conceptual primitive GO. This is not much better than representing the meaning of *pig* by a single binary feature [+PIG]. Jackendoff, however, argues that the concept GO happens to be a conceptual primitive. This makes the verb *go* a semantic primitive. The conceptual primitive GO is a component of concepts for all kinds of transitions. (Jackendoff's is a so-called localistic theory. Localism assumes that the linguistic concepts of space and motion are basic and serve as patterns for non-local concepts.) For instance, *John gave Bill $5* is represented as in (13a), brackets and subscripts omitted. The meaning of *give* itself would be (13b), with three empty argument places to be filled with concepts for the giver, the given and the recipient, respectively:

(13) a. *John gave Bill $5:*   CAUSE(JOHN, GO($5, TO(BILL)))
　　b. *give:*　　　　　　CAUSE(__ , GO(__ , TO(__)))

Embedded within the CAUSE concept, which has the same structure as the predicate **cause** in Dowty's analyses, we find the concept GO used to represent a transition of some object into the possession of Bill: the concept of motion in space is applied to a transfer of possession. The example may convey a first impression of the kind of generalizations a decompositional approach like this allows. In fact, it appears possible to reduce the meanings of thousands of verbs in English or any other language to a very limited number of general patterns composed out of a comparatively small set of basic conceptual components.

Again, the main asset of this approach lies in the possibility of forming complex meaning representations by way of embedding components into each other. Let me give you two more examples. The first one illustrates how selectional restrictions can be accounted for. The verb *drink* requires the object to be liquid. Jackendoff gives the analysis in (14a), simplified in (14b):

(14) a. *drink:*　$[_{Event}$ CAUSE($[_{Thing}$ __ $]_i$, $[_{Event}$ GO($[_{Thing}$ LIQUID$]_j$,
　　　　　　$[_{Path}$ TO($[_{Place}$ IN($[_{Thing}$ MOUTH OF($[_{Thing}$ __ $]_i$)]$)]$)]$)]$)]$

(14) b. *drink:*　CAUSE(__ $_i$, GO(LIQUID$_j$, TO(IN-MOUTH-OF __ $_i$)))

The structure of the meaning of *drink* is very similar to the structure of *give* in (13b).[10] The place for the 'moving' thing, i.e. the object that is drunk, is not just left open and categorized as Thing but specified by the concept LIQUID. The subscript '*j*' indicates that the argument is not implicit but has to be specified in the sentence. The specification of the object term is then 'fused' with the specification LIQUID (recall 6.7.2 for the process of fusion).

The other example is Jackendoff's analysis of the verb *butter*. The verb is obviously semantically related to the noun *butter*: it means ⟩spread (something) with butter⟨. In this concept, ⟩butter⟨ is an implicit argument of an underlying predicate (⟩spread with⟨). Jackendoff gives the following analysis for *butter* in a sentence like *Harry buttered the bread*, simplified in (15b):

(15) a. *butter:*　$[_{Event}$ CAUSE($[_{Thing}$ __ $]_i$,
　　　　　　$[_{Event}$ GO($[_{Thing}$ BUTTER$]$, $[_{Path}$ TO($[_{Place}$ ON($[_{Thing}$ __ $]_j$)]$)]$)]$)]$

　　b. *butter:*　CAUSE(__ $_i$, GO(BUTTER , TO(ON(__ $_j$))))

The sentence *Harry buttered the bread* can then be represented as in (16)

(16) *butter*:   CAUSE (HARRY, GO (BUTTER , TO (ON (BREAD))))

There are very many noun-verb pairs of this type in English. Of course, not all such pairs can be analysed in exactly the same way as *butter/butter*: think of *hammer/hammer* or *host/host*; obviously there are various patterns of decomposition and relations between the noun and the verb.

This may suffice as a sketch of the basic mechanisms and the explanatory power of what I would like to call 'formula' approaches to lexical decomposition. Both Dowty's and Jackendoff's approaches are parts of elaborated theories dealing with much more ambitious questions than just lexical decomposition. (For example, Jackendoff's approach also allows a derivation of the thematic roles of verbs from their meaning descriptions and a theory of linking.) Although their respective theoretical foundations and objectives are different, they use similar decompositional structures. Both work with abstract semantic primitives that have one or more arguments and thereby allow the embedding of other components. Thus it is possible to build up complex structures containing not only specifications of the referent – as BFA does – but of all arguments of the lexical item. An apparent restriction of the two approaches is the fact that they are only applied to verb meanings. There are, however, theories in a similar vein that deal with other lexical categories (cf. Bierwisch and Lang, 1989, for adjectives, and Pustejovsky, 1995, for his unified 'qualia' approach to nouns and verbs). What all formula approaches have in common is a formal apparatus (technically, a 'formal language') with a vocabulary of primitives and a precise syntax and semantics of its own that allows the formation of formulae as meaning representations.

7.5 Semantic primes: Wierzbicka's Natural Semantic Metalanguage

The last approach to decomposition to be discussed was developed by Wierzbicka. Her aim is the development of a system that allows the description of all meanings in all languages by means of a strictly limited set of 'semantic primitives' (or 'semantic primes', like 'prime numbers', in her terminology). She calls this system 'Natural Semantic Metalanguage', or NSM for short. NSM consists of a set of semantic primitives and a syntax for their combination. Let me give you her definition of the meaning of *envy* as a first example (Wierzbicka, 1996, p. 161):

(17)   X feels envy. =
          sometimes a person thinks something like this:
              something good happened to this other person
              it did not happen to me
              I want things like this to happen to me
          because of this, this person feels something bad
          X feels something like this

The defining part contains the semantic primitives, SOME, PERSON (= SOMEONE), THINK, (SOME)THING, LIKE, THIS, GOOD, HAPPEN, OTHER, NOT, I, WANT, BECAUSE, FEEL, BAD. They are combined into simple sentences following the syntactic rules of NSM.

For Wierzbicka and her followers the careful choice of semantic primitives is of central concern. An item qualifies as a semantic primitive under two conditions:

● It is *undefinable*, i.e. its meaning cannot be defined in terms of other expressions.
● It is *universal*, i.e. it is lexicalized in all natural languages.

Both requirements can only be met approximately. For example, many concepts appear to be interdefinable, e.g. ⟩eye⟨ and ⟩see⟨ (⟩eye⟨ = ⟩part of the body used for seeing⟨ and ⟩see⟨ = ⟩perceive with the eyes⟨). Which one is primitive can only be decided in practice. Universality is, of course, not verifiable. But the researchers adopting the approach did investigate a great number of languages, from Europe, Africa, Asia and Australia. So the primitives they sorted out on this basis are good candidates for universal primitives. Wierzbicka (1996, pp. 35f, 73f) lists 55 primitives, here rearranged; the list is constantly growing:

(18) I, YOU, SOMEONE (PERSON), SOMETHING (THING), PEOPLE; WORD
         THIS, THE SAME, OTHER, PART (OF), KIND (OF)
         ONE, TWO, MANY (MUCH), MORE, VERY, ALL, SOME (OF)
         THINK, KNOW, WANT, FEEL, SEE, HEAR, SAY
         GOOD, BAD; BIG, SMALL
         DO, HAPPEN; MOVE, THERE IS, (BE) ALIVE
         WHEN, BEFORE, AFTER; A LONG TIME, A SHORT TIME; NOW
         WHERE, UNDER, ABOVE; FAR, NEAR; SIDE; INSIDE; HERE
         NOT, CAN; IF, BECAUSE, LIKE, IF . . . WOULD, MAYBE

To the extent that the primitives are universal, every language is supposed to possess a corresponding set of lexemes, for example the words *I, you, someone* in English. If these lexemes are polysemous, they have to be taken in the relevant reading. For example, the English verb *want*, when considered the lexicalization of the NSM primitive WANT, must be taken as meaning 〉wish〈, not 〉lack〈. In addition, every language is supposed to possess syntactic rules for combining the lexical counterparts of the semantic primitives to the same effect as the primitives are combined in NSM. Thus the NSM meaning definitions can be translated into particular languages.

A few more examples may serve to show the kind of decompositional analysis possible in this framework. ABOVE and FAR are primitives that allow, among others, the definition of the meaning of *sky* (Wierzbicka 1996, p. 220):

(19) *sky*
>   something very big
>   people can see it
>   people can think like this about this something
>>   it is a place
>>   it is above all other places
>>   it is far from people

Once this concept is available, one can proceed to define the meaning of *sun* (Wierzbicka 1996, p. 220) and then of *blue* (Wierzbicka 1996, p. 309):

(20) *sun*
>   something
>   people can often see that something in the sky
>   when this something is in the sky people can see other things because of this
>   when this something is in the sky people often feel something because of this.

(21) *X* is blue. =
>   at some times people can see the sun above them in the sky
>   when one sees things like *X* one can think of the sky at these times

Let me finally illustrate how the NSM approach works for the kind of examples treated by Dowty and Jackendoff. Goddard (1998, p. 281) gives the following NSM definition of causative *break*, a verb that is of the same type as *open*$_{TV}$, discussed above.

(22) a. x_{Person} *break(s)* y (e.g. *Howard broke the window*) =
>   *a.* x does something to y
>   *b.* because of this, something happens to y at this time
>   *c.* because of this, after this y is not one thing any more[11]

Along the lines of Dowty and Jackendoff, the verb would be analysed as in (22b) and (22c), respectively:

(22)　b.　*x breaks y*:　　CAUSE(x, BECOME(**broken**(y)))
　　　　c.　*x breaks y*:　　CAUSE(x, GO(y, TO(BROKEN)))

The CAUSE component relates to an action of x that causes the change of y into the state of being broken. (The predicate **broken**/BROKEN in the two formulae is chosen just for convenience; for a non-circular definition it would have to be replaced appropriately.) This action, and the fact that it affects y, are expressed by the first two clauses in (22a). The change of state corresponding to BECOME(**broken**(y)) in (22b) and GO(y, TO(BROKEN)) in (22c) is expressed in a different, but equivalent way in the third clause of the NSM definition. Thus the analyses are very similar, although they look different.

Unlike the other approaches to decomposition, Wierzbicka's is not restricted to the analysis of certain word classes. It even offers meaning descriptions of emotion words like *envy* or colour terms or interjections (like *yuk!*), which other theories are unable to decompose. It is able to capture all sorts of meaning relations such as those that make up taxonomies (captured by means of the primitive KIND OF), or meronymies (captured by PART OF). More than any other approach, it allows the definition and comparison of word meanings in different languages. But the NSM method has its shortcomings too. First, it must be stated that NSM descriptions suffer from a certain lack of precision, as the primitives of NSM are very general and the definitions therefore rather vague. For example, the definition for *envy* given in (17) would also apply to self-pity or feeling neglected, etc. and the definition given for *break* also covers *cut, split, shatter* and similar verbs of destruction. For many NSM definitions, it is questionable whether they are sufficiently specific to capture the meaning of the terms defined. While this deficiency might be overcome by more elaborate definitions, a further drawback cannot be remedied: the approach is unable to explain meaning relations that hold between the primitives such as the antonymy of *big* and *small*, *good* and *bad*, *far* and *near*, or the directional opposition between *after* and *before*, or *under* and *above*. Their meaning relations are 'non-compositional' in this theory, i.e. they cannot be explained on the basis of meaning definitions in NSM, because these expressions have the status of undefinability.

7.6 Summary and evaluation of the approaches to decomposition

For the first time in this book, you have been exposed to theories (or parts of them). First, essentials of the structuralist approach were presented. Although no longer a leading paradigm in present-day linguistics, it still is very important. The method of analysing language as an autonomous

	BFA	Dowty	Jackendoff	Wierzbicka
Meaning	+	+	+	+
Basic meanings	(+)	(+)	(+)	+
Precision	(–)	+	+	(–)
Relations	(–)	+	+	(+)
Composition	(–)	+	+	(–)
Language comparison	(–)	(+)	(+)	+

Table 7.5 Evaluation of the approaches to decomposition

system, closed in itself, helped to establish linguistics as a science of its own. It also provided students of language and languages with the basic technique of determining the contrastive and combinatorial properties of units at different levels (from phonemes to sentences) in a systematic way. These methods are still valid.

Four approaches to decomposition were then introduced: BFA, which was developed in the tradition of structuralism, the formula approaches of Dowty and Jackendoff and Wierzbicka's NSM. Let us conclude the chapter with a brief evaluation (Table 7.5) of the four theories with respect to the objectives of semantic decomposition set out in the beginning:

M Providing models of word **meaning**.
B Reduction of word meanings to compositions of **basic** meanings.
P Allowing a **precise** interpretation of lexical items.
R Explaining meaning **relations**.
C Explaining the **compositional** properties of lexical items.
L Enabling meaning **comparison** across languages.

The approach that is still most popular (probably due to its simplicity), BFA, is the one with the most severe limitations. Being confined to very simple patterns of decomposition (i.e. conjunctions of one-place predicates), it is unable to account for all other types of meaning structures and, consequently, unable to capture meaning relations other than simple incompatibility, complementarity and hyponymy. Due to its insufficiency for semantic analysis in general it is of equally limited use for language comparison. The formula approaches perform equally well, due to their rich structures of meaning representations. They do not place too much emphasis on the basic nature of their primitives, hence the (+) ratings for Reduction and Language comparison. Their strength lies in the explanation of the compositional properties of verbs. Wierzbicka's is the only approach that makes basicness a central issue and focuses on language comparison. It is, however, less clear how the somewhat amorphous NSM definitions can be used for rigidly deriving meaning relations between lexical items, including the basic logical relations, and it remains open to what extent it is able to account for the compositional properties of lexical items. We also pointed out its lack of precision.

Checklist

decomposition
meaning component
structuralism
de Saussure
sign
arbitrariness
meaning
paradigm
   paradigmatic relations
   contrastive relations
   meaning relations
syntagm
   syntagmatic relations
   selectional restrictions
morpheme
lexeme
feature semantics
binary features
ideal properties of features
   primitive

general
universal
linguistically motivated
meaning postulates
kinds of features
   seme
   classeme
   marker
   distinguisher
semantic formulae
statives, inchoatives, causatives
Dowty
Conceptual Semantics
Jackendoff
Natural Semantic Metalanguage
Wierzbicka
semantic primitives/primes
   undefinability
   universality

Exercises

1   In which way is a linguistic unit integrated into, and defined by, the language system? What kinds of relations and properties determine the character of a linguistic unit?

2   What is the meaning of a lexeme according to the structuralist doctrine?

3   What is meant by the terms *syntagmatic relations* and *paradigmatic relations*? What, in particular, are syntagmatic and paradigmatic meaning relations? What do selectional restrictions have to do with these relations?

4   What is the difference between a lexeme and a morpheme?

5   How many and which morphemes make up the following words? For each morpheme (i) determine its input category and its output category (noun, verb, adjective) and (ii) find two more words that contain the same morpheme.

(a) *universality*   (b) *characterization*   (c) *unbelievable*

6   Which types of semantic features are distinguished in BFA? How do they differ? Try to give examples of expressions for which the different kinds of features can be considered meaning components.

7   Find ten more triplets of stative, inchoative and causative verbs (or adjectives, for the stative part). Check the entailments illustrated in (9). Try to find some examples in which not all items are morphologically related.

8   Discuss the advantages of formula approaches over BFA.

9   Discuss the differences between NSM and other approaches to decomposition.

Further reading

Saussure himself on structuralism (see Harris, 1983), also Lyons (1977, Chapter 12), more comprehensively Matthews (2001). Foley (1997, Chapter 4) on structuralism and its relation to linguistic anthropology. Dillon (1977) for an application of feature semantics. Lyons (1977, Chapter 9.9) for a criticism of feature semantics. Dowty (1979) requires a background in Montague Grammar, Jackendoff (1990) is somewhat easier to read, but cannot be fully understood without knowledge of Chomsky-type language theory and grammar. Goddard (1998) gives a survey of decompositional approaches and a very readable introduction into NSM analysis. Wierzbicka (1996) offers the essentials of NSM theory and its relation to semantic and cultural studies.

Notes

[1]   See Gussenhoven and Jacobs (1998, Chapter 1) for an explanation of the sounds. It is common practice in linguistics to write the phonetic pronunciation in square brackets [. . .] and with the symbols of the IPA (International Phonetic Association) alphabet, while the phonological form and phonemes (sound units of the language system) are written in slashes /. . . / using standard letters if possible.

[2]   This is a special use of the term *paradigm* in structuralist terminology. In morphology the term means something different, namely the set of all grammatical forms of a word.

[3]   See Haspelmath (2002) on the notion of morpheme and other basic concepts of morphology.

4 This only holds when the animal-related terms are used in their primary sense. Not surprisingly, these expressions can also be used derogatively for people. For example, 'saufen' applied to people means drinking greedily, excessively, etc. or being an alcoholic. *Halt dein Maul!* (lit. 'hold your [animal] mouth') has an extra negative expressive quality compared to the phrase *Halt deinen Mund!* with the neutral term for mouth. (Both expressions are rude.)

5 See Gussenhoven and Jacobs (1998, Chapter 5) for a phonological feature analysis.

6 In the view of more recent feature theories, the choice is a matter of markedness. Of the two alternatives, usually one is marked, or special, and the other unmarked, or normal, with clear linguistic criteria for markedness. Features and feature values are then chosen in the way that $[+\alpha]$ stands for the marked variant. In English, there is a certain tendency of marking expressions for female persons or animals (cf. *steward* vs *steward-ess*) by adding a special morpheme. This would provide a criterion for using the feature [±FEMALE] instead of [∓MALE].

7 From Latin *inchoare* 〉to begin〈.

8 The formulae used here are slightly simplified versions of the original ones given in Dowty (1979).

9 The following examples are taken from Jackendoff (1990).

10 The subscripts *i* and *j* are so-called referential indices. Identical indices indicate identical referents. Thus, the indexing in (14a) indicates that the drinking agent causes the object to 'go' into her or his own mouth. According to this analysis, the verb *drink* cannot be used for the action of pouring something into someone other's mouth, which is correct.

11 The original definition is in the past tense ('x *broke* y . . .'). The subscript PERSON on the variable x is used to distinguish this variant of the verb from the one in which the subject is an event, as in *the storm broke the window*.

Meaning and language comparison

8

If structuralism is right in assuming that every individual language is a
system of its own, we should expect that languages can be very different,
that they have terms for different things or different ways of naming the
same things and that similar situations are expressed in different ways and
from different perspectives. But how big are the differences between
languages? Are all languages essentially alike, allowing the expression of
the same thoughts, the communication of the same things, only differing in
their respective ways of formulation? Or are languages different to an
extent that it may be altogether impossible to express in one language what
can be expressed in another? Are the semantic systems completely
arbitrary, or are they constrained by universal principles?

We will start with simple examples that illustrate problems of translation. A closer look at different ways of expressing that someone has a
headache will take us a bit deeper into the matter of semantic comparison.
The second part will be devoted to studies of colour term systems across
languages. These studies played an important role not only for the understanding of the relationship between languages but also for the
development of semantics in general.

8.1 Translation problems

Everybody who seriously tries to learn a foreign language will sooner or
later realize how different languages are, not only with respect to grammar
and pronunciation but also with respect to their vocabulary and how it is
organized. When we naïvely begin to learn a new language, we will
probably start with the unconscious working hypothesis that for each word
in our native tongue there is a corresponding word in the target language.
But the more we get into the new language, the more this hypothesis will
crumble. People who have managed to master a foreign language to a

degree close to native-speaker competence would probably say that semantic equivalence of two lexemes is the exception rather than the rule.

There are different types of mismatch. One language may have two or more words where another language has only one:

(1) English   *mouse*   *rat*   *finger*   *toe*   *water*
     Japanese   *nezumi*   *yubi*   *mizu*   *yu*
                                                  ⟩cold w.⟨   ⟩warm w.⟨

But the relations can be more complicated. Consider the following lexical field in English and Japanese, and German for comparison:

(2) German   *Wald*   *Holz*   *Baum*
     English $wood_1$ $wood_2$ *tree*
     Japanese   *mori* ki_1 ki_2

English has a count noun $wood_1$ and a mass noun $wood_2$. A $wood_1$ consists of trees, while $wood_2$ is the substance trees largely consist of. Hence, the two meanings can be clearly distinguished on linguistic grounds. Likewise, the Japanese meanings of ki_1 and ki_2 are clearly different.[1] It follows that neither of the two English expressions matches either of the two Japanese words. They only match in one meaning variant, respectively.[2] In general, the ubiquitous polysemy of the vast majority of words suggests that (with the exception of number terms) there are almost no two expressions from different languages that have the same over-all meaning (cf. 3.3 for the parallel problem of total vs. partial synonymy).

In (2), the meanings of the English, German and Japanese terms at least (roughly) match in some of their possible readings. But in many cases, correspondences turn out to be more complicated. Even apparently basic and universal concepts such as ⟩eat⟨ and ⟩drink⟨ are differently lexicalized. A first glance at dictionaries will give us the following correspondences:

(3) German   *essen*   *trinken*
     English   *eat*   *drink*
     Japanese   *taberu*   *nomu*

But as was mentioned in 7.2.2, the German terms *essen* and *trinken* are reserved for people, unlike their English and Japanese counterparts. Even if we restrict the verbs to human agents, they do not match perfectly. In English and German, a (thin) soup can be either 'eaten' (*essen*) or 'drunk' (*trinken*), depending on whether a spoon is used or the soup is directly taken into the mouth. Japanese use the verb *nomu* regardless if the soup is drunk (which is the traditional technique) or consumed with a spoon. One might now think that the crucial criterion for using *nomu* is that the object be liquid. But this is not the case. The verb is also used for oral medicine, including pills. The crucial point appears to be that the object is directly swallowed without chewing. This is a different criterion from the one that regulates the use of English *drink* or German *trinken*. We cannot 'drink' a pill and we can eat a soup even if we do not chew it.

Still, these are cases where for every context appropriate translations are possible. But often a certain term in one language does not correspond to any term at all in the other language. This may be due to the fact that the things the term refers to simply do not exist where the other language is spoken, e.g. plants or animals or meals or artefacts or social institutions. But it also happens in semantic areas that are shared. Consider the area of working. English has a verb *to work* which, like German *arbeiten*, covers a broad range of activities, paid work as well as unpaid work (e.g. in one's own kitchen or garden). The work may be physical or intellectual work such as reading this book, learning German or studying linguistics. Japanese has no term that covers all these activities. The closest equivalent to the verb *work* is *hataraku*, but it does not cover intellectual work. On the other hand, Japanese has a verb *asobu* that can be used for any kind of activity that is *not* work: playing, any kind of entertainment or leisure including doing nothing at all. No simple verb with this meaning exists in English or German.

An insurmountable problem for adequate translations can be posed by differences in social meaning. Imagine an American movie of the type 'boy meets girl'. John, a yuppie real estate agent, meets Mary, a tough customer, and falls in love with her. If the dialogues are translated into German, the translators have to decide whether John and Mary address each other with *Sie* or *du* (2.4). They will have to start with *Sie*, because that would be adequate, to a German audience, for the business relationship between them, and will end up addressing each other with *du* once they have become intimate. The problem for the translator will be: when do they switch from *Sie* to *du*?

With Japanese, things are much more complex. First, there are several expressions available to render English *I* and *you*, respectively. Each one has a different social meaning, i.e. indicates different social relations. Second, in very many cases the use of pronoun-like expressions for self-reference and address is altogether inadequate in Japanese. For example, in a dialogue between mother and son, the son would normally address his mother with 'Mrs Mother' (*okâsan*), not with any variant of 'you'. Referring to himself he would either use a variant of 'I' or his own name(!), but not 'Mr Son'. His mother would refer to herself preferably as 'Mrs Mother' and address her son with a variant of 'you' or his name. For example, little Taro could ask his mother something of the form (4a) and his mother could answer (4b):

(4) a.   'Will Mrs Mother buy Taro an ice-cream?'
   b.   'Mrs Mother will buy Taro an ice-cream.'

Compare these forms to the adequate ways of expression in Western languages with the characteristic switch between the pronouns *I* and *you* for the same arguments of the predicate.

(5) a. 'Will **you** buy **me** an ice-cream?'

b. ' **I** will buy **you** an ice-cream.'

For Western ears, the sentences in (4) are formulated as though they were said about third persons. In fact, (4a) can as well be used, for example, by Taro's elder sister for asking a question to her father, *about* Taro and her mother, and her father could use (4b) as an answer.

Similar rules govern the forms of address and self-reference outside the family. Students would normally address their teachers as 'Teacher' (*sensei*) or 'name+Teacher' (e.g. *Yamamoto Sensei*), but not with 'you'. Direct translations of Western dialogue with personal pronouns would yield exchanges that sound grossly inadequate to Japanese. Conversely, if dialogues are to be translated from Japanese into English or other Western languages, a directly analogous translation would sound inadequate, if not misleading, while the choice of pronouns instead of relational terms and proper names would lead to an improper understanding of the social interactions and relationships between the protagonists.

8.2 Headache, international

Deeper in the language system we find differences in grammar. Examples are abundant once we compare historically unrelated languages, e.g. English and Japanese. In terms of structural differences, Japanese is not as 'exotic' as many other languages, for example native languages of the Americas, Australia or Papua New Guinea. But with respect to some semantic phenomena Japanese grammar differs considerably from English or other Western languages.

As an illustration, we will compare the ways in which having a headache is expressed in some European languages and in Japanese. A headache situation involves three ingredients: (i) an experiencer E who feels the headache; (ii) the sensation S, a pain that E feels; (iii) the body part B that aches: the head. Languages express the situations by a variety of grammatical patterns in which these three ingredients figure in different ways:

(6) a. English: *I have a headache*[3]

The English construction ties S and B, the pain and where it is felt, together into one concept 〉headache〈. In a possessive construction with the verb *have*, this entity B-S is said to 'belong' to E. The verb *have* can be used for a wide range of abstract relations, not only for possession. Somebody 'has' a peculiar name, a word 'has' an unknown origin or the bath water 'has' a certain temperature. What is expressed by *have* in (6a) is that the headache is in some way associated with E. Note that the relation would be much more specific if one said *I feel a headache* instead. The English construction is paralleled in German, with the slight difference that the sensations are in the plural, but there is also the synonymous *ich habe Kopfweh* (singular). The standard French phrase is also similar:

(6) b. German 1: *ich habe Kopfschmerzen*
          lit. 'I have headaches'
     c. French: *j'ai mal à la tête*
          lit. 'I've bad at the head'

French has a possessive construction with three argument terms, E in the subject position, S in the object position and B in a locative PP.

There is an alternative German construction that is similar to the standard Russian way of expressing the situation:

(6) d. German 2: *mir tut der Kopf weh*
          lit. '[to] me aches the head'[4]
     e. Russian: *u menya bolit golova*
          lit. 'at me aches head'

The main predicate, i.e. the verb, directly expresses the sensation itself, not some abstract association of E with S (the German verb *wehtun* 'ache/hurt' splits in two parts in this sentence type). The subject specifies the aching part B, while the experiencer term is put into an indirect object or PP position. Thus the head is what the statement focuses on, not the experiencer. A similar variant is used in Hungarian:

(6) f. Hungarian: *fáj*   *a*   *fej-em*
                      aches   the   head-POSS1SG, SG [5]
          lit. 'aches the head-of-mine '

Here the verb is used as a one-place predicate with B as its only argument. B, in turn, is specified with the possessive suffix as the B of E. B and E are tied into one.

The usual Japanese equivalent of the sentences in (6a-f) is (7a):

(7) a. Japanese[6] *atama*   *ga*   *ita-i*
                       head   NOM   feel aching-PRESENT TENSE
          lit. 'head feels aching'

Itai is a so-called verbal adjective (VA). Verbal adjectives carry a tense ending and can form the VP in predicative use. They function like a copula plus predicative adjective in English. Interestingly, the VA *itai* has only one argument, B, specified by the subject of the sentence. But what about the experiencer E? How do I know from a sentence like (7a) whose head it is that aches? The really interesting thing about Japanese is that one *does* know from the sentence, and this is a point where Japanese differs radically from English, German, French, Russian, Hungarian and many other languages.

The answer is simple: the experiencer in the case of (7a) is the speaker. There are only two exceptions. (i) The sentence could, with appropriate intonation, also be used as a question; it would then mean ⟩Do *you* have a headache?⟨. (ii) In a literary text with a central protagonist, whose eyes and mind the narration is told through, it could relate to that person. The crucial point is that *itai* means a subjective sensation, not an objective phenomenon. Subjective sensations, like the feeling of pain, itch, appetite, grief or longing, only exist for the experiencer. (7a) says something like 'the head feels aching'. E is the only one who can state this or answer the corresponding question. A specification of E can be explicitly added to the sentence, as in (7b, c), but it has to be semantically redundant. (7d) is unacceptable, except for the special literary reading mentioned. (TOP is the Japanese topic marker, which is hard to translate. It means something like 'as for . . .', but is less heavy.)

(7)	b.	*Watashi*	*wa atama ga itai.*	'As for me, head feels aching'
		I	TOP . . .	
	c.	*Anata*	*wa atama ga itai?*	'As for you, head feels aching?'
		you	TOP . . .	
	d.	*Mary wa atama ga itai.*		'As for Mary, head feels aching.'[7]

Sentence (7a) is syntactically complete. Words such as *itai* have an implicit argument for the direct experiencer. Thus Japanese represents the third logical possibility of tying together two of the three ingredients, this time S and E. It is worth noting that, wherever two ingredients are tied together, the combination is asymmetric in that it denotes primarily one of the two. In the B-S combination *headache/Kopfschmerzen* the component S is dominant (technically: the 'head' of the compound, 5.1.2), because a headache is an ache in the head rather than a head full of ache. The dominant element in the Hungarian B-E combination is the noun for B, in the Japanese S-E component the sensation S dominates, since the expression *itai* denotes a sensation.

The five patterns are compared in Figure 8.1. A rectangle indicates the central predicate expressed by the verb, circles represent its arguments; the subject is shaded. Where two ingredients are tied together, the dominating one is indicated by larger type.

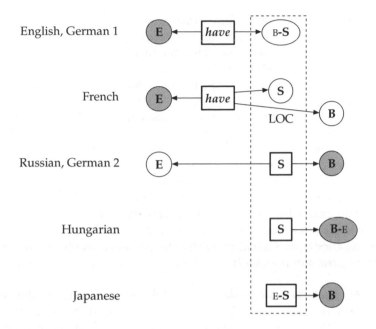

Figure 8.1 Headache constructions

These are not all the types that are logically possible. For example, our sample contains no constructions with B or E in predicate position. These, however, are unlikely. Given the typical function of verbs as denoting events and states of a temporary nature as opposed to nouns that tend to denote the more permanent objects of experience, we will expect that neither E nor B will figure as the verb of the construction. But there remain further plausible possibilities. Instead of a verb of the type *have* there might be constructions using *be* ('a pain is in my head') that put the sensation into the subject position. Also there may be languages where the pain is expressed by a two-place predicate with E in subject position ('I ache-feel my head'). And certainly there are languages that tie all three ingredients together into one complex predication of type **S**-ʙ-ᴇ.

As we have seen, the Japanese construction does not provide a syntactic position for the specification of the experiencer. How, then, is it possible to express that someone else has a headache? In the other languages considered, we can simply replace the experiencer 'I' by an appropriate NP and change the verb form if necessary. The resulting expressions are perfectly analogous to the first person variants (with the exception that the Hungarian construction needs an additional dative position for the possessor NP if it is not pronominal; the result is a construction very similar to German 2):

(8) a. English: *John has a headache.*
  b. German 2:   *John tut der Kopf weh.*
                           John-DAT aches the head
  c. Hungarian: *John-nak fáj a fej-e.*
                           John-DAT aches the head-POSS3SG,SG

Strictly speaking, Japanese has no way of saying this. But of course it has means of talking about third persons' headaches. The ways in which it can be done are interesting because they reflect a point that usually goes unnoticed to native speakers of languages such as English, Russian or Hungarian. Since all persons have their own body and their own sensations, we can never really *know* that someone else has a headache, not in the sense of knowing which experiencers themselves know. Knowledge about someone else's sensations is necessarily second-hand, and this is the way statements about such situations *must* be put in Japanese. (9) shows the three most common possibilities:

(9) a. *John wa atama ga itai-sô da.*   'John says he has a headache'
  b. *John wa atama ga ita-sô da.*   'John seems to have a headache'
  c. *John wa atama ga ita-gat-te iru.*   'John is displaying symptoms of
                                        having a headache'

In each case, the NP *John* is added to the basic construction as a topic and/or subject marked with the topic particle *wa*. In (9a) the nominal suffix *-sô* plus the copula verb *da* is added to the full form of the adjective *itai*, including the tense ending *-i*, to render the sense of John saying he has a headache. In (9b) the nominal suffix *-sô* plus copula is added to the bare stem *ita-* of the adjective, meaning something like the English *seem to* construction. The third pattern puts the experiencer into a more active role of displaying symptoms of, or behaving like, having a headache. The construction involves a verbal suffix *-garu* that turns a verbal adjective into a verb. It is here used in its progressive present tense form *-gatte iru*.

The grammar of Japanese strictly distinguishes between statements that we are entitled to make on the basis of first-hand knowledge and statements for which we rely on second-hand evidence. The so-called **evidential** constructions in (9) are widely used. There are about 70 adjectives for emotions, feelings, sensations and mental states that are used in the same way as *itai*, e.g. for feeling happy (*ureshii*), sad (*kanashii*), lonesome (*sabishii*), cold (*samui*) or hot (*atsui*), for liking (*suki*) and hating (*iya, kirai*), for being afraid (*kowai*), finding something cute (*kawaii*) or delicious (*oishii*).[8] One can only say of something that it is *oishii* if one has actually tasted it. Something that appears delicious would be said to be *oishi-sô* (cf. (9b)). This type of adjectives includes the volitional forms of verbs that are formed with the suffix *-tai* that turns verbs into verbal adjectives rendering the meaning

⟩want to V⟨. One can say 'I want to go' (*iki-tai*, from *iku* ⟩go⟨), but not with the same construction 'John wants to go' (**John wa iki-tai*). Again, one would have to use an evidential construction meaning ⟩John seems to want to go⟨ (*John wa iki-ta-sô da*, etc.)

The comparison of the way in which bodily sensations, feelings and wishes are expressed offers an insight into the nature of knowledge. Languages such as Japanese force upon the language user the distinction between first-hand and second-hand evidence. This insight could not be obtained from the analysis of languages such as English that treat feelings of oneself and the feelings of other persons alike and in the same way as any kind of objective observations, e.g. *John has red hair*.

8.3 Relativism and universalism

How different are languages? The possible positions regarding this question range between two extremes. One is called **universalism**. According to the universalist position, all languages obey the same principles. The structure of every language is some variant of universal grammar, and universal grammar is part of the human genetic equipment. Likewise, the cognitive system is genetically determined. For biological reasons, all human beings perceive themselves and their environments essentially in the same way, they form the same kinds of concepts and organize them into the same kind of complex model of the world. Consequently, languages can only differ within a limited range of variation. There do exist considerable differences between languages. The environment in which a linguistic society lives and the culture it has developed will be reflected in the language. For example, each language community will have a particularly elaborate vocabulary in those areas of life that are of central importance. But ultimately, the universalist would argue, all languages make use of the same mental resources. They differ only in the way in which these resources are used.

The opposite position is known as linguistic **relativism**. To an extreme relativist, each language is radically different. Due to its unique grammar and its uniquely structured lexicon, it represents a unique way of talking about the world and corresponds to a particular way of thinking. Each language represents, and causes, a world view of its own. The relativist position is connected with the names of two American linguists who worked on indigenous North American languages in the first half of the twentieth century, Edward Sapir (1884–1939) and Benjamin Whorf (1897–1941). The following passage from Whorf is often quoted as a formulation of the so-called **Sapir-Whorf hypothesis** (Whorf, 1956: 212–14, the original date of publication is 1940):

Formulation of ideas is not an independent process, strictly rational in the old sense, but is part of a particular grammar, and differs, from slightly to greatly, between different grammars. We dissect nature along lines laid down by our native languages. The categories and types that we isolate from the world of phenomena we do not find there because they stare every observer in the face; on the contrary, the world is presented in a kaleidoscopic flux of impressions which has to be organized by our minds – and this means largely by the linguistic systems in our minds. We cut nature up, organize it into concepts, and ascribe significances as we do, largely because we are parties to an agreement to organize it in this way – an agreement that holds throughout our speech community and is codified in the patterns of our language. The agreement is, of course, an implicit and unstated one, but its terms are absolutely obligatory; we cannot talk at all except by subscribing to the organization and classification of data which the agreement decrees.

Applied to the Japanese evidentials, this view would mean that the members of the Japanese speech community implicitly agree that second-hand evidence of emotions and perceptions is to be distinguished from first-hand knowledge. This claim is plausible, and there are many other phenomena where linguistic structures can be linked to the culture of a speech community. Take, for example, the Japanese terms for siblings which, in usual colloquial Japanese, force the language user to distinguish between younger and elder siblings. This trait of Japanese is not accidental. Japanese society is extremely hierarchical. No two persons that are in some social relation to each other are of the same rank. For example, those who are older rank higher than those who are younger and men rank higher than women. The ranking rules are deeply rooted in social behaviour *and* in language use and structure. For example, while siblings in Western societies address each other mutually by their first names, the mode of address between Japanese siblings of different ages is asymmetric. Elder siblings are addressed by their title, as it were, namely the polite versions of *ane* and *ani* (*onê-san* and *onî-san*, respectively, the latter literally meaning ⟩Mr elder brother⟨), but younger siblings are just called by their names.

The domain of sexuality provides another case of correspondence between culture and language. Due to a long history of sexual taboo enforced by the Christian Church, European languages exhibit remarkable lexical peculiarities. The taboo is reflected in the massive use of circum-scriptions, i.e. indirect ways of expression. The words for ⟩bra⟨ mentioned in 4.6.1 may illustrate the point. The French expression *soutien-gorge*, liter-ally meaning ⟩throat support⟨, avoids mentioning what is really 'supported' by referring instead to a neighbouring part of the body that is not taboo. The English term *bra* is even more indirect. It is an abbreviation of *brassiere* (a French loan word deriving from *bras* ⟩arm⟨) and originally means a short vest or top. The Spanish term *sujetador* (lit. ⟩subjugator⟨) reflects the sexual taboo in not mentioning the object of subjugation and in a negative attitude towards it as something to be subjugated. By contrast, the Tok Pisin notion ⟩prison of the breasts⟨ (*kalabus bilong susu*) mentions the breasts directly and reflects the loss of freedom that came with this particular item of Western culture and the foreign taboo that made it necessary.

Such phenomena, however, do not directly support the strong relativist position. Is it really language that forces Japanese into their hierarchical social thinking, or Westerners into observing sexual taboos? Rather, it appears, that language *reflects* social structure and cultural standards. It is true that it is not possible to talk directly about sexuality if the language does not provide the appropriate words. But the so-called sexual revolution in Western culture in the last decades has shown that speech communities rapidly develop socially acceptable expressions when the taboo loses force.

It must also be observed that particular grammatical traits of a language need not influence the world view of its users. For example, many European languages have grammatical gender. In French and Spanish each noun is either masculine or feminine, in German and Russian nouns are either masculine, feminine, or neuter. Gender determines, among other things, the form of the definite article (*le/la* in French, *der/die/das* in German). It would, however, be absurd to conclude that the gender classification imposes any kind of different world views upon the user. The fact that the German nouns for ⟩government⟨, ⟩street⟨ and ⟩banana⟨ (*Regierung, Straße, Banane*) are of feminine gender does not make speakers think of these things as having anything in common, in particular not female sex.

Although these observations point towards a differentiated position somewhere between universalism and relativism, the central questions remain. How different are languages? How deep are these differences? What do the observable differences indicate? Do they correspond to different ways of thinking? The questions are far from being settled. We will now turn to one field where extensive comparative research has been done: the field of colour term systems.

8.4 Berlin and Kay's investigation of colour terms

The spectrum of colours, the same for all human beings with normal vision, forms a continuum with no natural boundaries between the colours: red shades into orange, pink, purple, brown; orange into yellow and red, and so on. Thus it is to be expected that languages cut the colours up in different ways, into a different number of colour terms that denote different parts of the colour space. In fact it was held that languages lexicalize colours arbitrarily.[9] It was the investigation reported in Berlin and Kay (1969) which changed the scene dramatically.

The study covered approximately 100 languages from all over the world.

For 20 languages native speakers were interviewed. For the rest, Berlin and Kay drew on previous studies, grammars and dictionaries. They investigated how many colour terms these languages possess and to which range of colours each term refers. Such an investigation is only possible if it is restricted to what Berlin and Kay called **basic colour terms** (BCT, for short). English, for example, has hundreds of lexicalized colour terms (think of the vocabulary for the colours of lipsticks, eye-shadows, fashion accessories, cars, etc.). Only a few of them are basic. The main criterion for a basic colour term is:

BCTs are not subordinates of other colour terms.

This excludes terms like *olive* (a shade of green), *crimson* (red) or *chocolate* (brown). In addition, Berlin and Kay used the following criteria: BCTs are simple words, not compounds or derivations (like *greenish, dark green, mint-green, blue-green*); BCTs are not restricted to a narrow class of objects (cf. *blond* for hair); BCTs (not the colours they denote) are 'psychologically salient', i.e. they '[tend] to occur at the beginning of elicited lists of color terms', are stable across informants and across occasions and used by all informants.[10] Berlin and Kay also ruled out recent loan words (such as *aubergine*) and colour terms that are derived from the name of an object characteristically having that colour, such as *gold, silver, olive*, etc. *Orange* originally belonged to this class, but it qualifies as a genuine BCT since it fulfils the main criterion of being a term on a par with *red* and *yellow* rather than a subordinate of either.

Berlin and Kay let their subjects perform two tests. First, they elicited the set of BCTs. Then the informants were shown a chart of 329 colour chips (from the Munsell Color Company), 9 for black and white and different shades of grey, and 320 others, arranged in a field of 8 by 40 chips, that horizontally range from red via orange, yellow, green, blue, purple to red and vertically from near-white to near-black (see Figure 8.2, the original colour chart is depicted in Berlin and Kay, 1969 and in Palmer, 1996). They asked the subjects for each BCT (i) to point out the focal colour chip, i.e. the chip that was considered the best example for this BCT; and (ii) to indicate the outer boundary of the range of colours denoted by the BCT.

It turned out that informants of the same language narrowly agreed on the focal colours, but indicated the boundaries differently. The main result, however, was this: the languages vary in the number of BCTs from two to eleven.[11] But there are only eleven focal colours for the BCTs in all the different languages. These are focal (i.e. pure) white, grey, black, red, orange, yellow, green, blue, purple, pink and brown (indicated by the dots in Figure 8.2). These are the foci of the English BCTs *white, grey, black, red, orange*, etc. and of the corresponding words in all other languages with eleven BCTs. If a language has fewer BCTs, their foci are nonetheless among these eleven focal colours.

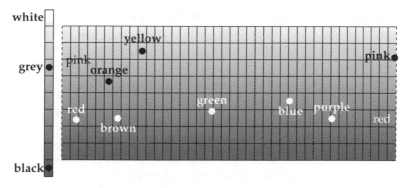

Figure 8.2 Munsell colour chart used by Berlin and Kay

For the BCTs in languages with less than the maximum number of terms, the range of colours a BCT denotes is wider, the smaller the number of BCTs. For example, in a language with five BCTs, focusing on focal black, white, red, yellow and blue or green, the red-term also applies to the greater part of orange and pink as well as to reddish purple and brown because there are no BCTs for orange, pink, purple and brown. If a language has no separate terms for blue and green, then one term covers both. In order to keep the different denotations of BCTs with identical focus apart, BCTs are denoted in the form BLACK/3, GREEN/5 etc. For example, BLACK/3 is a BCT in a three-BCT system with focus black. The findings of Berlin and Kay can then be represented as in Table 8.1. They distinguish seven stages of BCT

Stage	BCTs							
I	BLK/2	WHI/2						
II	BLK/3	WHI/3	RED/3					
IIIa	BLK/4	WHI/4	RED/4	YEL/4				
IIIb	BLK/4	WHI/4	RED/4		GRN/4			
IV	BLK/5	WHI/5	RED/5	YEL/5	GRN/5			
V	BLK/6	WHI/6	RED/6	YEL/6	GRN/6	BLU/6		
VI	BLK/7	WHI/7	RED/7	YEL/7	GRN/7	BLU/7	BRN/7	
VII	BLK/8	WHI/8	RED/8	YEL/8	GRN/8	BLU/8	BRN/8	GREY/8 *or* ORANGE/8 *or* PINK/8 *or* PURPLE/8
Focus	black	white	red	yellow	green	blue	brown	grey etc.

Table 8.1 The seven stages of colour term systems in Berlin and Kay (1969)

systems, depending on the number of BCTs. Languages with eight to eleven BCTs are all assigned to stage VII.

The findings show that the existing BCT systems are far from arbitrary. With the minor exception of stage III, languages with the same number of BCTs have BCTs for essentially the same colour categories. All stage-II languages have BCTs with the foci white, black and red. There are no white–black–green or yellow–red–blue languages. Furthermore, each system of a higher stage includes the system of all lower stages: if a language at a certain stage has a BCT with focus x, all languages of higher stages also have a BCT with that focus. Conversely, the presence of the BCTs of later stages implies the presence of all BCTs of earlier stages. For example, each language with a term for blue has BCTs for black, white, red, yellow and green.

From the distribution of BCT systems, Berlin and Kay drew the conclusion that the possible systems form evolutionary stages. The two BCTs of stage-I systems, WHITE/2 and BLACK/2, are terms for light/warm colours (white, yellow, red) and dark/cool colours (black, blue, green), respectively. In the transition to stage II, WHITE/2 splits into WHITE/3 for light colours (white) and RED/3 for warm colours (red, yellow), while BLACK/3 continues to denote dark/cool colours. When we proceed to stage III, in one variant yellow splits from RED/3 to form a category of its own, resulting in a system with WHITE/4 for light (white), RED/4 for red, YELLOW/4 for yellow and BLACK/4 still covering all dark/cool colours. Alternatively, green and blue together split from BLACK/3, forming a new colour category often called 'grue' that focuses on either focal green or focal blue (but never on turquoise). In the resulting system, yellow is still mostly denoted by RED/4. In the transitions to later stages up to V, the denotations of multicolour BCTs split further, e.g. grue into blue and green. The higher BCTs with foci on brown, grey, orange, pink and purple are not the result of splittings but of establishing terms for hues that lie between the foci of the six terms of stage V.

The findings of Berlin and Kay triggered a great number of follow-up studies. As a result, their findings were slightly revised. The larger categories of the early stages may have more than one focus, e.g. white, yellow, and red for WHITE/2 or green and blue for GREEN/4. It turned out that there are certain types that do not fit into the sequential chain, e.g. languages of stage III with a BCT for grue but yellow still going with white, while in stage-II systems yellow is already separated from white. Also the order of appearance of the 'higher' colours is less strict, and some languages have twelve BCTs.[12] But these are minor modifications. The main results were confirmed:

- The denotations of BCTs are best described in terms of focal colours.
- There is a limited universal set of eleven (or twelve) focal colours. The best representatives of BCTs are invariably among these focal colours.

- The possible types of systems form a sequence – starting with a contrast between WHITE/WARM and BLACK/COOL – in which the higher systems are extensions of the lower systems.

8.5 Consequences

What follows from the findings on colour terms for the structuralist view of language? The results certainly prove that the arbitrariness of lexicalization can be constrained. Still, languages differ largely in their colour terminology. Also, another doctrine of structuralism has been confirmed: the denotations of terms within the same field are interdependent and define each other: the range of a BCT with a given focus depends on how many other BCTs compete with it.

And what do the findings mean for the debate between relativism and universalism? Originally, the results were considered evidence against the Sapir-Whorf hypothesis. But are they really? It was claimed (Kay and McDaniel, 1978) that the universal constraints on the colour vocabularies are directly rooted in the nature of human colour perception. Even if this is right, this cannot be generalized to most other semantic domains. Most of the things languages have words for are not like colours. For example, we can see animals, but we do not have specialized dog cells and cat cells. Animal concepts, e.g. the meaning of the English word *pig*, are not based on sense data alone such as the visual appearance – although visual shape is probably part of the concept. In addition, animal concepts are based on cultural aspects. For example, the English ⟩pig⟨ concept will reflect that pigs are domesticated and eaten (witness the meaning relation between the words *pig* and *pork*). Thus, languages will associate culturally determined concepts with animal terms even if the terms refer to the same biological species. For other semantic domains, the findings on colour terms and colour perception have no significance at all. Many expressions do not refer to anything objective that can be perceived with our senses. Consider a word like *mistake*. The notion ⟩mistake⟨ appears quite natural and basic to us. But it presupposes complex cultural systems of rules that determine what is right and what is wrong and in which regard.

Relativism is certainly right in emphasizing the differences between languages. They do exist, they are the rule rather than the exception, they are deep – and they are fascinating. A relativist attitude is absolutely necessary for all who seriously try to understand other languages. It provides the only chance to escape the natural tendency of applying one's old views and categories to new things. Only when we expect other languages to be different from our native language, will we be able to recognize and understand the differences. Thus, relativism is the better working hypothesis. Once we are aware of the differences between languages, we may set out to satisfy the universalist by trying to determine the common denominator that makes a comparison possible. After all, it must exist, because otherwise we would not have been able to grasp the differences with our one and only mind.

Checklist

translation
   terms of address
relativism vs. universalism
Sapir-Whorf hypothesis
world view
   evidentials

basic colour terms (BCTs)
   Berlin and Kay
   colour terms
   focal colour
   stages of BCT systems

Exercises

1   When words are imported from other languages, their meaning is often changed more or less. For example, the German word *Arbeit* (›work‹) was borrowed into Japanese, where it was shortened to *baito*. Japanese *baito* has a narrower meaning, denoting part-time students' jobs such as giving private lessons.
   (a) Try to find three words in your native language that are borrowed from other languages. Consult dictionaries to determine their meanings in both languages.
   (b) Try to find an explanation why the meanings of loanwords so often differ from their origins – despite the fact that they are apparently borrowed for their meaning.

2   Try to determine the meaning relations that hold between the following pairs of words. First look up the translation of the English term in a bilingual dictionary, then cross-check with a reverse dictionary:
   (a) English *man*   vs   German *Mann*
   (b) English *blue*   vs   German *blau*

3   Another area that is subject to cultural taboos is death. Try to find a couple of English expressions that illustrate the influence the taboo exerts on language.

4   Ask three people to spontaneously list 20 or more colour terms in the order in which they come to their minds. Compare the results. Are the eleven BCTs among the words listed? Do they appear towards the beginning of the list? Which are the first five items?

5   Given that a BLACK/3 BCT covers not only black but also blue, green and other colours, why is it considered a case of BLACK/3 rather than, say, BLUE/3?

6   What are the essentials of the relativist and the universalist positions? Which position do you think is realistic? What is your own position in view of your own personal experience with foreign languages?

Further reading

Suzuki (1978, Chapter 5) for Japanese terms of address and self-reference, Kuroda (1973) for Japanese evidentials, Palmer (2001, Chapter 2.2) on evidentials in general. Whorf (1940) for a basic outline of the relativist position. Salzmann (1993, Chapter 8) for a discussion of the Sapir-Whorf Hypothesis and the relation between language and culture. Palmer (1996, Chapter 6) on language and world view. Berlin and Kay (1969) for the original report of their investigations of colour term systems; Kay and McDaniel (1978) for an explanation of the universals in terms of colour perception; Wierzbicka (1996) for an alternative account in the framework of NSM. Foley (1997, Chapter 7) for an up-to-date discussion of the research in colour terminology, Chapter 6 on kinship term systems in the context of the relativism vs. universalism debate. Lee (1996) offers a careful reconstruction of Whorf's original theory and its fate in the relativist–universalist debate. See also Lucy (1992) for a comprehensive discussion of the relationship between language(s) and thought including a critical evaluation of the colour term experiments.

Notes

[1]   It should, however, be noted that it is not justified to assume that a word in one language is polysemous *whenever* there is another language that has two or more expressions covering the same denotation. For example, one would not assume that the English word *brother* is ambiguous between ⟩elder brother⟨ and ⟩younger brother⟨ just because there are languages with two separate terms (cf. Table 7.1). Polysemy must be linguistically relevant within one language, and there is no evidence in English for the word *brother* behaving differently if it is used to refer to a younger brother than referring to an older brother. In the case of English *wood* and Japanese *ki* the assumption of polysemy is linguistically justified.

[2]   Curiously, the title of the Beatles song *Norwegian wood* (on the LP *Rubber Soul*) was translated into Japanese as *Norway no mori* (⟩forest⟨), although in the song and its title *wood* is clearly meant in the sense of *wood₂* (= ki_1).

[3]   This is the most common construction. Alternatively, headaches can also be expressed by the variants *my head is aching*, or *my head is hurting me*, which are similar to the Hungarian construction (6f) and German 2 (6d), respectively.

[4]   The two German constructions are not completely equivalent, the latter being more generally applicable to any kind of pain felt in or at the head, but that does not matter for the present discussion.

[5]   *-em/-am* is a noun suffix that indicates possession to the speaker and singular number of the noun.

[6]   In order to keep the grammatical structures of the sentences as transparent as possible, Japanese examples are given in the so-called plain style lacking all formality markers (cf. 2.3.2).

7   The sentence may, perhaps, be read as meaning something like ⟩when I think of Mary, I'm getting a headache⟨, but it cannot mean ⟩Mary has a headache⟨.

8   See Martin (1975, p. 361) for a survey.

9   See Berlin and Kay (1969, n.1, p. 159f) for quotations of this position.

10 See Berlin and Kay (1969, p. 6) for the details.

11 The maximum number was later corrected to 12 (see below).

12 For example, Russian has two BCTs for lighter and darker blue, Hungarian has two for red.

Meaning and cognition

9

During the past three decades, the development of a new branch of science, cognitive psychology, or more generally **cognitive science**, has given important fresh impetus to linguistics in general and semantics in particular. Cognitive science is concerned with how the human mind works, how it receives information from the environment via the senses and processes this information, recognizing what is perceived, comparing it to former data, classifying it and storing it in the memory. It tries to account for the complex ways in which the vast amount of information is structured in our minds, how we can operate with it when we think and reason. Language plays a central role in these theories. On the one hand, speech perception and production and the underlying mental structures are major objects of investigation. On the other hand, the way in which we use language to express what we 'have in mind' can tell much about how the human mind is organized.

The importance of cognitive psychology for semantics lies in its emphasis on the exploration of the concepts and categories we use. While semantics in the wider tradition of structuralism aims at a description of meaning relations, the cognitive approach focuses on meanings themselves. It tries to provide positive descriptions of the word meanings, and thereby to account for why and how words denote what they denote. In terms of the semiotic triangle, a cognitive approach to semantics can be characterized as focusing on the base of the triangle, the meaning and how it determines the denotation (Figure 9.1).

You will be introduced to the basic notion of **categorization**, the mental act of classifying things and forming categories that underlies cognition in all its aspects (9.1). Traditionally, categorization was held to be a matter of necessary and sufficient conditions (for example, a bird belongs to the category of penguins if and only if it fulfils the particular set of conditions that define this category). This view was challenged by the proponents of so-called Prototype Theory. These cognitivists argued that categories are

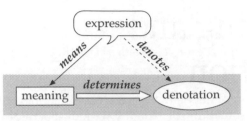

Figure 9.1 The focus of cognitive semantics

essentially defined by prototypes, i.e. those examples of a category that come to mind first and represent the most typical cases. Prototype Theory led to a radically different view of categorization implying, for example, fuzzy category boundaries and gradual membership (9.2). Another important innovation was the investigation of the hierarchical organization of our category system (9.3) with the result of establishing what came to be called the basic level of categorization. This is a medium level of generality that is preferred in thinking and communicating.

The chapter will then take a rather critical turn, investigating the assumptions of Prototype Theory from a semantic point of view. Is it in accordance with the semantic data? Does it help to provide better explanations than other approaches? As we will see, many of the central claims of Prototype Theory, in particular fuzzy category boundaries and gradual membership, are problematic (9.5). The last major section (9.6) will address another central question relevant for the relationship between meaning and cognition: the distinction between the meaning of a word and the total knowledge we connect to the word in our minds. Put more technically, we will discuss the distinction between semantic knowledge and cultural knowledge and why the distinction is important for semantics.

9.1 Categories and concepts

The fundamental notion of cognitive science is **categorization**. In his introduction to cognitive psychology, Barsalou describes it as follows:

> Upon walking into a home, people know instantly what is present. They recognize chairs, stereos, plants, dogs, friends, guacamole, wine, and just about anything else they happen to perceive. . . . When people interact, they recognize friends, facial expressions, actions, and activities. When people read, they categorize letters and words. Categorization occurs in all sensory modalities, not just vision. People categorize the sounds of animals and artifacts, as well as the sounds of speech; they categorize smells, tastes, skin sensations, and physical movements; and they categorize subjective experiences, including emotions and thoughts.

Categorization provides the gateway between perception and cognition. After a perceptual system acquires information about an entity in the environment, the cognitive system places the entity into a category.

(1992a, p. 15)

Categorizing something that we perceive (or imagine, or remember) means to perceive it *as* something of a kind. If we look at a photograph of a person, we will categorize it as an object of the kind 'photograph' that displays something of the kind 'person', and if we recognize the person, we will categorize him or her as that person. We assign everything that enters our minds to one or more **categories**. The category DOG (we will use SMALL CAPITALS for categories) consists of all those things we would categorize as dogs. It includes not only the real existing dogs but also former and future dogs or fictitious dogs in novels, jokes, etc. Entities belong to different categories at the same time. Our common friend John belongs to the categories PERSON, MAN, FICTITIOUS, BICYCLE OWNER and maybe (we just do not know) LOUSY DANCER along with countless other categories. The single entities that belong to a category are called **exemplars** or **members** of the category. (John is an exemplar of the category BICYCLE OWNER.) Larger, more general categories include smaller, more specific ones. These are **subcategories** of the former: MAN and WOMAN as well as BICYCLE OWNER are subcategories of the category PERSON. All members of a subcategory are also members of the more general category. Note that the subcategories of a category are not *members* of it. Rather, both share members. If you are familiar with set theory, it may help to realize that categories are sets, subcategories subsets and members elements.

We encountered categories before. **denotations** (2.2.2) are categories. The descriptive meaning of a word defines a category, the set of all its potential referents. When we refer to Donald using the word *duck*, we treat him as a member of the category DUCK.

Categorization is only possible if the respective categories are in some way available in the cognitive system, i.e. in our mind. In the terminology of cognitive science, categorization requires **mental representations** of the categories. There are various theories concerning the nature of category representations. Here the view will be adopted that categories are represented by **concepts** for their exemplars. The category DOG is represented in the mind by the concept ⟩dog⟨.[1] When we encounter an object, our cognitive apparatus will produce a preliminary description of it, which consists of what we perceive of the object, e.g. its size, shape, colour, smell, etc. The description will be compared with the concepts we have in our mind and if the description happens to match with the concept ⟩dog⟨, the object will be categorized as a dog.

Two things must be kept in mind when we think of word meanings and concepts. First, word meanings do not coincide with our concepts for actual categories. For example, the meaning of the word *bicycle* is a relatively abstract concept that is just rich enough for defining the category of bicycles but you will probably have a richer concept depending on your individual knowledge of bicycles and your personal experiences. Thus, the bicycle concept that constitutes the meaning of the word is only part of the concept that in *your* mind defines your personal category of bicycles. The meaning of the word must be a much leaner concept that is shared by all English speakers who know the word and its meaning.

Second, we do not have a word for every category we have a concept for. Trivially there are infinitely many concepts which can be expressed only by complex expressions, e.g. the concept ⟩expensive sushi restaurant closed on Saturdays⟨ – the syntactic possibilities of language reflect this potential. However, there are also categories and concepts which cannot be verbalized at all, or only insufficiently. Many concepts for bodily sensations, feelings, emotions, for facial expressions and physiognomies, for flavours and odours, for melodies and harmonies, etc. can hardly be put into words, if they can at all. For example, a verbal description of a face can never be as accurate as a photograph. Words can never fully describe the taste of an orange, the smell of carnations or the sound of a violin. In fact, it is plausible to assume that only the lesser part of our concepts can be expressed in language.

The system of lexical meanings is only part of the overall system of concepts. And a lexicalized concept is only part of the richer concept that defines the category we actually connect to the word. In this regard, a distinction will later be drawn between semantic concepts (word meanings), cultural concepts (richer concepts shared by a cultural community) and personal concepts (cf. 9.6).

9.2 Prototype Theory

9.2.1 The traditional model of categorization

The traditional view of categorization is shaped by the model of 'necessary and sufficient conditions' (**NSC model** for short) that goes back to Aristotle. According to the NSC model, a category is defined by a set of necessary conditions, which together are sufficient. For example, if we assume that the category WOMAN is defined by the three conditions of being human, female and adult, each one is *necessary*. If someone is not human or not female or not adult, he or she is not a woman. On the other hand, the condition of being human and female and adult, is *sufficient* for membership in the category WOMAN. It does not matter what other conditions someone or something may fulfil. Being a woman or not depends on these three conditions.

As you will have noticed, the NSC model of categorization, also called the check-list model, exactly matches with the BFA notion of meaning (7.3).

The binary features that make up the meaning of a word according to BFA directly correspond to the necessary conditions of the NSC model.

The Aristotelian model can be characterized by the following points:

- Categorization depends on a fixed set of conditions or features.
- Each condition is absolutely necessary.
- The conditions are binary (yes-or-no) conditions.
- Category membership is a binary (yes-or-no) issue.
- Categories have clear boundaries.
- All members of a category are of equal status.

That categories have clear boundaries is a direct consequence of the fact that the defining conditions are binary. Everything either fulfils this set of conditions or it does not. If it does, it belongs to the category, otherwise it does not. As a consequence, categories have clear boundaries, and within their boundaries all members enjoy the same status of full members. Each single point of the NSC model was challenged in Prototype Theory, the result of the first extensive studies in categorization undertaken by cognitive psychologists and semanticists.

9.2.2 Prototypes

The findings on colour terms, which at the same time were findings on colour categorization, did not seem to fit the NSC model at all. Clearly, the subjects did not categorize the colour chips by checking a list of binary features. The basic colour categories are primarily defined by focal colours. A definite boundary between neighbouring categories cannot be drawn. 'Category boundaries ... are not reliable, even for repeated trials with the same informant' (Berlin and Kay, 1969, p. 15). When one moves from focal red to focal brown in a system that has BCTs for both, one somewhere leaves the range of red hues and enters that of brown hues. Furthermore, the categories RED and BROWN intuitively overlap. Brownish red is predominantly red but still more or less brown, and reddish brown is vice versa. Thus, it appears, a colour belongs to a category if it is sufficiently similar to the focal hue, i.e. the best example. Since, however, similarity is a matter of degree, category membership too is a matter of degree, rather than a yes-or-no issue.

Linguists and psychologists set out to investigate other areas for similar phenomena. They found that for many different categories best examples can be empirically established. These come to mind first and are consistently considered 'better members' than less typical cases. Such central examples came to be called **prototypes**. Experiments were carried out to examine whether category membership in general is a matter of similarity to the prototype and hence a matter of degree; whether categories have fuzzy boundaries; whether the defining conditions, or features, are binary and always strictly necessary.

It soon turned out that, apparently, many categories have a 'graded structure'. They contain prototypical exemplars that represent the category best and other exemplars that do it to a lesser extent but are still good examples, while others only enjoy a marginal status. For example, in a famous study cited in every textbook on cognitive semantics, Eleanor Rosch, whose name is inextricably linked with the early development of Prototype Theory, established a ranking within the general category BIRD. The subjects participating in the study were asked to rate on a scale from 1 (for best) to 7 the 'goodness-as-example' of different kinds of birds. The results were surprisingly consistent. Robins were considered the best examples, followed by doves, sparrows and canaries; owls, parrots, pheasants and toucans occupied a medium position, ducks and peacocks were considered even less good examples, while penguins and ostriches ranked lowest. Similar results were obtained for the categories FURNITURE, FRUIT, CLOTHING, etc. Furthermore, the rankings were consistent with other findings, such as the time it took the subjects to answer questions of the type 'Is a penguin a bird?', 'Is an eagle a bird?', etc.; the less typical the examples were, the longer the reaction time.

Since prototypical examples are what we think of first, we will exclude other cases when a category is mentioned, as long as there is no reason to do otherwise. Thus prototypes play an important role in what is called **default reasoning**, i.e. reasoning in terms of assumptions which replace specific actual information as long as none is provided. For example, when Mary tells John,

(1) *Look, there's a bird on the window sill.*

John will think of a prototypical bird, not of an owl, a condor, an ostrich or a penguin. If someone mentions a 'car', we will not think of a truck or a veteran car. It is therefore misleading to use the general terms for non-prototypical cases, misleading – but not semantically incorrect. Penguins *are* birds and we can refer to them as birds in appropriate contexts. For example, (2a) and (2b) are perfectly acceptable:

(2) a. *The only birds that live in the Antarctic are penguins.*
  b. *Penguins come ashore to nest. The birds lay one to three eggs.*

9.2.3 Fuzzy boundaries

Other experiments were performed in order to assess the fuzziness of category boundaries. The linguist William Labov presented pictures similar to those in Figure 9.2 to students and asked them to name the objects depicted. The subjects categorized objects like 3 as a cup, 10 as a vase and 6 as a bowl, but produced inconsistent answers for vases or bowls with a handle – 1 and 5 – or exemplars with intermediate height:width ratio such

Figure 9.2 Cups, bowls, vases

as 2, 4, 7 and 9. The subjects were also asked to imagine that the objects are filled with coffee or standing on a shelf with cut flowers in them, etc. This had a strong influence on the categorization (for example, more objects were categorized as cups when they contained coffee.) The experiment showed that prototypical cups are about as high as they are wide, have a handle and are used for drinking hot drinks such as coffee, while prototypical vases are higher than they are wide, lack a handle and are used for putting flowers in. If we encounter an object where these features are shuffled into a different combination, the criteria for categorizing it as a cup, a vase or a bowl may come into conflict with each other. Is object 1 a cup because it has a handle or is it a vase because it is much higher than it is wide? Likewise the criterion of the height:width ratio may cause problems if an object's ratio lies somewhere between that of cups and vases (2 and 9) or between that of cups and bowls (4 and 7).

9.2.4 Family resemblance

The prototype phenomena cast a new light on the features that define a category. If a category is primarily defined through its prototype, the conditions that define the prototype need not be necessary conditions for the rest of the category. (If they were, all members of the category would be equally prototypical.) For example, members of the category CUP may lack a handle although the prototype has one; the prototype of the category BIRD is small and able to fly, but other members may be unable to fly or be much bigger. For the case of cups, let us assume that they are distinguished by (i) being used for drinking coffee or other hot drinks; (ii) having a handle; and (iii) having a balanced height:width ratio. In Figure 9.3 the ten objects are arranged in accordance with these features. If we accept that all objects except 6 and 10 (the prototypical bowl and vase) are in some sense cups, the resulting category is not defined by any common condition. Some of the objects fulfil one condition, others two, prototypical cups all three. What ties the objects together in one category is what is called a **family resemblance**. The philosopher Wittgenstein (1958) introduced the notion in connection with his famous example of the category GAME. He argued that there is no property shared by all games. Rather, some games share

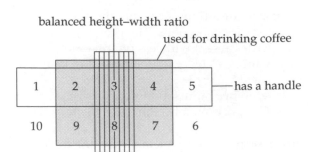

Figure 9.3 Family resemblance and the distribution of cup features

properties with certain others, e.g. the property of being played on a board or being competitive. Others may share no properties at all, but the whole domain of games is interconnected by similarities between the members. Applied to our simple example, we see that object 1 resembles object 2 in having a handle, object 2 resembles object 9 in that we would drink coffee from it; but object 1 and object 9 share none of the three properties, yet they belong to the same category, due to the linking element 2.

9.2.5 Degrees of membership

Still, the ten objects in Figure 9.2 do not seem to be simply cups or not. We may count object 1 as a cup, but it certainly resembles a vase more than a cup. Other objects such as 7 seem to fall right between the categories CUP and BOWL. The many cases of uncertain category membership and the ranking results in the tests mentioned suggested that category membership is not a yes-or-no question but a matter of degree. Degrees of membership can be determined by ranking experiments. Or they could be calculated on the basis of the prototypical properties, weighting the features and reducing the degree of membership if a certain property is missing. For example, one might rate the prototypical cup 3 as a 1.0 cup and 2, 4 and 8 as 0.8 cups (= pretty good cups), 7 and 9 might be 0.5 cups (half-cups) and 1 and 5 0.2 cups (very marginal cups); but the prototypical bowl 6 and the prototypical vase 10 would be 0.0 members of the category, i.e. definitely non-cups.

9.2.6 The prototype model of categorization

The characteristics of the resulting new model of categorization can be summarized as follows:

- **Graded structure**. The members of a category are not of equal status.
- **Prototypes are best examples**. There are prototypical members that are consistently considered the best examples of the category.

- **No set of necessary conditions**. Category membership is not a matter of a fixed set of necessary conditions. The prototype of a category may be defined by properties absent with less typical examples.
- **Family resemblance**. Category members are connected by family resemblance.
- **Prototypes are reference points**. Prototypes serve as reference points for categorization. Category membership is a matter of similarity to the prototype.
- **Graded membership**. Category membership is a matter of degree.
- **Fuzzy boundaries**. Categories have fuzzy boundaries.

As we shall see in the next section, most of these claims are not unproblematic. However, when they were first established, they appeared suggestive and plausible and proved very influential. In fact they still are, despite the fact that researchers like Rosch herself soon revised her initial views. Before we turn to a critique of PT (henceforth short for *Prototype Theory*), we will take a closer look at the notion of the prototype. In order to make the argumentation in the following more transparent, Figure 9.4 displays the central points and how they are interconnected in Prototype Theory.

According to PT, prototypes have two crucial properties. First, they are the **best examples** for their category. This point is due to the **graded structure** of categories, i.e. the existence of better and poorer examples. Conversely, the existence of best examples, along with less good examples, entails graded structure. Second, PT claims, prototypes serve as **reference points** for categorization, the crucial criterion for membership in the category being similarity to the prototype. The two properties are seen as mutually dependent: prototypes are the best examples because they serve as reference points, and they do so because they are the best examples. Similarity itself is a matter of degree. Hence the second property of prototypes implies **graded membership**: category membership is not a yes-or-no matter but a matter of degree. As a consequence of graded membership, categories have **fuzzy boundaries**. Conversely, fuzzy boundaries are

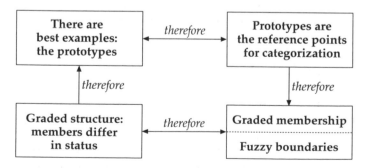

Figure 9.4 Central claims of prototype theory and how they are connected

understood as giving rise to graded structure: the clear members of a category are better members than those that form the fuzzy boundary area of the category. Graded structure and graded membership are seen essentially as two sides of the same coin. If something is a poorer member, it is less similar to the prototype and hence belongs to the category to a lesser degree, and vice versa. For the sake of simplicity, family resemblance and the role of necessary conditions are not included in the schema.

In the following the network of assumptions and claims of PT will be subjected to a critical evaluation from a semantic point of view. As it will turn out, the picture gives rise to a couple of serious questions.

9.2.7 What kinds of entities are prototypes?

The informal definition of prototypes as the 'best examples' suggests that prototypes are distinguished individual members of the category. This makes sense in some cases, for example for the colour categories. The prototype of GREEN is one particular colour, i.e. one member of the category, but if prototypes are to be not only best examples but also reference points for categorization, then for most categories they cannot be exemplars. If, for example, a certain dog exemplar had to serve as the prototype of the category DOG, one would have to know this particular dog in order to be able to categorize anything as a dog, because potential members would have to be compared with it. Exemplar prototypes may work in very early stages of language and concept acquisition where we first learn what a dog is by being shown a particular dog, but later we will replace the representation of the first dog we knew by a more abstract general representation of 'the' prototypical dog.

In the ranking experiments by Rosch and others, the subjects were asked to judge the representativeness not of exemplars but of subcategories of a given category. For example, they were asked to rank subcategories of birds. However, identifying the prototype with a particular subcategory does not work either. First, the problem is only shifted. If ROBIN is the prototype of BIRD, what is the prototype of ROBIN? Most of us do not know subcategories of robins, but certainly there are better and poorer examples of robins too. Also, the question arises as to whether all robins are prototypical examples of the category BIRD or only prototypical robins. If the latter, the prototype of ROBIN would be identical with the prototype of BIRD and the categories would coincide. If we decide instead that any robin whatsoever counts as a prototypical case of a bird, we have to include extraordinary big fat monster robins unable to fly among the prototypical birds. Second, robins exhibit distinctive features such as having a red breast which we would not include among the features of the prototypical bird.

It makes much more sense to assume that the prototype is an abstract case defined by a concept that fixes certain features and leaves others open. The concept for the prototypical bird contains a specification of its appearance and anatomy and of the most prominent features of its behaviour. Other traits may be unspecified, such as their diet, the exact shape of the beak, the colour of the feet or the markings of the feathers. Such a concept is different from the concept for an individual bird, which would have to be specified for all features. Therefore, the prototype is not an exemplar. It is not a subcategory either, because these would also be specified for some of the features left open, e.g. the four mentioned. An individual bird will count as prototypical if it exhibits all the features that make up the prototype. Prototypical birds may differ in the features left open. If a certain subcategory, e.g. ROBIN or SPARROW, matches the concept of the prototype for its normal members, it may be roughly identified with the prototype but strictly speaking, it is something different.

It must be noted, however, that for more abstract categories, such as the biological category ANIMAL that includes not only mammals, prototypes cannot be defined in this way. There are certainly best examples for the category, probably cats and dogs.[2] But dinosaurs, birds, fish, insects, worms, coral polyps and amoebae are also animals. The category is much too general to fix any concrete anatomical or behavioural properties of the kind that make up the prototype. Rather, for such categories the choice of best examples is not a matter of exemplariness but of familiarity. It is therefore questionable if this kind of prototype can possibly serve as a reference point for categorization with respect to such categories.

9.2.8 Which features make up the prototype?

One is tempted to answer: the typical features. Some features of birds are intuitively considered essential and typical features of birds, e.g. having wings and feathers and being able to fly as well as the properties of singing, having a beak, laying eggs and hatching them in a nest. Others, like having a particular colour, a certain weight and size may be characteristic for certain kinds of birds but not for birds in general. Having feathers is a 'good' feature because it well distinguishes birds from non-birds. The feature is therefore said to have a high **cue validity** for the category BIRD which means that it applies to a high proportion of members and to a low proportion of non-members. The features of having wings, being able to fly and laying eggs have a lower cue validity because they are shared by other kinds of animals, e.g. most insects. They are, however, of higher cue validity within the narrower domain of vertebrates. Here, the feature of having wings and being able to fly is very distinctive, since except for birds only bats share it. Thus, a prototype must be defined by a combination of features that together maximize the cue validity. Features of low cue validity that distinguish birds and other vertebrates from insects have to be included in order to enhance the cue-validity of the features such as having wings and being able to fly.

9.2.9 Similarity

Prototype theory claims that membership in a given category is a matter of similarity to the prototype. While this seems a clear and simple criterion, a closer look shows that it is anything but that. When thinking of applications, we will think of comparing, for example, various kinds of birds to a prototypical bird with respect to physical appearance, primarily shape, size and colour. However, similarity in this concrete sense of resemblance is not relevant in most cases. Consider, for example, a wolf, a husky and a poodle. Wolves and huskies are physically very similar and both very different from poodles. Yet the husky and the poodle belong to the same category DOG and the wolf does not. The categorization of dogs and wolves is not only a matter of physical similarity. Membership in the category DOG must be a matter of similarity to the prototypical dog in some other respects. The question, then, arises: *in which regard* is a would-be member of a given category to be similar to the prototype? Which of its properties are relevant for the comparison? The answer is far from trivial.

Consider a second case. Mary has two cousins, Marc and Tom. They are brothers and physically very similar. Let us assume that we know that Marc is a fairly prototypical member of the category MAN. The physical resemblance of Tom would then entitle us to categorize him too as a man. Yet if Marc is a butcher, Tom's physical similarity to Marc does not entitle us to conclude that he has the same profession. Rather, the relevant aspect of Marc and Tom would be the kind of job they have or they are qualified for. Categorization in the category MAN requires similarity to the prototype in quite different respects from categorization in the category BUTCHER, or in the category BACHELOR or NEIGHBOUR or HIP-HOP FREAK, for that matter.

These considerations show again that in order for prototypes to serve as reference points of categorization they must be defined by a set of crucial features. And it is these features that must be checked in order to judge the similarity to the prototype. The features may be of different weight or interdependent. For example, for birds the feature of being able to fly may depend on the body weight and the form and relative size of the wings. In this sense, the resulting model of categorization is not the same as the simple checklist model of NSC, where each feature is supposed to be necessary, independent of the other features, but the difference is not as radical as PT made it appear.

Another difficult question concerns the relevant scale of similarity on which the degree of membership depends. Let us assume similarity is measured in values between 0 and 1. Given a prototype and the set of criteria relevant for the comparison, it is clear which cases have the value 1 on the scale of similarity: all those that completely agree with the prototype in all relevant aspects. However, in the other direction the scale is undefined and, in fact, indefinable. Consider again the case of the category DOG. Since wolves are definitely non-members of the category DOG, they must be assigned the value 0.0 on the scale of similarity. But some of the crucial defining properties of the prototypical dog must also be properties of wolves. Certainly wolves are more similar to dogs than to cows. For that reason, the categories WOLF and DOG belong to the same superordinate category CANINE while COW does not. It then appears we should assign cows the value 0.0 and wolves some value reasonably greater than 0.0. Of course, this kind of adjustment of the scale can be repeated arbitrarily. Cows are more similar to dogs than crabs are, because both cows and dogs are mammals; crabs are more similar to dogs than potatoes, potatoes more similar than stones, and stones more similar than, say, French personal pronouns. The more kinds of cases we include in the assignment of similarity values, the greater the value of wolves becomes and the more similar (in terms of the scale) they become to dogs. It is just impossible to fix, for a given category, a general zero point of the scale and degrees of membership for potential and actual members – except for uncontroversial members. Apparently the degree of similarity and membership depends on the given context, namely on the range of rival categories.

The considerations about the nature of the prototype, its defining properties and the notion of similarity show that PT is not as unproblematic as it appears at first sight. The claim that categorization is a matter of similarity to the prototype raises a lot of non-trivial questions.

9.3 The hierarchical organization of categories

9.3.1 The basic level

Look at Figure 9.5. What do you see? Your spontaneous answer will probably be, 'A lion!'. Although your answer is not hard to guess, the fact that it is not is far from trivial.[3] The reason why the unanimous answer is not trivial is that 'A lion' is by no means the only possible answer to the question. You could have categorized the entity referred to more specifically as a 'male lion', an 'adult male lion', a 'prototypical male lion' or a 'marching male lion with a big mane', 'a marching big lion in side view', and so on. Alternatively it would be correct to use more general terms such as *feline, mammal, animal, living thing* or *entity*. In the given context, the question can also be taken as referring to the picture rather than what it

Figure 9.5

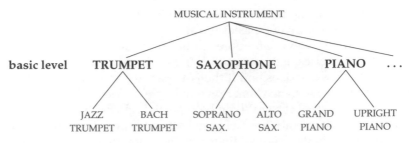

Figure 9.6 Categories of musical instruments – basic level

depicts. So what you see when you look at Figure 9.5 is as well a 'picture', a 'picture of a lion', the 'MS Office™ ClipArt's lion in black and white', an 'illustration', an 'example', etc. Even if we disregard the latter kind of answers, the phenomenon remains that an object can always be categorized at different levels of generality. What the little experiment shows is that there is obviously one level of categorization that we prefer, an intermediate level somewhere between very specific and very general categorization.

Berlin and others studied large plant taxonomies in a Mexican language and managed to establish this preferred intermediate level. Rosch applied this kind of research to other areas such as clothing and furniture. The main result is this: there is an intermediate level, the so-called **basic level** which is in several regards distinguished and privileged. Figure 9.6 shows a minor part of the taxonomy of English terms for musical instruments. The basic level is occupied by the categories TRUMPET, SAXOPHONE, PIANO (as well as all those not depicted here, such as VIOLIN, FLUTE, GUITAR, DRUM, ORGAN, CLARINET, etc.). The subordinate level is by no means complete. Of course, it is not the lowest level that exists. On the second subordinate level there are special categories of jazz trumpets or soprano saxophones, and so on. Yet it should be noted that there is a limit to levels of categorization as far as lexicalized categories are concerned. The subordinate level displayed here is probably

Level	Categories			
superordinate	GARMENT	VEHICLE	ANIMAL	COLOUR
basic level	TROUSERS, SKIRT, SHIRT, DRESS, BRA, JACKET, . . .	BICYCLE, CAR, BUS, TRUCK, MOTORBIKE, . . .	DOG, CAT, HORSE, BEAR, PIG, RABBIT, TIGER, LION, . . .	WHITE, BLACK, RED, YELLOW, GREEN, BLUE, BROWN, . . .
subordinate	BLUE JEANS . . .	RACING BIKE . . .	COLLIE . . .	OLIVE GREEN . . .

Table 9.1 Examples for the basic level

the lowest level of categories in non-expert terminology. Table 9.1 gives some further examples of the basic level.

9.3.2 Properties of the basic level

The psychological aspect: properties of basic level categories

The basic level (BL) is privileged in the cognitive system in various ways. It operates faster than higher and lower levels: in psychological experiments, response times for BL categorizations are the shortest. Apparently it is the level at which most of our general knowledge is organized. For example, the knowledge of what people normally wear is in terms of BL garment categories, the composition of a jazz band is in terms of BL instruments, and so on.

The BL is the highest level at which category members have a similar overall shape. (Trumpets have a common shape and saxophones have, but not musical instruments in general.) The overall shape is not only a matter of the visual appearance. An important aspect of shape is the characteristic parts the object consists of. Most BL terms have their own meronymy (5.3.4). For example, a 'piano' has a 'keyboard'; the keyboard in turn consists of white and black 'keys' which each serve to move a felt 'hammer' inside the piano that hits one to three 'strings' thereby producing a tone of a certain pitch. Similarly, the category of birds is characterized by having 'feathers' and a 'beak'. No such common parts necessarily exist for higher level categories such as ANIMAL or MUSICAL INSTRUMENT. In the case of visible categories it is possible to draw a general picture of the members of BL and lower categories, e.g. a picture of a pig, a piano or a car, but not so for any higher level categories.

BL categories are partly defined in terms of the ways in which we interact with their members. For example, a trumpet, a piano and a harp are each played in their own way and used for different kinds of musical activities. Shirts are put on and worn in particular ways that distinguish them from coats or socks. For artefacts, the characteristic parts (keys, wheels, sleeves) are intrinsically connected to the ways in which we use the objects or in which they function. (Therefore not any arbitrary *piece* of an object counts as a *part* of it, but only such that are linked to the way in which the object functions or is handled. A key of a piano is a part of it, but not the middle part of its lid.) Likewise, members of natural categories play a different role in human life. In Western cultures, pigs are kept for slaughter, and cats as pets. Tigers mostly live in the wild and if we encounter one we will act differently than if facing a reindeer, an ant or a snail.

The linguistic aspect: properties of basic level terms

The preference for BL categories in our cognitive system is reflected by the terms we have for BL categories and the privileged role they play in communication. They are mostly simple, short, native and old (except for terms for new categories of artefacts). If BL terms are complex, long or of foreign origin, they are likely to be shortened and assimilated (note the origins of *bra* < *brassiere*, *bus* < *omnibus*, *piano* < *pianoforte*, *bike* < *bicycle*). In contrast, lower level category terms are often composite (cf. *wonder-bra*, *jazz trumpet*, *racing bike*, *olive green*) and sometimes borrowed from other languages. BL terms are learned first. And they are the ones used most frequently. Their use complies with one of the fundamental rules of communication, the demand to be as informative as required and not to be more informative than necessary.[4]

The basic level and prototypes

The concept of prototypes works best for BL categories. The common overall shape and the uniform ways in which we interact with the members of BL categories make up the most part of the prototype. BL categories combine a high degree of distinctness from others with a rich specification of characteristics, thus exhibiting what was called a high cue validity.

9.4 Challenges to Prototype Theory

In this section and the next, some issues will be pointed out that present challenges to PT. The discussion offers the opportunity of addressing a number of basic questions. The critical points are those of the right part of the schema in Figure 9.4:

- the role of prototypes as reference points for category membership and, consequently, the abandonment of necessary conditions;
- the notion of graded membership;
- the fuzziness of category boundaries.

It will be argued that these points are not as firmly established and as closely interconnected as was suggested in early PT. The phenomena PT addresses allow for alternative interpretations and explanations. It should be emphasized, however, that the critique does not concern the results concerning the hierarchical organization of categories.

9.4.1 Graded membership vs graded structure

Some experiments of cognitive psychologists produced evidence in conflict with PT. One such finding is that there are best examples even for categories with clear boundaries and binary membership. For example, it was proved by experiments that for the category ODD NUMBER the smaller odd numbers 1, 3, 5, 7 and 9 were considered the best examples. Yet there are no borderline cases, and in no sense is 18764098376542141 less of an odd number than 3.

There are two defining conditions: an odd number must be a natural number > 0, i.e. a member of the set {1, 2, 3, 4, ...} and it must not be divisible by 2. Both conditions are necessary. Hence there is no room for more or less similarity to the prototype(s); 4 is somehow similar to an odd number in that it is not divisible by 3 (instead of 2), but this does not count. Likewise, 12.999999 is almost identical with an odd natural number, but it is no more of an odd number than 2 or π. Thus, the concept of similarity boils down to the trivial borderline case of absolute equivalence. And as for that, *any* member of the category would obviously do as an object of comparison. The main point, of course, is that categorization in this case does not involve *comparison* at all. If we want to decide whether a number is odd or even, we usually think of its decimal form and check if the last digit is 1, 3, 5, 7 or 9. Thus, these five cases do play a crucial role in categorization but not the role PT provides for them, i.e. not the role of serving as reference points of comparison. The best examples of the category ODD NUMBER may be considered prototypes (they certainly come to mind first and represent the category best) and consequently the category itself has a graded structure. However, if these cases are prototypes, they do not play the role of reference points for categorization. And although the category has a graded structure, it has clear boundaries.

Similarly, in the case of the much-cited category BIRD one must admit that penguins, although certainly odd birds, nevertheless *are* birds, not quarter-birds or something. Likewise for superordinate categories such as the broad category ANIMAL, membership cannot be a matter of comparison with the prototype. There is no similarity between an amoeba and a dog, not in any intuitive sense, yet an amoeba is a 100 per cent animal. For such categories, membership is a matter of definition, i.e. of necessary conditions, although there are prototypes in the sense of best examples. In general, the prototype model of categorization seems to work at the basic level and below, but not above it. As a consequence, we have to state the following qualifications of PT:

- A category may have prototypes, but they need not be reference points for categorization.
- Graded structure is not necessarily linked with graded membership.
- Category membership is not necessarily a matter of similarity to the prototype.
- Category membership may be a matter of necessary conditions as assumed in the NSC model.

The case of categories such as ODD NUMBER and ANIMAL shows that the two criteria for prototypes – being the best examples and serving as reference points for categorization – are, in fact, independent. Consequently, graded structure and graded membership are not two sides of the same coin. Even if some members of a category are more representative than others, all

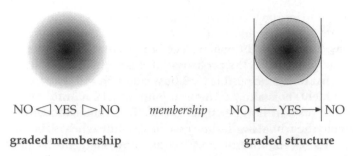

NO ◁ YES ▷ NO   *membership*   NO ◄—— YES ——► NO

graded membership   **graded structure**

Figure 9.7 Graded membership vs graded structure

members may be 100 per cent members separated from non-members by a well-defined boundary. Figure 9.7 schematically illustrates the case of a category with graded membership on the left, which is necessarily accompanied by graded structure and a fuzzy boundary. The right figure shows a category with yes-or-no membership and a resulting clear boundary, yet with graded structure (such as ODD NUMBER or BIRD).

9.4.2 Fuzzy boundaries

From a semantic point of view, the question of fuzzy category boundaries and graded membership is more important than the existence, nature and role of prototypes. It will be argued in 9.5 that for semantic categories, i.e. word and sentence denotations, the assumptions of graded membership and fuzzy boundaries are generally unacceptable. Since all examples hitherto mentioned (BIRD, CUP, etc.) are semantic categories, this is indeed a strong claim. We will therefore take a closer look at this part of PT.

There seem to be two reasons for the wide acceptance of the fuzziness claim. First, the claim appears to be in accordance with our intuitive impression that category boundaries very often are *in some sense* fuzzy, unclear, variable or fluid. The impression has several sources and, in fact, concerns different phenomena, which do not all bear on the issue in the same way. The sources include:

- variation of word meanings within a language community;
- partial knowledge of word meanings (ignorance);
- sloppy use (pragmatism);
- inherent flexibility of word meanings (vagueness).

The second reason is, of course, the evidence produced in experiments such as the cup test by Labov. The evidence, however, is not as conclusive as it appears at first sight. First, the outcomes of the experiments are in part a consequence of the test designs. Second, the results allow for alternative interpretations.

Sources of fuzziness

Meaning variation. As you will certainly have experienced countless times, people's use of terms actually differs. For example, one might have an argument with others about where blue ends and green begins. Disagreement is even the rule for all subjective categories such as BEAUTIFUL, BORING or FUN, which depend on personal attitudes and evaluations. The application of personal standards for what is boring, fun, etc. does, however, not mean that the resulting *individual* categories are fuzzy. Apart from such subjective notions, there are words with which people connect similar but different concepts, think of categories such as ADULT. For some people, age is the main criterion for adulthood, for others maturity, for yet others economic independence.

Meaning variation plays a role in our intuitive notion of fluid category boundaries, because in addition to the knowledge of word meanings we have a 'theory of common usage', i.e. a theory of how other people use the words and how their uses vary. Such a theory is an important part of our communicative competence, because in order to make ourselves understood we must be able to anticipate how other people will interpret what we say.

Ignorance. We all use so many words whose meaning we do not really understand. Obviously, the resulting kind of uncertainty about the exact denotations of words is not at issue in a general theory of categorization. PT is meant as a model for the categories we have, not for those we have not. Nevertheless, the fact that there are so many words we do not really understand contributes strongly to our subjective notion that categories are fuzzy, and hence to the plausibility of the general fuzziness claim of PT.

Pragmatism. Whether something belongs to a category is one question, whether it can be successfully referred to with the corresponding word is another. The first issue concerns the order of things in one's mind, the other is a matter of successful communication. Since we do not have categories and words for everything we may happen to want to talk about, we often find ourselves in the need of referring to something outside our system of shared categories. If we then choose an expression that in the strict sense does not apply to the intended referent but yields a description that fits it approximately and best among the expressions available, this may well pass as regular language use. In actual communication, we can expand the range of application for a given word well beyond its original limits, provided we do not come close to the denotations of other words. We often choose our terms rather sloppily. Thus, the *practical* denotation of a word, i.e. the range of objects it can actually be used for, depends on the CoU and is wider than the denotation defined by its lexicalized meaning.[5]

Vagueness. If all these sources of fuzziness are excluded, the question remains of how the proper source of fuzziness, variability of a particular, fully known, uncontroversial category is to be modelled. PT has provided one model: categorization in terms of graded similarity to the prototype. In 9.5.3 we will see that there is an alternative explanation – vagueness – which is reconcilable with simple yes-or-no membership.

Test design and interpretation of the experiments on category fuzziness

In part, the results of the crucial experiments were predetermined by the very test designs. When subjects are asked in a scientific experiment to assign membership ratings to different types of furniture, they will produce a scale of the kind they feel is required. The results will, however, not so much reflect their individual categorizations as their willingness to compromise (pragmatism) and their theories of common usage. Such an experiment is not suitable for testing whether for the subjects membership is a yes-or-no matter or a matter of degree.

Another criticism concerns the nature of the features chosen for the tests. It is questionable if the shape criterion which played such a prominent role in Labov's cup experiments is of much importance for the categorization of cups, bowls and vases. Human artefacts are created for certain purposes. Cups, for instance, are made for drinking coffee, tea, hot chocolate and other hot drinks. This is the central and crucial feature of cups: ⟩for drinking hot drinks⟨. From this single feature all other characteristics of cups can be derived. As these drinks are hot, the material must be sufficiently heat-resistant and insulating. A handle is a good idea if one does not want to burn one's fingers. The normal quantity of such beverages consumed at a time determines the size of cups. The wish to have the drink while it is still hot restricts the diameter of the container, and so on. The derivative features follow from practical experience. Their presence optimizes the suitability for drinking hot drinks from the objects. That is why they are features of the prototypical cup. None of the derivative features constitutes a necessary condition. And there is no need to consider any of them an extra part of the concept that defines the category CUP. However, then the question of whether one or more of them is absent has nothing to do with the categorization. Likewise, the category VASE is defined by the feature that vases are for putting cut flowers in. Thus, the impression of a continuum of membership degrees between different categories such as CUP and VASE is an artefact of an experiment that emphasized the derivative feature of shape rather than the primary feature of function. The test design also suggested that the categories tested should be mutually exclusive. In fact, the same object can be used both for drinking coffee and putting flowers in (a fact that was confirmed by Labov's results). When it is used for coffee, it is a cup, when it hosts a bunch of flowers, it is a vase. Thus what the experiments really show is that categorization is flexible and context-dependent because it is, for things like cups, *not* primarily a matter of physical features; but they do not prove that category boundaries are fuzzy.

9.4.3 Summary

What do the considerations in this section amount to? One of the basic observations of PT cannot be denied. Certainly for many categories there are prototypes in the sense of best representatives. More generally, many categories have more central and more marginal members. In this respect the findings on colour terms carry over to a large range of other categories. Also, category boundaries are variable and flexible. We have, however, to distinguish between variability in different senses. Meaning variation, ignorance and sloppy use may contribute to our subjective notion of category fuzziness, but only inherent variability of single categories in our individual cognitive systems is relevant for a model of categorization. And this type of variability can be explained differently, as will be argued in the next section.

Thus, while the observations are valid and challenging, the conclusions are not necessarily those drawn in early PT. The experimental findings do *not* compel us to accept that

- necessary conditions play no role in defining categories;
- category membership is generally a question of similarity to the prototype;
- category membership is generally a matter of degree;
- category boundaries are generally fuzzy.

Meanwhile, many cognitive semanticists have abandoned the original PT model. Instead of prototypes they talk of 'prototype effects' in connection with graded category structure. Richer and subtler models of categorization account for the graded structure of categories (cf. the notion of ICM, 'idealized cognitive models' in Lakoff, 1987). The structure then gives rise to prototype effects, for example typicality of certain members of the category. In this volume, we will not go into these more detailed developments of cognitive semantics.

9.5 Semantics and Prototype Theory

9.5.1 Cognitive semantics

When we transfer the notions of cognitive science to semantics, we obtain the version of the semiotic triangle displayed in Figure 9.8. The proposition of the sentence is a concept for the category of situations potentially referred to, and the meanings of the referential phrases are concepts for their potential referents. In relating a sentence to a particular situation and particular referents, we categorize them accordingly. For example, if Mary says to John:

(3) *The tea is lukewarm.*

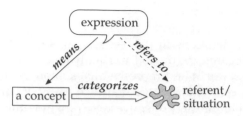

Figure 9.8 Cognitive version of the semiotic triangle

she categorizes the situation as a the-tea-is-lukewarm situation, the beverage she refers to as tea, its temperature as lukewarm. In general, each predication contained in a sentence represents a categorization of its arguments and the complex predication expressed by the whole sentence amounts to a categorization of the situation (recall 6.8).

In a very general sense, **cognitive semantics** can be used as a general term for any semantic approach that adopts this perspective on meaning and reference (i.e. for mentalistic semantics in general). The range of cognitive semantics is smaller than the range of cognitive science because, as was noted above, the categories and concepts that can be expressed by words are only a subset of the categories and concepts that form our cognitive systems. It is therefore useful to have specific terms for **semantic concepts**, i.e. meanings, and **semantic categories**, i.e. denotations.

So-called **prototype semantics** (PS) applies PT directly to semantic categories. If the notion is adopted that category membership is a matter of degree, then the suitability of certain words for certain things is also a matter of degree. In the PS perspective, we cannot say that we can or cannot use the word *cup* for referring to some object x, but rather that x can well or hardly be called a cup. Graded membership carries over to the whole sentence. A sentence is therefore not simply true or false. If we identify true with 1.0 and false with 0.0, truth values lie somewhere on a scale between 0.0 and 1.0 (including the two endpoints). For example, if Fido passes for a 0.7 member of the category MONSTER, the sentence *Fido is a monster* will receive a truth value of 0.7. As will be argued, this consequence is unacceptable from a semantic and pragmatic point of view.

9.5.2 Polarization

Back in Chapter 4, in connection with Donald Duck, the Principle of Polarity was introduced: 'In a given CoU, with a given reading, a declarative sentence is either true or false.' The principle, which we took as an apparent truism there, now appears in a new light. As it stands, it plainly rules out graded membership. Is it wrong? A simplification? Or is there evidence for it?

Yes, there is evidence. First of all, if there is any semantic universal, then it is negation. Every language has grammatical and lexical means for negating a given sentence. Thus, the possible sentences of a language, apart from a few exceptions which need not bother us here, come in pairs of positive sentences and their respective negations. As we saw in 4.1.3, determining the respective pairs is not always trivial, because we may tend to mix up negation with contraries, e.g. when we first think of the negation of *always* as being *never* rather than *not always*, but it is possible, if the methods of logical analysis are properly applied. The availability of negations for all (positive) sentences has the effect that whatever we say constitutes a choice between two alternatives. When Sheila tells Mary, 'The dog has ruined my blue skirt' she does so rather than using the negative counterpart 'The dog hasn't ruined my blue skirt.' When we decide to say, 'Donald is a not duck', we decide against the option of saying 'Donald is a duck.' This makes anything we say a matter of Yes or No. Language forces us into a simple black-and-white mode. The phenomenon is best captured with the term **polarization**, which means a partition of everything into two polar alternatives, Yes or No, true or false.[6]

Polarization is not restricted to declarative sentences. It applies as well to all other sentence types such as interrogative or imperative sentences:

(4) a. *Why is there beer in the fridge?* vs *Why is there no beer in the fridge?*
    b. *Please, put beer into the fridge!* vs *Please, don't put beer into the fridge!*

In this respect, it is even more general than the Principle of Polarity, which only applies to declarative sentences. Polarization does, of course, not only apply at sentence level, but it concerns every single predication contained in a sentence. Imagine, for example, Mary telling John:

(5) *The mouse is eating a big grain of corn.*

In doing so, she not only decides for the positive alternative of the sentence as a whole, but also for the positive alternative of the predications 'is a mouse', 'is eating', 'is a grain of corn' and 'is big': (5) would not be true unless each of the predications is true. Thus, when using predicate terms in composing a sentence, one puts a plus or minus sign before each one and as a result also before the total predication expressed with the sentence.

The general availability of negation is one piece of evidence for polarization. The other one, equally universal, is the possibility of transforming any declarative sentence into an interrogative sentence. For *Donald is a duck*, there is the interrogative counterpart *Is Donald a duck?*, and so on. The resulting questions require a simple type of answer: Yes or No. Since the interrogative sentence has the same proposition as its declarative counterpart (see 2.2.3), the fact that the possible answers to such questions are just

Yes or No proves that there are only two truth values for propositions, TRUE and FALSE, and not a whole scale between them.

Consider now what would happen to polarization if membership in semantic categories were a matter of degree. For example, let us assume that the creature referred to in (5) is only a 0.8 mouse, that it is only 0.7 eating and the grain of corn is only 0.3 big. Weighting the single predications appropriately, we might obtain a value of, say 0.5, for the whole situation. (In models with graded membership, 0.5 is usually considered a pretty high value, which justifies the categorization.) But under these circumstances, we could with the same right claim the contrary of (5), namely that the mouse is *not* eating a big grain of corn. Clearly this is not what we mean when we opt for the positive sentence. We mean that *it* is true and not its negation. Even if the situation we refer to is not exactly as we say, the way we put it is as we say it and not the other way round. And this is what we will be taken to have said and is therefore to be considered the meaning proper of our utterance.

Polarization is inescapable, but it would not be, and probably would not even exist, if membership in semantic categories were graded. It is therefore concluded that semantic categories are binary.

Two questions arise now: (i) How can we account for flexible category boundaries, if membership is yes-or-no? (ii) How does language cope with the obvious fact that the world does not come divided into black and white but rather as a continuum of phenomena without natural partitions? The answer to the first question is inherent vagueness, the answer to the second is the availability of various linguistic means of differentiation.

9.5.3 Flexible concepts: vagueness

The crucial point concerning the flexibility of semantic categories is the fact that it is built into the very word meanings. Let us consider a simple example, the adjective *big*. It presents a prototypical case of what was already introduced as **vague** meaning in 3.2.3. The vagueness of the adjective has two sources. First, whether we categorize something as big or not big is a matter of a norm. If we consider the 'big grain of corn' in (5) once more, the object may be called big if it is big for a grain of corn or big for a mouse to eat or big for a grain of corn for *this* mouse to eat (the mouse may prefer grains of corn of a certain size). These are three different norms. Once we have chosen a particular norm, we next have to fix a borderline that separates big grains from grains that are not big, i.e. we have to fix the criteria for a categorization by size in terms of the chosen norm. Size is an attribute of objects that allows ordering on a scale, with smaller objects ranging lower than bigger objects. Somewhere on this scale there is a point beyond which everything is big, while everything below it is not. This is illustrated in Figure 9.9. Six objects of different size are shown in the upper part. In the lower part, they are ordered on a scale of increasing size. We

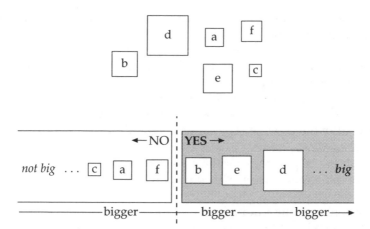

Figure 9.9 The *big* categorization

may draw the critical line between f and b as well as at a different point of the scale. This is a matter of contextual appropriateness. But wherever the line is drawn, it creates a yes-or-no division on the scale. Thus, semantic concepts may be vague in the sense that the boundaries of the resulting categories can be fixed in a flexible way, but in each given context they *must* be fixed somehow and will then yield a simple yes-or-no categorization.

In the case of colour terms too categorization is a matter of norms. In the neutral case, these are defined by the focal colours, but the norms may differ for certain kinds of objects (cf. red ears, blue lips, green apples, yellow leather, etc.). When we use a colour term in a particular context, we choose the appropriate focus hue and draw some circle, as it were, around it that marks the boundary of the resulting denotation.

Many concepts owe their vagueness to single vague meaning components. For example, among the three components of the semantic concept ⟩boy⟨ – ⟩human⟨, ⟩male⟨, ⟩not adult⟨ – the component ⟩not adult⟨ is vague since it requires and allows a line to be drawn within the continuum between youths and adults. In the case of ⟩cup⟨, the central criterion of suitability for hot drinks is vague, because the suitability depends on secondary features that may vary considerably. The mathematical concept ⟩odd⟨ is not vague, while the everyday concept ⟩odd⟨ is. In fact, probably the majority of semantic concepts are in some sense vague. This is not a flaw of natural language but a great achievement because it allows a very flexible use of the semantic material.

Vague concepts are not deficient. On the contrary, the meaning of *big* is quite precise. Its flexibility is due to its adjustability to context. Like an adjustable lens, it can be focused for the given purpose but whatever focus we choose in a given context, the concept then *has* a certain focus and polarizes accordingly.

The observation of inherent vagueness allows a different explanation for the flexibility of category boundaries. The PT model explains it with a fixed prototype and allowance for more or less similarity to it, with flexible use of fixed means, so to speak. The inherent-vagueness model explains it as variable use of adjustable means. A vague semantic concept such as ⟩big⟨ allows us to choose an appropriate norm in the given context (e.g. the average size of grains of corn or the average size of things mice eat). Consequently, the concept ⟩big⟨ determines a different category in each context of use, e.g. BIG FOR A GRAIN OF CORN or BIG FOR A MOUSE TO EAT. Thus, the concept ⟩big⟨, in practice, provides us not with one category but with clusters of categories, each cluster corresponding to the choice of a norm and alternative decisions as to where to draw the exact borderline. Such concepts can cope both with the requirement of flexibility *and* of polarization.

The PT model and the vague-concepts model may be symbolized as in Figure 9.10. In the PT model (left side), the arrows point to single candidate members, thicker arrows indicating a higher degree of membership. In the other model, circles and ellipses represent possibilities of drawing boundaries for the category, reflecting, for example, different choices of norms for size combined with choices of drawing the borderline between 'big' and 'not big'.

category defined by   category cluster defined by
prototype and similarity   an adjustable concept

Figure 9.10 Prototypes vs vagueness

If PS is to maintain the position of widespread graded category membership, the phenomenon of polarization presents a serious challenge. PS would have to postulate and model a general mechanism that turns the assumed underlying fuzzy categories into binary semantic categories, whenever the respective words are used in a natural language sentence in a particular CoU. This challenge, however, has not yet been addressed in PT or later developments.

9.5.4 Means of differentiation

Language has several means to cope with the black-and-white nature of the semantic category system. Three of them will briefly be mentioned.

Hedges

So-called hedges are often cited in PT as evidence for fuzzy category boundaries. These are expressions that allow a general modification of a categorization that yields either an expansion, (6a), or a narrowing of the categorization, (6b):

(6) a. *A futon is* kind of *a mattress / ... is* something like *a mattress.*
  b. *John is a* real *bike freak.*

Such phenomena do not prove that category boundaries are fuzzy and memberships graded. (6a) does not simply mean that a futon is a mattress; rather it describes a futon as something that is *not* a mattress, albeit similar to one. ⟩Kind of a mattress⟨ is a vague concept *derived* from the concept ⟩mattress⟨.

Lexical differentiation

Apart from these general means of differentiation, a language community and individual language users have the possibility of adopting the lexicon to the needs of categorization in communication. For example in the domain of colours, the system of basic colour terms is supplemented in various ways. There are:

- expressions for categories half-way between others: *green-blue, blue-grey,* etc.;
- lexicalized hedge categories: *whitish, reddish, bluish, greenish;*
- terms for more special categories: *crimson, scarlet, vermilion, fiery red, blood-red,* and hundreds more.

Quantification

Another general means of differentiation is provided by what is called quantification. Let us consider first a simple example without quantification:

(7) a. *The eggs are raw.*
  b. *The eggs are not raw.*

Together, the sentences form a clear alternative. The eggs referred to either fall into the category RAW or they do not. The alternative represents the simple all-or-nothing contrast symbolized in Figure 9.11 (where we assume that there are nine eggs; black dots represent raw eggs). The alternative of (7a) vs (7b) obviously suits only the cases 0 and 9. Pragmatism may allow the use of the sentences also for cases like 1 and 8, but this is not what is literally asserted. The intermediate cases with some of the eggs raw and some not are simply cut out, as it were. The alternative constitutes a system

the eggs are **not** raw	○○○ ○○○ ○○○	○○● ○○○ ○○○	○○● ○○○ ○●○	○○● ●○○ ○●○	●●○ ●○○ ○●○	●○● ●○○ ○●○	●○● ●●○ ○●○	●○● ●○● ○●●	●●● ●●○ ○●●	●●● ●●● ●●● *the eggs are raw*
	0	1	2	3	4	5	6	7	8	9

Figure 9.11 All-or-nothing contrast

of two categories that covers only the extreme cases. These are at the same time the simplest cases in that all the eggs are alike. Although this may seem rather drastic, the strategy of focusing on simple phenomena and disregarding the more complex is quite representative of the way in which we make use of semantic categories. A certain degree of simplification serves communicative economy.

We are not, however, forced to use this black-and-white mode of speaking. For the grey shades, we can specify the quantity of raw eggs, or more generally, the number or portion of cases for which the VP is true. The general phenomenon is called **quantification**. It consists of using expressions, so-called quantifiers, that specify numbers, portions, frequencies and the like.

(7) c.   *Some of the eggs are raw.*
    d.   ***Many** of the eggs are raw.*

(7c) is true if at least one egg is raw and false if none is. (7d) specifies the number as great. Like *big*, the adjective *many* is vague and its truth depends on the choice of a norm. If we compare the number of raw eggs to the rest, we may fix ⟩many⟨ as ⟩five or more⟨. In other cases it might be appropriate to draw the division line at a lower or higher number.[7] In any event, two things happen when we quantify. First, the whole range of possible cases between all and nothing is opened up and arranged on a scale of quantity. Second, at some point of the resulting scale a division is introduced between truth and falsity of the new sentence. Thus we receive a binary alternative of categorizations that together cover also the intermediate cases. This is illustrated for *many* in Figure 9.12. Note that the resulting

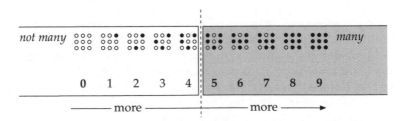

Figure 9.12 Quantification with *many*

picture is analogous to the one for *big* in Figure 9.9. The possible locations of the crucial line that separates true from false, or membership from non-membership for the quantifier category, primarily depends on the choice of the quantifier. If we replace *many* by *some*, the borderline would shift to between 0 and 1; for *all*, it would have to be placed between the maximum and the one immediately below (8 and 9 here).

9.5.5 Summary

The adoption of the cognitive perspective as such is no doubt very useful. However, one central point of PT, graded membership and the resulting concept of fuzzy category boundaries, is inappropriate for semantic categories. Human language forces upon its user the application of any categorization in a binary yes-or-no mode (polarization). Word and sentence meanings nevertheless allow a highly flexible use because many meanings are vague and therefore adjustable to the particular CoU. Since flexibility is built into the meanings themselves, variable boundaries are compatible with yes-or-no membership. Apart from the availability of expressions with a vague meaning, language has several devices that allow for a differentiation of available categories.

Figure 9.13 shows the main results of our discussion of PT. If you compare this to Figure 9.4 above, you will realize that the right half of the original claims of PT are questioned. What remains of the original picture is the notion of graded structure, reflected in the existence of better and less good examples. This observation is very valuable and its explanation is the objective of much, and promising research in the area. What is to be refuted, however, is the idea that the graded structure is just a direct reflection of different degrees of membership. Furthermore, it is certainly necessary to provide for more than one model of categorization. There may be categories for which membership is a matter of matching with the prototype (in certain, relevant respects). For other categories, the NSC model may be more adequate. Yet other models may be necessary for further types of categories. The notion of fuzziness is not altogether inadequate for semantic

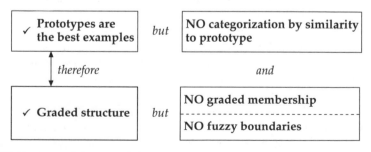

Figure 9.13 Revision of the central claims of Prototype Theory

categories, as vagueness and context-dependence give rise to 'fuzziness' in *some* sense, but the variability of category boundaries must be reconciled with polarization, i.e. with binary membership.

9.6 Semantic knowledge

9.6.1 Personal knowledge vs cultural knowledge

In his textbook *Language*, written long before the emergence of cognitive science, Sapir characterized the role of semantic categories in language use as follows:

> The world of our experiences must be enormously simplified and generalized before it is possible to make a symbolic inventory of all our experiences of things and relations and this inventory is imperative before we can convey ideas. The elements of language, the symbols that ticket off experience, must therefore be associated with whole groups, delimited classes, of experience rather than with the single experiences themselves. Only so is communication possible, for the single experience lodges in an individual consciousness and is, strictly speaking, incommunicable. To be communicated it needs to be referred to a class [= category, S.L.] which is tacitly accepted by the community as an identity.
>
> (1921, p. 12f)

The passage illustrates the necessity of distinguishing between personal knowledge and the knowledge that defines the category for the community we are a member of. For example, everyone of us knows several things about apples. Some of what we know is personal knowledge, e.g. how the particular apples we ate tasted, which role which sorts of apples play in our personal diet, where we can buy apples in our neighbourhood, etc. Only part of our knowledge is common property of the cultural community we belong to. It includes the knowledge that apples are fruits, what they look like, how they taste, that they contain vitamins, where they come from, how they are eaten or prepared, how they are traded, what they cost, that they are used to produce apple juice, etc. Let us call this knowledge **cultural knowledge** as opposed to our **personal knowledge**. Cultural knowledge defines what can be called cultural categories, the categories which are 'tacitly accepted by the community as an identity'. Names of cultural categories will be marked with a subscript 'C'. For example, $APPLE_C$ is the cultural category of apples, defined by our present cultural knowledge of apples. Cultural knowledge is not to be taken as 'everything that is known about the category'. It does not include expert knowledge. For example, knowledge of the complex biochemistry of apples is not part of the cultural concept. Personal knowledge usually includes the greater part of cultural knowledge, depending on the range of experience of the individual, but we are all some way apart from commanding *all* cultural knowledge, as we all have little experience in many areas of everyday life.[8]

Given that the speech community makes use of cultural categories, the question arises of how much of it constitutes the meaning of words. Is the meaning of the word *apple* the concept for the cultural category APPLE$_C$? If so, every detail that belongs to the cultural knowledge of apples is part of the meaning of the word. If not, the meaning of a word is only part of the cultural concept. Aspects such as what apples normally cost in the supermarket, what sorts of apples one can buy there and how one prepares baked apples might then not be considered components of the word meaning.

The distinction between **semantic knowledge** and 'world knowledge' (i.e. cultural and personal knowledge) is a doctrine of traditional semantics. It can be plausibly argued that we do not need to have the total cultural knowledge about apples, computers, mice or alcohol in order to know the meaning of the words *apple, computer, mouse* and *alcohol*. Many researchers of the cognitive orientation are, however, pleading for abandoning the distinction. They argue that our semantic categories are interwoven with our overall cognitive system in a way that does not allow their separation. Also, they argue, the full meaning of a word can only be grasped in the context of larger parts of the cognitive system. This view resembles the structuralist position in emphasizing the interdependence of categories, but it does not primarily relate to semantic categories. Rather, it aims at the way in which our categories, among them the semantic categories, are integrated into a full model of the world, the world as we perceive and interpret it, in which we are placed ourselves, interacting with it. In the following, we will nevertheless argue that a distinction between cultural knowledge and semantic knowledge is necessary, important and feasible.

9.6.2 The apple juice question

Ungerer and Schmid (1996), a recent introduction to cognitive linguistics, which focuses on cognitive semantics, explicitly subscribes to an approach that tries to capture meaning in terms of the experiential knowledge that laypersons connect with words. The approach is representative for a position contrary to a distinction between cultural knowledge and semantic knowledge. Let us call it the 'cultural knowledge approach' (CKA, for short). The authors report on an experiment for determining what makes up the category APPLE JUICE (Ungerer and Schmid, 1996, pp. 88 ff.). Lay subjects were asked to list features of apple juice. It was then checked whether these features can also be assigned to either or both or neither of the categories APPLE and JUICE, in order to determine where the features stem from. The result is given in Table 9.2. In addition to these properties, ›made from apples‹ is listed as 'salient specific attribute' (Ungerer and Schmid's

---

Salient specific feature: ⟩made from apples⟨

---

features that the category APPLE JUICE shares with the categories . . .

1 . . . JUICE	⟩liquid⟨
	⟩no alcohol⟨
	⟩thirst-quenching⟨
	⟩supplied in bottles or carton⟨
	⟩served in glasses⟨, *etc.*
2 . . . JUICE and APPLE	⟩sweet or sour-sweet⟨
	⟩healthy⟨
	⟩tastes good⟨
3 . . . APPLE	⟩yellow or similar colour⟨
	⟩fruity⟨, *etc.*
4 with neither	⟩mixed with soda water⟨
	⟩naturally cloudy⟨

Table 9.2 Features of the category APPLE JUICE according to Ungerer and Schmid (1996)

term *attribute* is replaced by *feature* in order to keep to the terminology chosen here).

The word *apple juice* is a regular compound of the two nouns *apple* and *juice*. According to the 'classical' analysis briefly sketched in 5.1.2, its meaning is the meaning of the head noun plus a specification added by the modifier. In favour of CKA, Ungerer and Schmid argue that their results provide evidence against the traditional analysis. If it were correct, they claim, most features of the category APPLE JUICE should be shared with the head category JUICE, only one should be contributed by the modifier (⟩made of apples⟨) and no extra features should apply to the category APPLE JUICE only. The latter requirement follows from the fact that the meaning of regular compounds should completely derive from the meanings of their parts. Ungerer and Schmid point out that, however, the category APPLE JUICE is linked to the category APPLE by quite a number of further common features (rows 2 and 3) and exhibits some genuine features of its own (row 4).

While the results of the experiment are as they are, it must be questioned if the subjects described what for them constitutes the meaning of the word *apple juice*. Apparently they described the cultural knowledge they commanded and held relevant. However, a critical look at the features listed shows that most of the features elicited cannot be considered parts of the meaning of the word.

How can we decide if a particular feature of a category is part of the meaning of the corresponding word? There are (at least) two tests. First, we can check if it is necessary to know that this is a feature of the category in order to know what the word means. Second, we can carry out the following thought experiment: if the members of the category happened to lack the feature in question, could we still use the word for referring to them? Such thought experiments are relevant because the meaning of a word must fit all *potential* referents. There is no way of exploring concepts other than by asking oneself what they would *possibly* cover.

Let us apply the tests to the critical features in Table 9.2, i.e. those in rows 3 and 4, which according to Ungerer and Schmid contradict the classical analysis. For the thought experiment, imagine the food industry decides that apple juice needs a radical change in order to sell better. Thus they filter the stuff, add blue colour and heavy peppermint flavour and promote it as a definitely-no-soda drink. It would cease to have any of the critical features and would yet be apple juice, because it would still be made from apples. The result of the experiment is in accordance with what we find when we ask ourselves what one needs to know about apple juice (the stuff) in order to be entitled to claim knowledge of the meaning of the word *apple juice*. One does not need to know its colour or if it is cloudy. In fact, as anybody knows, there is cloudy as well as clear apple juice. Did you know that potato juice of ordinary potatoes turns reddish in a few minutes? If not, would you say you did not understand the word *potato juice* in the previous sentence? The other features have the same status. One need not know the taste of apple juice in order to know the word meaning. (Have you ever tasted potato juice?) And one need not know the soda water thing. There is one feature that really carries the whole load: ⟩made of apples⟨. The word *apple juice* means ⟩juice made of apples⟨. Period. If one knows that, one knows the meaning of the word. Apple juice being a quite common sort of drink, the other features are likely candidates for the cultural knowledge about apple juice, but they do not form components of the meaning of the word *apple juice*. Thus, the classical semantic analysis of compounds is not disproved by the experiment. Rather, the discussion proves the importance of distinguishing between cultural knowledge and semantic knowledge.

9.6.3 Cultural knowledge vs semantic knowledge

From this the following picture emerges. To any word that we know (e.g. *apple juice*), we connect in our personal cognitive system a semantic concept, its meaning (⟩apple juice⟨ = ⟩juice made of apples⟨). The meaning determines a fairly broad category, the denotation of the word. Let us mark denotations, or semantic categories, with the subscript S for 'semantic'. The category APPLE JUICE$_S$ contains all possible variants of apple juice including the clear, blue, mint-flavoured, no-soda variant of our thought experiment. The category APPLE JUICE$_S$ is broader than the presently valid cultural category APPLE JUICE$_C$ which is characterized by additional features such as those elicited in the experiment reported in Ungerer and Schmid (1996). The cultural concept that represents APPLE JUICE$_C$ is correspondingly more specific

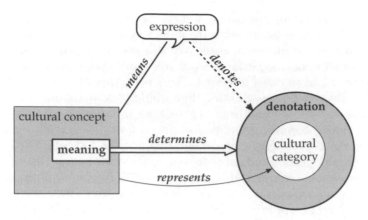

Figure 9.14 The semiotic triangle integrating cultural knowledge

than the leaner concept that constitutes the word meaning. This is an iron law of cognition: the more specific a concept, the narrower the category it represents, and vice versa. Thus, the meaning of the word *apple juice*, the semantic concept ›apple juice‹, is part of the cultural concept for apple juice, but the cultural category APPLE JUICE$_C$ is a subcategory (!) of the semantic category APPLE JUICE$_S$. In Figure 9.14, the cultural concept and the cultural category are integrated into the semiotic triangle. Note how the more specific cultural concept includes the leaner semantic concept, while, conversely, the cultural category is only a subset of the semantic category.

The cultural category can be roughly equated with the *actual* denotation of the word, i.e. those members of the total denotation that we encounter, or expect to encounter, in actual life. These form only a subset of those we might conceive of, i.e. all *potential* referents of the word. Theorists that equate semantic knowledge with cultural knowledge, equate the actual denotation with the total denotation.

An approach that distinguishes between semantic knowledge and cultural knowledge, or between the meaning of a word and the cultural concept into which it is embedded, is superior to CKA in offering an explanation for the following points:

- The **stability** of word meanings as compared to cultural concepts.
- The **abstractness** of word meanings as compared to cultural concepts.
- The communicational **economy** of word meanings.
- The simplicity of **meaning relations** between words.

Let us conclude this section with a brief illustration of these points.

Stability

Cultural knowledge is subject to constant change. For example, certain categories of artefacts such as TELEPHONE$_C$ or COMPUTER$_C$ have changed to a degree that people of, say, two generations back, would have been unable to anticipate. Nevertheless, the telephones and computers of the 1950s are no less members of the respective semantic categories than today's telephones and computers. Both are 100 per cent members of the semantic categories TELEPHONE$_S$ and COMPUTER$_S$. While the cultural categories have shifted, e.g. with the invention of the mobile telephone or the personal computer, we do not feel that the words *telephone* and *computer* have changed their meanings. Rather, word meanings form a stable core of the changing cultural concepts. Constant meanings allow for communication with constant means in an ever-changing world. Of course, meanings are not completely constant. The lexicon keeps adapting to the changing communicational needs, but at a much larger temporal scale.

Abstractness

The lack of many concrete features that narrow down the cultural categories also accounts for the abstractness of semantic concepts which allows their application to uncommon cases outside the familiar cultural categories. One example was the applicability of the semantic concept ⟩apple juice⟨ to exotic fictitious varieties of apple juice. Similar thought experiments could be conducted for almost all other semantic categories.

Economy

Although the greater part of cultural knowledge does not form part of the word meaning, it is nevertheless relevant for communication. In conversation, we draw heavily on all sorts of common knowledge. This allows us to keep our messages semantically to a minimum. For example, if John says (8a) to Mary, indicating thereby that Mary should bring him some apple juice, he will rely upon his and Mary's common cultural knowledge about the packaging of apple juice. If John's apple juice is usually packed in bottles, he need not say (8b), yet Mary will understand as much and be able to locate the juice among the things on the balcony.

(8) a.   *There is apple juice on the balcony.*
    b.   *There is apple juice in bottles on the balcony.*

The fact that Mary understands something like (8b) when John says (8a) does not mean that ⟩is in bottles⟨ is part of the meaning of the word *apple juice*. On the contrary, the feature need not be part of the word meaning *because* it is part of the additional cultural knowledge.

Meaning relations

Last but not least, it must be stated that CKA approaches blur rather than explain meaning relations such as those between a compound and its parts. The simple meaning relation between the head and the compound is buried under a heap of cultural features.

9.7 Summary

This chapter took us through a series of fundamental issues. First, the notions of meaning as a concept and denotation as a category were embedded into the larger context of cognitive science. Here the most basic issue is the general nature of categorization. The traditional view, represented for example by the BFA approach, considers membership in a particular category a matter of a fixed set of necessary conditions to be fulfilled by its members. The view implies that membership in a category is a clear yes-or-no issue. Given a particular category, anything either belongs to it or it does not. Hence, all members of a category enjoy equal member status. As a consequence, a sharp category boundary separates members from non-members (9.2.1). This view was challenged by PT. No!, PT says, category boundaries are not sharp but fuzzy; there are better and poorer members, in particular there are best examples: the prototypes. On the other hand, categories may have very poor members. Thus, no clear distinction can be drawn between members and non-members, rather membership is a matter of degree. As for the defining 'necessary' conditions, even the most typical ones such as ability to fly in the case of birds may be violated. So: dispense with necessary conditions! Categorization is not a matter of checking conditions but is carried out by a comparison with the prototype (9.2).

While all this has its appeal, the PT approach proves problematic under closer scrutiny. Its results do not apply to categorization as generally as was claimed and are not as cogent as it first appeared (9.4). If PT is applied to semantics, severe problems arise with the notion of graded membership: it is in direct conflict with polarization, probably the most fundamental semantic phenomenon (9.5.2). Polarization totally pervades word and sentence meaning. It underlies each predication – and therefore almost all word meanings. And since each sentence contains at least one predication (because it must contain a finite verb and all verbs are predicate terms), each single sentence is subject to polarization. Consequently, categorization by verbal means is always binary, i.e. a yes-or-no matter. Despite such problems, PT did contribute valuable results to semantics. The observation that for most categories we operate with prototypes, for example as default cases when no further specification is available, is an important result. A further important contribution of PT is the detection and specification of the basic level (9.3).

In tackling the PT claims about fuzzy category boundaries and graded membership we obtained insights into the nature of word meanings and the ways in which language, this polarizing (or polarized) cognitive equipment, copes with the non-binary character of the 'world'. For one thing, vague meanings enable a flexible categorization. There is no need for concepts that would provide fuzzy category boundaries, because the word meanings available enable us to adapt category boundaries to the requirements of communication (9.5.3). In addition to flexible word meanings, other linguistic devices such as lexical differentiation or quantification allow for compensation of what would otherwise be heavy black-and-white thinking (9.5.4).

No doubt the main merit of PT is its focus on the conceptual level. The other two mainstreams of semantics, the structuralist tradition and formal semantics (to be introduced in the next chapter), avoid addressing meaning itself. The structuralist tradition approaches meaning indirectly via the investigation of meaning relations. (Recall the claim of structuralism that the meaning of an expression is the sum of its relations to other expressions within the system.) Formal semantics tries to capture meaning equally indirectly by studying reference and truth conditions.

Addressing the conceptual level itself raises another fundamental problem, the role of linguistic meaning within our overall cognitive system (9.6). Are the concepts that are assumed to constitute the meanings of words identical with the concepts that define our everyday categories? Given that language is a general means of communication within a cultural community, a distinction must be drawn between the knowledge at our personal disposal and that part of it which we may assume to be (by and large) shared by the other users of the language. The latter was dubbed 'cultural knowledge' as opposed to 'personal knowledge'. A closer consideration of regular compounds led to the conclusion that cultural knowledge must be further distinguished from semantic knowledge. Semantic concepts are much leaner than the corresponding cultural concepts. Only this assumption allows an account of basic phenomena such as simple meaning relations and the stability of word meanings.

Within the given limits, it is not possible to present all of the major cognitive approaches to semantics in a way that would do justice to the whole field. One area should be mentioned where modern developments of cognitive semantics are very successful: the investigation of polysemy and, closely related, semantic change. In particular, it was shown that metaphor and metonymy are general cognitive mechanisms that play a central role in meaning variation and historical meaning shifts. In very many cases, meaning variants of the same word are linked by a metaphorical or metonymical relation (or both). The matter was briefly touched upon at the end of Chapter 3 and will not be pursued here any further.

We focused on the earlier claims of PT because this allowed us to address several issues of central importance. Meanwhile 'Cognitive Semantics' is an established field of research and theory. Yet it must be stated that it is still far from a fully-fledged semantic theory. Central fields of semantics have never been elaborated within the cognitive framework. These include meaning relations and semantic composition. In part this is a consequence of particular assumptions. The assumption of wide-spread graded membership would render an account of the composition of sentence meaning very difficult. Similarly, the identification of semantic knowledge with cultural knowledge impedes the proper treatment of meaning relations (9.6.2). Yet none of these assumptions are necessary components of a cognitive semantic theory. A theoretical account of meaning relations and composition is not impossible within a cognitive framework – it just has not been developed yet.

Checklist

cognition
  categorization
  category
  member
  subcategory
  concept
  mental representation
  NSC model
Prototype Theory (PT)
  prototypes
  graded structure
  fuzzy boundaries
  prototypes as reference points
  graded membership
  family resemblance
  cue validity

basic level
Prototype Semantics (PS)
  meaning, denotation
  polarization
  vagueness
  hedges
  lexical differentiation
  quantification
semantic knowledge
  semantic concepts/categories
  cultural knowledge/
    concepts/categories
  cultural knowledge approach (CKA)
  regular compounds
  personal knowledge

Exercises

1 Explain the difference and relation between concepts and categories.
2 Explain the difference between *mushroom*, MUSHROOM and ⟩mushroom⟨.
3 What kind of entity is a prototype?
4 What is the role of prototypes in PT?
5 What is problematic with the notion of 'similarity to the prototype'?
6 What is meant by 'polarization' and why does it pose a serious problem to Prototype Semantics?
7 Perform an experiment asking several people a question like that in the beginning of 9.3.1 Discuss the result.
8 Consider the following terms. Using the criteria mentioned in 9.3.2, try to assign the terms to the basic level, to a more general (higher) or to a more specific level.
   television set, radio, toaster, washing machine, portable TV, cassette player, Walkman, household appliance, PC, notebook (electronic), electrical appliance

9   Ask three people to spontaneously write down 30 terms for clothing in
    the order in which they come to mind.
    a.   Try to assess which kinds of clothing are prototypical.
    b.   Try to arrange the terms in a taxonomy. Which ones are basic level
         terms?
10 Discuss the distinction between personal knowledge, cultural knowl-
    edge and semantic knowledge, using the word *money* as an example.
    Try to find features that (a) are part of your personal knowledge about
    money, but not of the cultural knowledge; and (b) are part of the
    (present) cultural knowledge but not necessarily part of the meaning of
    the word *money*.

Further reading

For a discussion of PT see Aitchison (1987, Chapter 5), Ungerer and Schmid
    (1996, Chapter 1), Lakoff (1987, Chapter 2) for its history. On the
    hierarchical organization of the category system see Ungerer and Schmid
    Chapter 3. On the role of metaphor and metonymy in cognitive
    semantics: Ungerer and Schmid, Chapter 4, Palmer (1996, Chapter 8),
    Foley (1997, Chapter 9) and the case study on the category ANGER in
    Lakoff (1987, pp. 380–415).

Notes

[1]   Henceforth, ⟩ ⟨ quotes are used not only for meanings but for everything on the
      conceptual level, i.e. meanings, concepts and components of concepts.

[2]   Along with this category, there is a much narrower category ANIMAL, roughly the
      same as QUADRUPED, that does not include birds, fish, reptiles, etc., let alone insects
      and amoebae. Here and below, the category ANIMAL is not meant in the narrow
      sense.

[3]   You can test it yourself: show 20 people a toothbrush, ask them to answer
      spontaneously to the question 'What is this?', and 20 people will answer 'A tooth-
      brush.'

[4]   The so-called 'Maxim of Quantity', one of four conversational 'maxims' of Paul
      Grice. See Chapter 1, Further reading, for references.

[5]   For a much more elaborate and systematic account of the ways in which we
      make use of our linguistic means in actual communication, see the discussion of
      'variability', 'negotiability' and 'adaptability' in Verschueren (1999), Chapter 2.

[6]   This is a point where a remark about **presuppositions** is in order. Many, if not all,
      sentences carry what is called semantic presuppositions. These are logical
      preconditions for the sentence to make sense in a given CoU. Semantic presup-
      positions originate from the lexemes used as well as of the structure of the

sentence. In 6.7 we discussed selectional restrictions as one sort of presupposition. When a sentence contains a predicate term, the use of the term in a given CoU requires that the argument fulfils the selectional restrictions. For example, if one says *this is green* or *this is not green*, where *this* refers to some entity x, it is required that x is a visible object (if *green* is to be taken in its colour predicate sense, that is). If x is invisible, we cannot decide whether it is green or not and the sentences are both neither true nor false. The Principle of Polarity notwithstanding, there is always the possibility that a sentence or, more generally a predicate, yields no truth value at all. Failing to have a truth value, however, is not on a par with being true or being false. In particular, it does not constitute a case somewhere between TRUE and FALSE. Therefore, the fact that sentences have a truth value only if their presuppositions are fulfilled, does not affect the argument we are developing here. In the cognitive semantics literature this general problem of categorization is not addressed (although it is known as 'category failure' in more traditional approaches). For the sake of simplicity we will ignore the issue of presuppositions in the following.

7 You may wonder why case 0 is included within 'not many' and case 9 in 'many'. If one knows the exact number, one would express case 0 with *no* and case 9 with *all* or use the quantifier-free sentences in (7a, b). Yet the fact that it is acceptable to say 'not many, if any, . . .' and 'many, if not all, . . .' proves that the two extremes *no* and *all* are logically compatible with *not many* and *many*, respectively, and hence included in their meanings.

8 The term *cultural knowledge* was chosen here in order to avoid the terms *world knowledge* and *encyclopaedic knowledge*, which you may frequently encounter. Often the notion *world knowledge* is used indiscriminately for cultural knowledge and personal knowledge, while 'encyclopaedic knowledge' is understood as including expert knowledge.

Sentence meaning and formal semantics 10

Building on the results of Chapters 4 and 6, this last chapter deals with semantic composition. More precisely, it offers an introduction to formal semantics (alternatively: model-theoretic, truth-conditional, referential, logical or possible-world semantics). Whatever the name, it is semantics based on reference and truth conditions. It is the most technical and difficult variety of semantics, very mathematical, but it is the main framework in which sentence semantics has been developed.

You will be introduced step by step to its central notions and methods. We will start with an analysis of Japanese numerals. Numeral systems are a good example to use when demonstrating the mechanism of semantic composition and how it is treated in formal semantics. In 10.2 we will develop a semantic analysis of some simple types of English sentences. The example is far from the real complexities of sentence semantics, but will suffice to introduce the basic idea of analysing sentence meanings by translating them into predicate logic. The resulting formulae are then given a precise compositional interpretation in a 'model', i.e. an assignment of referents and truth values. The definition of the model will serve as an example of model-theoretic semantics (10.3). In 10.4 the model-theoretic method is extended into what is commonly called *possible-world semantics*. In 10.5, we discuss the scope and limits of this approach.

10.1 Japanese numerals: a simple example of a compositional analysis

10.1.1 The system of numerals

Japanese has two sets of numerals, a native set of expressions for the numbers 1 to 10, 20 and a couple of greater numbers such as 100 and 1000. The numeral system proper is of Chinese origin. It is chosen here because it is perfectly regular, unlike the system of number names in English or those of any other European language. The basis of the system for the first 99 numerals are just ten lexical units, the expressions for the first ten numbers:

(1) *ichi* *ni* *san* *yon* *go* *roku* *nana* *hachi* *kyû* *jû*
    1   2   3   4   5   6   7   8   9   10

When we attach the word for 10 *jû* to the words for the digits 2 to 9 we obtain the terms for the tens:

(2) *jû* 10   *nijû* 20   *sanjû* 30   *yonjû* 40   . . .   *kyûjû* 90

Thus, 30 is expressed as 'three ten'. Terms for the numbers 11, . . ., 19, 21, . . . 29 and so on are formed by attaching the words for the digits 1, . . ., 9 to the terms for the tens including *jû*. 11 is expressed as 'ten one' and 21 as 'two ten one'. The complete system for 1 to 99 is given in (3). The overall system continues in the same economic fashion, but we will confine the analysis to the numerals for 1 to 99:

(3)   *jû*   10   *ni* *jû*   20   . . .   *kyû* *jû*   90

    ichi 1   *jû* *ichi* 11   *ni* *jû* *ichi* 21   . . .   *kyû* *jû* *ichi* 91

    ni 2   *jû* *ni* 12   *ni* *jû* *ni* 22   . . .   *kyû* *jû* *ni* 92

    san 3   *jû* *san* 13   *ni* *jû* *san* 23   . . .   *kyû* *jû* *san* 93

    . . .   .

    kyû 9   *jû* *kyû* 19   *ni* *jû* *kyû* 29   . . .   *kyû* *jû* *kyû* 99

10.1.2 Formal description

How can this neat little system be described? There are two types of composite expressions, the terms for the tens in (2) and the terms for the numbers between the tens in (3). Both types are formed by the same morphological operation, called concatenation. Concatenation (from Latin 'chain together') forms one expression out of two by attaching the second to the end of the first. While both types of composites are formed by concatenation, the interpretations of the combinations differ. The word *sanjû* ⟩three ten⟨ for 30 means ⟩three *times* ten⟨, but *jûsan* ⟩ten three⟨ for 13 means ⟩ten *plus* three⟨. If the first part denotes a smaller number than the second, concatenation is interpreted as multiplication. Otherwise concatenation stands for addition. For those numerals that involve both types of combination, the order of the two steps matters. For example, *sanjûroku* could, for its mere form, be derived in two ways:

(4) a.   (3 10) 6: First concatenate *san* 3 with *jû* 10 to form *sanjû*, then concatenate *sanjû* with *roku* 6.

    b.   3 (10 6) First concatenate *jû* 10 with *roku* 6 to form *jûroku*, then concatenate *san* 3 with *jûroku*.

When we follow (4a), we obtain the interpretation 30 for *sanjû* (smaller number 3 times greater number 10) and 36 for *sanjûroku* (greater number 30 plus smaller number 6). But with (4b) we obtain the interpretation 16 for *jûroku* and would then have to multiply this by 3, obtaining 48. Only the first derivation is correct: first form the ten word and then attach the digit word. We are now in a position to give a compositional description of the system. A compositional description always consists of four components.[1]

FB   Formation Base
A list of the basic expressions.
IB   Interpretation Base
A specification of the interpretations[2] of the basic expressions.
FR   Formation Rules
A specification of the formation rules for complex expressions.
IR   Interpretation Rules
A specification of the corresponding interpretation rules for complex expressions.

FB was defined in (1):

FB   Basic expressions are *ichi, ni, san, yon, go, roku, nana, hachi, kyû, jû*

FR consists of two rules:

F1   form 'XY'   where   X = *ni, san, yon, go, roku, nana, hachi* or *kyû*
            and   Y = *jû*
F2   form 'ZX'   where   Z = *jû, nijû, sanjû, . . . , kyûjû*
            and   X = *ichi, ni, san, yon, go, roku, nana, hachi* or *kyû*

We will use square brackets denoting interpretations: [A] is 'the interpretation of A'. IB assigns interpretations to the ten basic expressions:

IB   [*ichi*] = 1, [*ni*] = 2, [*san*] = 3, . . . , [*kyû*] = 9, [*jû*] = 10

IR consists of two interpretation rules, I1 and I2, that correspond to F1 and F2, respectively:

I1   If XY is formed according to rule F1,
          then [XY]   =   [X] × [Y]
I2   If ZX is formed according to rule F2,
          then [ZX]   =   [Z] + [X]

We can now 'compose' the meanings of the complex numerals. In (5), this is done for *nanajûroku* 76. On the basis of the given rules, the expression can only be derived by first applying F1 and then F2: *nana* and *jû* combine to *nanajû* 70, then *nanajû* is concatenated with *roku* 6. If we first derived *jûroku* 16 by F2, we could not concatenate this with *nana*, as neither formation rule allows for *jûroku* as the second part.

(5) a. **formation** of *nanajûroku*
      F1: *nana, jû → nanajû*
      F2: *nanajû, roku → nanajûroku*
  b. **interpretation** of *nanajûroku*
      I1: [*nanajû*]   = [*nana*] × [*jû*]
                 = 7 × 10   (IB)
                 = 70
      I2: [*nanajûroku*] = [*nanajû*] + [*roku*]
                 = 70 + 6   (above, IB)
                 = 76

Figure 10.1 shows the parallel steps in deriving the form and the interpretation of *nanajûroku*.

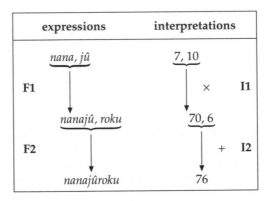

Figure 10.1 Formation and compositional interpretation of *nanajûroku*

10.1.3 The general scheme

The formal treatment of the numeral system illustrates the general scheme of compositional semantics as given in Figure 10.2. The essence of composition is the stepwise parallel formation of a complex expression and its interpretation. The basis of the system consists of the components FB and IB. These constitute the lexicon: a list of the lexical items with specified interpretations (= lexical meanings). Unlike in our example, the lexical items are usually categorized as, for instance, nouns, intransitive verbs, prepositions, etc. Such grammatical categories are sets of expressions with

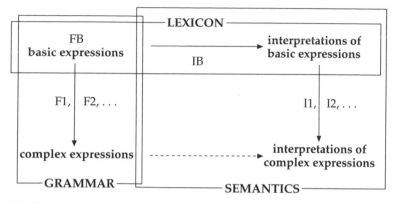

Figure 10.2 The general scheme of semantic composition

the same combinatorial properties. They are needed for the formulation of the formation rules, because these usually apply only to certain categories of expressions. The components FB and FR form the grammar of the system, i.e. the part that determines which expressions, basic or complex, are **regular** expressions and to which categories the regular expressions belong. FB and IB form the lexicon. The interpretation of the basic expressions, IB, and the set IR of interpretation rules I1, I2, . . . constitute the semantics of the system, i.e. the apparatus that provides each regular expression with an interpretation. The basic expressions receive an interpretation directly by IB while the interpretations of complex regular expressions are derived step by step from the interpretations of the basic expressions they contain. Each time a formation rule applies to derive a new expression, the corresponding interpretation rule applies to derive the interpretation. The broken-line arrow in Figure 10.2 represents the resulting assignment of interpretations to complex expressions.

10.2 A small fragment of English

In formal semantics, the description of composition is usually broken down into two steps. The first consists of a 'translation' of natural language sentences into an appropriate formal language, usually some variant of predicate logic. This step itself is compositional in the sense that the translations are systematically derived step by step in the same sort of parallelism as semantic composition. In a second step, these logical formulae receive a standard compositional interpretation. While the two-step procedure may seem complicated at first sight, it is in fact of great advantage. The translation into a logical language is the essential step of the analysis. Since logical formulae are, to the trained eye, semantically completely transparent, the translation of a sentence reveals its semantic structure as far as it can be expressed in the logical language. The second step, a compositional interpretation of the logical language, is standard and trivial, once the general rules are defined; actually it is usually omitted. The logical formulae are therefore practically considered as meaning representations. It would technically be possible to skip the translation into logic and supply the natural language sentences directly with the interpretations the translation formulae would receive. But the result would be clumsy and the semantic analysis of the sentence meanings less transparent.

Since semantic theory is still far from being able to provide such an account for even the major part of any language, the analysis is always restricted to a 'fragment', a limited set of lexemes and a limited set of formation rules, for which the corresponding interpretation rules are set up. Compositional analysis of natural language is difficult because syntactic combinations tend to allow for several semantic interpretations. In what follows we will treat a small fragment of English containing just a handful of basic expressions. For the sentences of the fragment, we will derive translations into predicate logic formulae similar to those used in 6.5.

10.2.1 The grammar of the fragment

The lexicon of the fragment is minimal, just designed to contain representatives of the major word classes and to allow for minimal variation. In order to keep the intermediate level of free grammatical forms (1.2.1, Figure 1.1) out of the system, the forms are simply fixed: all nouns are singular, all adjectives in their positive form, and all verbs in simple present tense, third person singular, indicative, active. The basic expressions are categorized in the traditional way.

FB	Basic expressions are the members of the following categories:	
NP	noun phrases	*Mary, John*
N	nouns	*person, fox*
A	adjectives	*fat, busy, wicked*
D	articles	*a*
VP	verb phrases	*squints, smokes*[3]
TV	transitive verbs	*knows, dislikes*
CV	copula verb	*is*

Formation rules

A formation rule specifies three things: (i) the categories of the input expressions, (ii) the form of the output expression, and (iii) its category. According to the first rule, a sentence may consist of an NP followed by a VP. This is the only rule for forming a sentence. It supplies the VP with a subject NP, i.e. a specification of its first argument:

F1   NP VP → S

The notation of the rule represents the general format used here. On the left side of the arrow, the input categories are specified. The form in which they are arranged indicates the form of the resulting expression. Thus, the rule takes as input an NP and a VP and forms a string consisting of the NP followed by the VP. On the right side of the arrow, the output category is specified. F1 reads as follows: take an NP and let it be followed by a VP; the result is of category S (sentence). Members of S are always complex expressions. If we had only this formation rule, it would allow us to form four sentences:

(6) | **NP** | **VP** | result: **S** |
|---|---|---|
| *Mary* | *squints* | *Mary squints* |
| *Mary* | *smokes* | *Mary smokes* |
| *John* | *squints* | *John squints* |
| *John* | *smokes* | *John smokes* |

In addition to the basic NPs *Mary* and *John*, complex NPs can be formed by combining nouns (N) with the indefinite article (D).[4]

F2   D N → NP

F2, so far, allows the formation of the complex NPs *a fox* and *a person*. F2 enlarges NP, an input category of F1. So we are able now to derive four more sentences: *a fox smokes, a person squints*, etc.

With F3, we can combine adjectives with nouns:

F3   A N → N

When we apply this rule once, we can form six AN combinations, among them *fat fox* and *wicked person*. But since the output of rule F3 is again of category N, the rule can be applied repeatedly. It allows for the formation of *fat wicked person* out of the derived N element *wicked person* and the adjective *fat*, and so on. Consequently, an N can be preceded by any number of adjectives, for example, *fat wicked fat fat fat wicked fox*. This consequence of the rule, though looking strange, is harmless. There is nothing ungrammatical to such formations. F3 also indirectly enlarges the number of NPs and sentences, since all N elements provide input to rule F2 and the output of F2 is input to F1. With F1, F2, F3 we can form sentences such as *a fat busy person smokes*.

Let us now turn to the rules for forming complex VPs. Both transitive verbs and the copula *is* can be combined with an NP to form a VP. There are two different formation rules F4 and F5 because, as we will see, the interpretation of the two types of VPs differs. The last rule allows the formation of a VP by combining the copula with an adjective:

F4	TV	NP	→	VP
F5	CV	NP	→	VP
F6	CV	A	→	VP

Now the grammar of the system is complete. Using F4, F5, and F6, we can form sentences like those:

(7) a. *John is busy*
   F6: CV *is*, A *busy* → VP *is busy*
   F1: NP *John*, VP *is busy* → S *John is busy*
 b. *Mary is a busy person*
   F3: A *busy*, N *person* → N *busy person*
   F2: D *a*, N *busy person* → NP *a busy person*
   F5: CV *is*, NP *a busy person* → VP *is a busy person*
   F1: NP *Mary*, VP *is a busy person* → S *Mary is a busy person*
 c. *a fat fox dislikes John*
   F3: A *fat*, N *fox* → N *fat fox*
   F2: D *a*, N *fat fox* → NP *a fat fox*
   F4: TV *dislikes*, NP *John* → VP *dislikes John*
   F1: NP *a fat fox*, VP *dislikes John* → S *a fat fox dislikes John*

Small though it is, the system already poses a reasonable set of compositional problems. To begin with, the translation of the basic expressions must be carefully arranged in order for the rest of the system to work out properly. Then there are a number of problems concerning the system of composition rules.

1 **NPs** can be used in two different ways (6.4.1). If they are used according to F1 or F4, they are verb complements with a referent. If F5 is applied, the NP is part of a copula VP, *is a fat fox*, *is Mary*, etc. and has no referent of its own (6.4.3).
2 There are NPs of two different forms, **proper names and indefinite NPs**. As verb complements, the two kinds of NPs seem to function differently. In 6.5 we would have represented the meaning of (7c) as (8):

(8) $\mathbf{fat}(x) \land \mathbf{fox}(x) \land \mathbf{dislike}(x, j)$

The proper name NP *John* directly provides the second argument of the verb **dislike**. In contrast, the indefinite NP *a fat fox* contributes two further predications, $\mathbf{fat}(x)$ and $\mathbf{fox}(x)$, about the first argument of the verb. The translation system has to take care of the difference. At the same time, however, it should manage to treat both types of NPs in a uniform way: for each of the three formation rules F1, F4 and F5, there should be only one translation rule.

3 A parallel problem arises with **adjectives**. How can they be analysed in a uniform way that covers their attributive use (F3) as well as their predicative use (F6)?

4 A more general problem is a proper account of **argument sharing** as illustrated by (7c): the analysis must result in a translation like (8) where the verb shares its first argument with the adjective and the noun.

10.2.2 The predicate logic language PL-F: its grammar

For the translation of the fragment, we define an appropriate predicate-logic language, PL-F. All PL languages make use of the same repertoire of formation rules, but they differ in the choice of the basic expressions, i.e. predicate terms and individual terms (recall 6.5).

PL-F contains just the basic expressions we need: individual constants for Mary and John, one-place predicate terms for the adjectives, nouns and intransitive verbs and two-place predicate terms for the transitive verbs. In addition, we will need two variables for individuals. Both individual constants and individual variables belong to the category T of [individual] terms. In addition, individual variables form a category of their own, V (variables). When specifying FB for PL-F, bold face is used for the constants that correspond to lexical items of the natural language fragment. As PL-F does not obey the rules of English syntax, the ending -s is omitted for the predicate terms that correspond to verbs:

FB	Basic expressions of PL-F are the members of the following categories:		
T	individual constants, terms	**m j**	
V, T	individual variables, terms	x y	
P1	one-place predicate terms	**fox person**	
		fat busy wicked	
		squint smoke	
P2	two-place predicate terms	**know dislike**	

The formation rules for PL-F are only a subset of the usual PL system. F1 and F2 allow the formation of so-called prime formulae by attaching the right number of argument terms to predicate terms (recall the description of PL formulae in 6.5):

F1 $P1(T) \rightarrow S$
F2 $P2(T, T) \rightarrow S$

S, again, is the category of sentences (or formulae). The two rules allow the formation of a limited number of formulae (60 in total), among them:

(9) a. **person(m)**　　　**fat(x)**　　　**squint(j)**
 　b. **dislike(j,y)**　　**know(x,m)**

In addition to this type of prime formulae we can form identity statements by connecting two terms with the 'equals' sign, yielding formulae such as 'x=m':

 　F3　T=T → S

Semantically, the equals sign is just another two-place predicate constant. It could be introduced as such and treated syntactically as the others. We would then write '=(x,m)' instead of 'x=m'. The usual way of writing identity statements is commonly preferred in PL. However, as you see, the price of doing so is an extra syntactic rule.

　　Next, we conjoin two formulae by logical conjunction. More connectives are used in richer PL languages, such as ∨ for 'or' and → for 'if . . . then . . .'. But we can do without them here. We also do not include negation.

 　F4　S ∧ S → S

F4 can be applied repeatedly. It allows the formation of complex formulae:

(10) a. **fat(j) ∧ wicked(j)**
 　 b. **fox(x) ∧ fox(y)**
 　 c. **fox(x) ∧ fat(x) ∧ dislike(x,y) ∧ y=m**

(10a) says that John is fat and wicked, (10b) is a way of expressing that both x and y are foxes, while the longish formula (10c) tells us the following: x is a fox and fat and dislikes y and y is Mary. In other words: x, a fat fox, dislikes Mary.

　　The last formation rule introduces the **existential quantifier** ∃. This operator, combined with a variable, is used as a prefix to a formula. The formula is enclosed into parentheses in order to mark the part of the total expression to which the quantifier applies, its so-called **scope**.

 　F5　∃V (S) → S

The existential quantifier is to be read and interpreted as 'there is at least one V such that S'. Usually, the 'at least' part is omitted in reading (but nevertheless to be understood). The rule gives us formulae like these:

(11) a. $\exists x\ (\textbf{fat}(x))$ there is an x that is fat
   b. $\exists x\ (\textbf{fat}(x) \wedge \textbf{person}(x))$ there is an x that is fat and a person
                                            = there is an x that is a fat person
   c. $\exists y\ (\textbf{know}(x,y) \wedge x=\textbf{m})$ there is a y such that x knows y and x is
                                            Mary
                                            = there is a y that Mary knows

Both F4 and F5 can be applied repeatedly and in combination with each other. The formation potential of the system is considerable, but we will confine our examples to such cases as will actually occur as translations of English fragment sentences, for example:

(12) $\exists x(x=\textbf{m} \wedge \exists y(\textbf{dislike}(x,y) \wedge \textbf{fox}(y)))$

The formula reads as follows: 'there is an x such that x is Mary and there is a y such that x dislikes y and y is a fox'. (12) is somewhat complex, so we will give its derivation in full detail. First the prime formulae are generated (steps 1 to 3). Then they are packed according to the structure of the total formula. Following the bracketing, we first conjoin the second and the third subformulae (step 4) and then apply $\exists y$ in step 5. Next, we conjoin 'x=$\textbf{m}$' to the $\exists y$-subformula (step 6). $\exists x$ is applied in the last step.

(13)   step 1   F3 $x=\textbf{m}$
      step 2   F2 $\textbf{dislike}(x,y)$
      step 3   F1 $\textbf{fox}(y)$
      step 4   F4 $\textbf{dislike}(x,y) \wedge \textbf{fox}(y)$
      step 5   F5 $\exists y(\textbf{dislike}(x,y) \wedge \textbf{fox}(y))$
      step 6   F4 $x=\textbf{m} \wedge \exists y(\textbf{dislike}(x,y) \wedge \textbf{fox}(y))$
      step 7   F5 $\exists x(x=\textbf{m} \wedge \exists y(\textbf{dislike}(x,y) \wedge \textbf{fox}(y)))$

The formation rules of PL allow for two different uses of variables. First, by F5, they can occur in the scope of an existential quantifier with that variable. Such occurrences are called **bound** by the quantifier. Alternatively, a variable may occur in a formula without being bound by a quantifier. It is then called **free**. To see the difference, consider the stepwise derivation of the formula in (13). In step 1, x is free and it remains free until it is bound by $\exists x$ in step 7. The variable y is introduced in step 2 as a free variable. It is eventually bound in step 5 by $\exists y$. Note that in step 5 $\exists y$ only binds y.

It is important to note that free variables are interpreted on a par with individual constants. They stand for a particular individual, functioning roughly like 'the x'. Existentially bound variables, however, achieve the reading of 'some x'. Therefore, steps 4 and 5 are interpreted as follows:

(14) a. **dislike**$(x,y) \land$ **fox**(y) the x dislikes the y and the y is a fox
    b. $\exists y($**dislike**$(x,y) \land$ **fox**$(y))$ there is *some* y that the x dislikes and y
                                          is a fox
                                          i.e. there is some fox that the x dislikes

Note that the bound variable can be eliminated when the formula is expressed in ordinary language (*there is some fox . . .*). The free one cannot, because it essentially functions like a proper name.

10.2.3 Translating the fragment into predicate logic

The translation of the fragment into PL-F follows the scheme of semantic composition. The notion of *interpretation* is to be replaced by *translation*. The general schema is given in Figure 10.3. The translation base TB fixes the translations of the basic expressions. Those given here will not be regular expressions of PL-F inasmuch as they contain empty slots for argument terms. In the course of applying the translation rules, these empty slots are properly filled with individual terms. In the end, each fragment sentence receives a regular PL-F formula as its translation. The use of empty slots helps us to keep track of the translation steps. There are two basic expressions of the fragment that do not receive a translation, the indefinite article and the copula. These will be taken care of in the translation rules concerning the categories **D** and **CV**. An underlined expression stands for the translation of the expression. (*John* is the translation of *John*, *Mary is a fat person* is the translation of *Mary is a fat person*.)

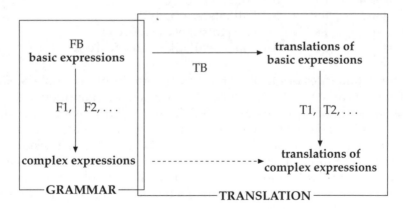

Figure 10.3 The general scheme of the translation procedure

The translation base

Except for the copula and the indefinite article, we treat all basic expressions including proper names as predicate expressions:

TB	NP	_John_ :	_=j
		Mary :	_ = m
	N	_fox_ :	fox(_)
		person :	person(_)
	A	_fat_ :	fat(_)
		busy :	busy(_)
		wicked :	wicked(_)
	VP	_squints_ :	squint(_)
		smokes :	smoke(_)
	TV	_dislikes_ :	dislike(_ , _)
		knows :	know(_ , _)

You may wonder why the proper names _John_ and _Mary_ are not translated into one-place predicate terms, rendering the translations **John**(_) and **Mary**(_). The reason is that proper names correspond to particular individuals. Translating _Mary_ as '_=**m**' takes account of both aspects of proper names, their being predicate terms and there being a unique individual to which the name applies. Other one-place predicate terms such as ordinary nouns, verbs and adjectives, may be true of any number of individuals, zero, one or more. For a predicate term such as _person_ there is no particular individual **p** such that 'x is a person' would be tantamount to 'x=**p**'.

The translation rules

The simplest rules are those handling the indefinite article and the copula. As a matter of fact, both expressions are treated as semantically zero:

T2	_a_ **N**	=	**N**
T5	_is_ **NP**	=	**NP**
T6	_is_ **A**	=	**A**

A noun, e.g. _fox_, constitutes a one-place predicate term that is true of all foxes. An indefinite NP such as _a fox_ provides the same predication. If an indefinite NP is combined with the copula, the result is a one-place verb phrase, another predicate term with the same meaning.[5] Similarly, an adjective like _busy_ provides the same predicate as the copula expression _is busy_. The three rules lead to the results in (15):

(15) a. _a fox_ = _fox_ = **fox**(_) (same for _a person_)
  b. _is a fox_ = _a fox_ = _fox_ = **fox**(_) (same for _is a person_)
  c. _is Mary_ = _Mary_ = _=**m** (same for _is John_)
  d. _is wicked_ = _wicked_ = **wicked**(_) (same for _is fat_, _is busy_)

We interpret the combination of A and N as logical conjunction, which is adequate for the adjectives in the fragment.

T3 $\underline{A\,N} = \underline{A} \wedge \underline{N}$

Together with T2 and T5 we get for example:

(16) a. <u>*busy person*</u>   = <u>*busy* ∧ *person*</u> = **busy**(_) ∧ **person**(_) T3
  b. <u>*a busy person*</u>   = <u>*busy person*</u>   = **busy**(_) ∧ **person**(_) T2, a
  c. <u>*is a busy person*</u> = <u>*a busy person*</u> = **busy**(_) ∧ **person**(_) T5, b

The rules of combining a verb with an argument, T1 and T4, introduce an existential quantifier for the argument.

T1 $\underline{NP\,VP} = \exists x(\ |\underline{NP}|\text{-}x \wedge |\underline{VP}|\text{-}x\ )$

The notation '| … |-x' stands for the expression that we obtain when we insert the variable x in the last empty slot of each predicate term within | . . .|. Thus, for example, |**fat**(_)|-x is **fat**(x) and |**know**(_ , _)|-y is **know**(_ ,y). The procedure will be referred to as **variable insertion**. So far, all predicate terms are one-place. Thus, the last argument slot is the only one. Let us apply T1 to the sentence *Mary squints*.

(17) <u>*Mary squints*</u> = $\exists x(\ |\underline{Mary}|\text{-}x \wedge |\underline{squints}|\text{-}x\ )$ T1
        = $\exists x(\ |\ \_ = \mathbf{m}|\text{-}x \wedge |\mathbf{squint}(\_)|\text{-}x\ )$ TB
        = $\exists x(\ x = \mathbf{m} \wedge \mathbf{squint}(x)\ )$ x insertion

Note that x insertion can only be performed when the resolution of the translation is down to the basic translations with the empty slots. Next, we combine the NP *Mary* with the VP *is a busy person* from (16):

(18) <u>*Mary is a busy person*</u> =
        = $\exists x(\ |\underline{Mary}|\text{-}x \wedge |\underline{is\ a\ busy\ person}|\text{-}x\ )$ T1
        = $\exists x(\ |\ \_ = \mathbf{m}|\text{-}x \wedge |\mathbf{busy}(\_) \wedge \mathbf{person}(\_)|\text{-}x\ )$ TB, (1)
        = $\exists x(\ x = \mathbf{m} \wedge \mathbf{busy}(x) \wedge \mathbf{person}(x)\ )$ x insertion

The translation rule for the combination of a transitive verb with its object NP is similar to T1. Instead of x, the variable y is used for the object referent. Rule T4 is applied before T1 (because the VP must be formed before it can be combined with the subject NP). Therefore the provision that the variable be inserted into the last empty slot of each argument term ensures that the object argument slot is filled first.

T4 $\underline{TV\,NP} = \exists y(\ |\underline{TV}|\text{-}y \wedge |\underline{NP}|\text{-}y\ )$

One example, *a fox dislikes John,* may suffice to show how this rule works in combination with T1. The formation of the sentence is given in (19f), its translation in (19t).

(19) f. F4: TV *dislikes,* NP *John* → VP *dislikes John*
       F2; D *a,* N *fox* → NP *a fox*
       F1: NP *a fox,* VP *dislikes John* → S *a fox dislikes John*

(19) t. *a fox dislikes John* =

=	$\exists$x(| *a fox* |-x $\land$ | *dislikes John* |-x)	T1
=	$\exists$x(| *fox* |-x $\land$ | *dislikes John* |-x)	T2
=	$\exists$x(| *fox* |-x $\land$ |$\exists$y(| *dislikes* |-y $\land$ | *John* |-y) |-x)	T4
=	$\exists$x(| **fox(_)** |-x $\land$ |$\exists$y(| **dislikes(_,_)** |-y $\land$ |_=**j**|-y) |-x)	TB

Now that we are down to the translations of the basic expressions with empty slots for arguments, we perform the variable insertions, first, the inner insertions of y and then the outer insertions of x.

(19) (contd.) = $\exists$x(\| **fox(_)** \|-x $\land$ \|$\exists$y(**dislikes(_,y)** $\land$ y = **j**) \|-x) y insertion
            = $\exists$x(**fox(x)** $\land$ $\exists$y(**dislikes(x,y)** $\land$ y = **j**)) x insertion

Discussion

How does the system cope with the problems addressed at the end of 10.2.1? To begin with, TB assigns the proper types of translations, i.e. one-place or two-place predicate terms, to the basic expressions of the fragment. The four problems are then taken care of as follows:

1 T1 and T4 introduce referents only for **referential NPs, i.e.** NPs in subject or object position. For each referent there is a variable bound by an existential quantifier. This is adequate since reference necessarily involves existence of the referent. Rule T5 for predicative NPs does not introduce an existential quantifier but leaves the argument slot(s) of the NP unoccupied (rules T1, T4, T5).
2 The system treats **proper names and indefinite NPs** in the same way. They uniformly add a predicate conjunct to the verb predication or to the zero meaning of the copula.
3 The system treats **attributive and predicative adjectives** alike. T3 for attributive and T6 for predicative adjectives both add the adjective meaning as a predicate conjunct to the meaning of N or to the zero meaning of *is.*
4 The system properly accounts for **argument sharing** among predicate terms. Terms that are to share an argument are first conjoined and then the same variable is inserted into their empty slots (rules T1 and T4). For the sentences in (18) and (19), Figure 10.4 displays argument assignments for the predicate terms and referent assignments for the NPs (recall the analyses in Figure 6.2 and Figure 6.4).

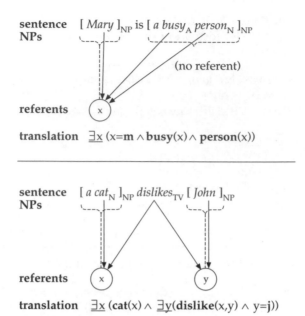

Figure 10.4 Referents and arguments of two sentences

The translation system yields PL **representations** that essentially correspond to the intuitive representations we used in 6.5. At first glance, the
translations are different. For example, *a fox dislikes John* would have been
analysed there as (20a) instead of our actual result (20b):

(20)   a.   **fox**(x) ∧ **dislike**(x,j)
       b.   ∃x(**fox**(x) ∧ ∃y(**dislike**(x,y) ∧ y=j))

The difference between the two formulae is due to two properties of the
translation system. First, **m** and **j** are not directly inserted into the empty
argument slots. This is why our translation has (21b) where (20a) simply
has (21a):

(21)   a.   **dislike**(x,j)
       b.   ∃y(**dislike**(x,y) ∧ y=j)

These two subformulae, however, are logically equivalent. According to
(21b), there is an individual y such that x dislikes y and y is John. As there
is only one John, there is only one such individual y, namely John. Thus
(21b) actually says that x dislikes John, i.e. what is directly expressed by
(21a). Our way of translating the proper name NPs, thus, leads to a more
complex representation but is logically correct, because the additional
quantifier can be eliminated without changing the truth conditions. When

we make use of the equivalence of (21a) and (21b) for simplifying (20b), we obtain (20c):

(20) c. $\exists x(\textbf{fox}(x) \wedge \textbf{dislike}(x,j))$

The result still differs from the original formula (20a) in that it encloses it in an existential quantification $\exists x(\ )$. The translation system generates no formulae with free variables, because variables exclusively come with a binding existential quantifier. This is the correct procedure. In fact, the use of free variables in 6.5 was sloppy, to say the least. The intended reading of 'some x' can only be achieved by binding the variable with an existential quantifier.

Let me add a few critical remarks about this system. First, while the system illustrates the general way in which formal semantics operates, it involves the unusual employment of empty slots and argument insertion. This allowed me to avoid additional formalism (such as λ operators, for those who know). But due to this, only sentences receive regular PL-F expressions as translations: translations of everything below sentence level contain empty argument slots, which are not provided for by the syntax of PL-F. Second, the reader must be cautioned that the system takes advantage of considerable restrictions of the lexical input. For example, not all types of one-place adjectives can be treated in that way, as was pointed out in 6.4.2. None of the rules applies to *all* adjectives, one-place nouns, NPs, intransitive or transitive verbs.

10.3 Model-theoretic semantics

We will now undertake the next major step, the introduction of a formal semantics for the PL language and thereby indirectly for the fragment. A formal semantics for a PL language serves one purpose: the assignment of a truth value to every formula. The interpretation base of such a system is a so-called **model**. It fixes the interpretations of all individual terms and predicate terms. The truth values of formulae derive from these fixings by means of general rules valid for all PL languages. For each language an infinity of different models can be defined. We will first fix a model for PL-F and then introduce the general interpretation rules.

10.3.1 A model for PL-F

A model for a PL language consists of two components, a so-called universe and an interpretation base. The **universe** is needed for the interpretation of quantifiers and predicate terms. The basic idea of interpreting an existential quantification is this: there is a given domain of cases; these cases are checked for the condition formulated in the scope of the quantifier; if there is at least one case in the domain for which the scope formula is true, then the existential statement is true, otherwise it is false. The universe of the model provides this domain of cases. If no such domain were fixed in advance, it would be impossible to assess that an existential quantification is false. Even if all cases checked so far were false, there would be others yet to be checked and therefore possibly true.

The universe indiscriminately provides the domain of cases for all quantifying formulae. (The technical term for this domain is *domain of quantification*.) What are the 'cases'? They are the potential arguments of the predicates used in the language. For example, if we are to determine the truth value of the formula $\exists x(\textbf{fox}(x) \wedge \textbf{dislike}(x,j))$, the cases to be checked are the entities the variable x can stand for, and these are the possible arguments of the predicates denoted by **fox** and **dislike**. It is common practice to use the general term *individuals* for all those abstract or concrete things that might be arguments of the predicates of the PL language. Depending on the model, i.e. on the application of the PL language, the individuals may be persons, or numbers, or points in time or sets or whatever.

---

(22) **IB**   The **universe** U of our model of PL-F is the set consisting of the following four individuals:

Ken: a squinting dog

Fritz: a fat, wicked fox

Mary: a person, neither fat nor busy nor wicked nor squinting nor a smoker

John: a fat, busy, wicked smoker

Having fixed the universe, we can assign interpretations to the basic expressions. Each individual term receives one of the individuals in the universe as its interpretation. We fix the interpretations as follows. There is no need to assign a different interpretation to each term or to provide a term for each individual, but we will do so:

(23) **IB**   [j] = John   [m] = Mary   [x] = Ken   [y] = Fritz

The model must fix interpretations for the variables too because they can occur freely in formulae such as '**fox**(x)' or 'x=y'. If no interpretations for variables were fixed, it would not be possible to determine the truth value of such formulae.

The interpretations of predicate constants are entities that assign a truth value to every individual in the model. As a convenient notational convention, from here on small capitals are used for the interpretations of predicate constants, FOX for [**fox**], KNOW for [**know**] and so on. FOX assigns 1 to Fritz and 0 to Ken, Mary and John, because in our model Fritz, unlike Ken, Mary and

John, is a fox. The table in (24) displays the assignments of truth values to
individuals for PERSON, FOX, FAT, BUSY, WICKED, SQUINT and SMOKE.

(24)				Ken	Fritz	Mary	John
IB	[person]	=	PERSON	0	0	1	1
	[fox]	=	FOX	0	1	0	0
	[fat]	=	FAT	0	1	0	1
	[busy]	=	BUSY	0	0	0	1
	[wicked]	=	WICKED	0	1	0	1
	[squint]	=	SQUINT	1	0	0	0
	[smoke]	=	SMOKE	0	0	0	1

Two individuals, Mary and John, are persons, one is a fox. Two individuals
each are fat and wicked (Fritz and John). FAT and WICKED assign the same
truth value in every case, as do BUSY and SMOKE. Apart from specifying Ken as
neither being a person nor a fox, the model leaves open what species Ken is
(he must have two eyes, though, because he squints).

In mathematics, such assignments are known as functions. Functions
assign 'values' to their 'arguments'. Since FOX, FAT, WICKED, etc. assign truth
values to individuals, they are functions. The particular type of function
that assigns truth values to its arguments is called a *predicate* in mathematics. Since we have been using the term *predicate* for a certain type of
concept, we will call predicates in the mathematical sense *m-predicates*.[6]

DEFINITION

An **m-predicate** over a set A is a function that assigns a truth value to
every element of A.

M-predicates resemble predicates-as-concepts in that both yield truth values
when applied to their arguments. But while predicates-as-concepts are part
of our cognitive systems, m-predicates are abstract set-theoretical constructs,
namely pairings of arguments and truth values. For example, the function
FAT is the set of the four pairs Ken–0, Fritz–1, Mary–0 and John–1. That is why
m-predicates can be defined in the form of tables that list the truth values for
all arguments as we did in (24). If two m-predicates (or functions in general)
assign equal values to all arguments, they are identical. Hence, in our model,
FAT = WICKED and BUSY = SMOKE. The corresponding mental predicates ⟩fat⟨ and
⟩wicked⟨, or ⟩busy⟨ and ⟩smoke(r)⟨, are of course by no means identical.
They just happen, in this model, to be true of the same individuals. In Table
10.1, the seven m-predicates of our model are depicted as what they just are:
sets of argument–value pairings.

1 [person]	2 [fox]	3 [fat] [wicked]	4 [busy] [smoke]	5 [squint]
Ken → 0	Ken → 0	Ken → 0	Ken → 0	Ken → 1
Fritz → 0	Fritz → 1	Fritz → 1	Fritz → 0	Fritz → 0
Mary → 1	Mary → 0	Mary → 0	Mary → 0	Mary → 0
John → 1	John → 0	John → 1	John → 1	John → 0

Table 10.1 The five one-place m-predicates of the model

There are one-place and more-place functions. Two-place functions assign a value to pairs of arguments, and so on. The interpretations of the two-place predicate constants **know** and **dislike** are two-place m-predicates. Their definition requires a different form of table. In (25) a1 stands for the first argument, the subject of the corresponding transitive verb, a2 for direct-object argument.

(25)

IB	a1 \ a2	Ken	Fritz	Mary	John		a1 \ a2	Ken	Fritz	Mary	John
	Ken	0	1	1	0		Ken	1	1	1	1
	Fritz	1	0	0	1		Fritz	1	1	0	1
	Mary	1	0	0	1		Mary	1	0	1	1
	John	1	1	1	0		John	1	1	1	1
		DISLIKE						KNOW			

According to (25), Ken dislikes Fritz and Mary, Fritz dislikes Ken and John, and so on. In connection with m-predicates we use the common mathematical notation 'f(x)=y' :

(26)   FOX(Fritz)=1   for: FOX assigns 1 to Fritz
       DISLIKE(Ken, Fritz)=1   for: DISLIKE assigns 1 to Ken and Fritz
                                      (in this order, i.e. Ken dislikes Fritz)

With the definition of the universe and interpretations for all basic expressions of PL-F, the model - one possible model - is complete. Since the same interpretation rules apply to all PL languages, these rules are not part of a particular model.

10.3.2 Interpretation rules for PL-F

Since all complex expressions in PL-F are formulae, we can give the interpretation rules in a uniform format:

[S]=1   *iff*   *(condition)*

The condition on the right side of *iff* is a condition for the sentence S being true, i.e. its **truth conditions**. The first three interpretation rules take care of the prime formulae. T and T' are used when two terms must be distinguished:

I1	[P1(T)]=1	*iff*	[P1]([T])=1
I2	[P2(T,T')]=1	*iff*	[P2]([T],[T'])=1
I3	[T=T']=1	*iff*	[T]=[T']

In (27), rule I1 is applied to 'fox(j)':

(27)   [fox(j)]=1   *iff*   [fox]([j])=1   by I1

This step takes us down from the interpretation of the formula to the interpretations of the predicate constant and the term. [fox] is the m-predicate fox, [j] is the individual John. In the next step, these are inserted:

[fox(j)]=1   *iff*   fox(John)=1   by IB

We now have to check the truth value of the m-predicate fox for the individual John. It is 0 (see (24)). Thus, the statement on the right side is false, and consequently the one on the left side is too. In other words: [fox(j)] = 0 (because, if a formula is not true, it is false).

An application of I2 is given in (28). (29) illustrates the interpretation of identity statements:

(28)   [dislike(y,m)]=1   *iff*   [dislike]([y],[m])=1   by I2
    iff   dislike(Fritz,Mary)=1   by IB
    Since dislike(Fritz,Mary)=1, [dislike(y,m)]=1.

(29)   [m=x]=1   *iff*   [m]=[x]   by I3
    iff   Mary=Ken   by IB
    Since Mary is not Ken, [m=x]=0.

Two rules are left. The interpretation of conjunction is straightforward. It states that a conjunction is true iff both conjuncts are true (cf. the definitions in 4.4):

I4 $[S \wedge S'] = 1$ *iff* $[S] = 1$ and $[S'] = 1$

(30) $[\textbf{wicked}(x) \wedge \textbf{know}(x,y)] = 1$

iff	$[\textbf{wicked}(x)] = 1$	and	$[\textbf{know}(x,y)] = 1$	by I4
iff	$[\textbf{wicked}]([x]) = 1$	and	$[\textbf{know}(x,y)] = 1$	by I1
iff	$[\textbf{wicked}]([x]) = 1$	and	$[\textbf{know}]([x],[y]) = 1$	by I2
iff	WICKED(Ken) = 1	and	KNOW(Ken,Fritz) = 1	by IB

Since WICKED(Ken) = 0 and KNOW(Ken,Fritz) = 1, the conjunction is false: $[\textbf{wicked}(x) \wedge \textbf{know}(x,y)] = 0$

Rule I5 for existential quantification is in need of some explanation. Grasping the sense of such formulae is one thing, giving a precise interpretation rule, another. Let us consider an example first:

(31) a. $\exists x(\textbf{fox}(x) \wedge \textbf{wicked}(x))$

In a given model, the formula is true if there is at least one individual in the universe that is both a fox and wicked. How can this be put on terms with the general design of the interpretation rules? What we have to do in order to check whether (31a) is true is check the truth value of the formula $\textbf{fox}(x) \wedge \textbf{wicked}(x)$, for different possible interpretations of x. Is it true if we assume that [x] = John? Is it true for [x] = Mary? And so on for each individual in our universe. If the formula is true for at least one individual, then the existential quantification is true. This yields the following formulation of I5, where **V** represents the bound variable.

I5 $[\exists V\,(S)] = 1$ *iff*   there is at least one individual u in U such that, for $[V] = u$, $[S] = 1$

Applied to (31a), the new rule yields the following derivation:

(32) $[\exists x(\textbf{fox}(x) \wedge \textbf{wicked}(x))] = 1$

iff	there is at least one u in U such that, for [x] = u, $[\textbf{fox}(x) \wedge \textbf{wicked}(x)] = 1$	by I5
iff	there is at least one u in U such that, for [x] = u, $[\textbf{fox}(x)] = 1$ and $[\textbf{wicked}(x)] = 1$	by I4
iff	there is at least one u in U such that, for [x] = u, $[\textbf{fox}]([x]) = 1$ and $[\textbf{wicked}]([x]) = 1$	by I1
iff	there is at least one u in U such that, for [x] = u, FOX([x]) = 1 and WICKED([x]) = 1	by IB
iff	there is at least one u in U such that FOX(u) = 1 and WICKED(u) = 1	

Since Fritz is such an individual, the formula is true.

We can now see why employment of an existential quantifier makes a big difference. Compare (31a) with the 'naked' (31b):

(31) a.   ∃x(**fox**(x) ∧ **wicked**(x))
   b.   **fox**(x) ∧ **wicked**(x)

The quantifier-free formula in (31b) is just about a single case, namely about the individual we happened to fix as the interpretation of the variable x in case it is used as a free variable. In our model, (31b) thus happens to be false because [x] is Ken, and Ken is neither a fox nor wicked. If (31b) were true, it would be a coincidence. The existential formula (31a) is about the whole universe of the model, stating that it contains at least one wicked fox. (31b) is about *the* interpretation of x in the model, while (31a) is about *all its possible* interpretations in the model. This is why only existential formulae have the 'some' quality with respect to the variable, saying roughly, 'there is *some* x such that . . .'.

Now that the interpretation system for PL-F is complete, let us have a look at how it works and what it buys us. It yields the assignment of an interpretation (in the technical sense) to every basic or complex expression of the language. Thus, in mathematical terms, an interpretation system is a complex definition of the function [ ] which assigns each expression its interpretation in the model. Different categories of expressions receive different types of interpretations: we assign individuals to individual terms, m-predicates to predicate terms and truth values to sentences. The interpretation base and the rules are designed in a way that everything works out properly, different types of interpretations combining in just the right way. For example, the interpretation rule I1 for the formula type P1(T) produces a truth value by the following mechanism. It takes the individual [T] and the m-predicate [P1] and lets the m-predicate work on the individual to produce a truth value. This, then, is the resulting interpretation of the formula, its truth value in the model. Table 10.2 displays the general picture for PL-F and how it works out for such a formula.

category	*individual term*	*predicate term*	*formula/sentence*
expression	**m**	**busy**	**busy(m)**
interpretation	**Mary**	Ken → 0 Fritz → 0 **Mary** → **0** John → 1	**0**
type of interpretation	*individual*	*m-predicate*	*truth value*

Table 10.2 Categories of expressions and types of values

10.3.3 Application to the translations of fragment sentences

With the interpretation system for PL-F, a first formal semantics for our fragment of English is complete. The semantics consists of two steps. First, sentences from the fragment are translated into PL-F. In a second step, their truth values in the given model are determined in the interpretation system for PL-F. We will illustrate the process for one sentence of the fragment, *a fox dislikes John*. The example is somewhat complex because we have to deal with double quantification.

(33) a. *a fox dislikes John*
   b. translation (cf. (19)): $\exists x(\textbf{fox}(x) \wedge \exists y(\textbf{dislike}(x,y) \wedge y=\textbf{j}))$
   c. truth value :
   $[\exists x(\textbf{fox}(x) \wedge \exists y(\textbf{dislike}(x,y) \wedge y=\textbf{j}))]=1$

   iff there is at least one u in U such that, for [x]=u,
   $[\textbf{fox}(x) \wedge \exists y(\textbf{dislike}(x,y) \wedge y = \textbf{j})]=1$ by I5

   iff there is at least one u in U such that, for [x]=u,
   $[\textbf{fox}(x)]=1$ and $[\exists y(\textbf{dislike}(x,y) \wedge y=\textbf{j})]=1$ by I4

   iff there is at least one u in U such that, for [x]=u,
   $[\textbf{fox}(x)]=1$ and there is at least one v^7 in U such
   that, for [y]=v, $[\textbf{dislike}(x,y) \wedge y=\textbf{j}]=1$ by I5

   iff there is at least one u in U such that, for [x]=u,
   $[\textbf{fox}]([x])=1$ and there is at least one v in U such
   that, for [y]=v, $[\textbf{dislike}]([x],[y])=1$ and
   [y]=[j]   by I1, 2 ,3, 4

   iff there is at least one u in U such that
   FOX(u)=1 and there is at least one v in U
   such that DISLIKE(u,v)=1 and v=John   by IB

   iff there is at least one u in U such that
   FOX(u)=1 and DISLIKE(u,John)=1

Since the condition is fulfilled – Fritz dislikes John, see (25) – the sentence *a fox dislikes John* is true in the model.

What is the benefit of all this formal apparatus? After all, the results look utterly trivial. Is not the result of the formal analysis of the sentence *a fox dislikes John* just a somewhat more cumbersome way of saying the same thing? Yes, it is. But the crucial point is: it *must* be that way. If the resulting truth conditions were not recognizably those of the original sentence, the analysis would be wrong. After all, semantic analysis is to reproduce our semantic intuitions, and these are with respect to the sentence *a fox dislikes John* just that the sentence says 'a fox dislikes John'. The main achievement of the analysis is a description of *how the truth conditions come about*. In the course of deriving the truth conditions for the sentences of the fragment, we had to settle a number of semantic questions that are far from trivial. What are the meanings of the basic expressions and what are their respective contributions to the truth conditions of a sentence? How do their meanings combine with those of the other parts of a sentence? How can expressions of different meanings and forms but of the same syntactic category, e.g. proper names and indefinite NPs, be analysed in a uniform way? The answers to these questions are nothing less than a description of central composition rules – the main objective of sentence semantics.

10.3.4 Model-theoretic semantics

The interpretation system for PL-F is an example of a so-called model-theoretic semantics. Model theory is a branch of mathematics concerned with the interpretation of formal languages such as PL. It provides general definitions of possible models and the general rules of deriving truth conditions for the formulae of such languages on the basis of a given model. A model-theoretic semantics is a semantics in a technical sense in that it assigns non-linguistic entities to linguistic expressions, entities such as referents, m-predicates and truth values which are at least somehow related to meaning in the usual sense. When natural language sentences are translated into a formal language and then given a model-theoretic inter-pretation (see Figure 10.5 for the general scheme), this kind of 'semantics' is

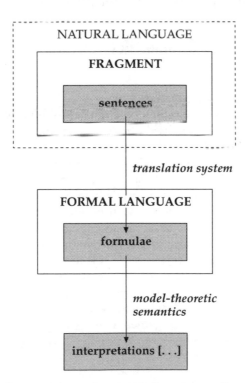

Figure 10.5 Two-step interpretation assignment in formal semantics

applied to, or supplied for, natural language. 'Meanings' in model-theoretic semantics are whatever interpretations the function [ ] assigns to natural language expressions. Let us take a look at what kind of semantics we have achieved so far.

The first thing to observe is that the expressions receive interpretations only for a given model. What is such a model? It is something that fixes referents for the individual terms of the PL language and truth values for the individuals with respect to each predicate term of the language. For natural language sentences, the choice of a model essentially means the choice of one concrete CoU (out of an infinity of possible CoUs).

Clearly, the truth values of a sentence in one particular CoU is not its meaning. If it were, all sentences true in that CoU would have the same meaning. Likewise the referent of an NP cannot be equated with its meaning. Nor does an m-predicate that assigns a truth value to every individual in a given CoU constitute the meaning of a predicate term. Recall how the interpretations of *fat* and *wicked* coincided in our model. Therefore, these interpretations cannot be considered the meanings proper.

What we need in order to account for the meanings of natural language expressions is more: a description of the potential of the expressions with respect to *all* possible CoUs. The model-theoretic approach will therefore be extended to so-called possible-world semantics.

10.4 Possible-world semantics

10.4.1 Possible worlds

Let us assume we are dealing not with a small fragment of English but have managed to set up a fully-fledged formation system of English, a complete lexicon and grammar. Let us further assume that we have a translation system that yields representations of arbitrary English sentences into an appropriate logical language LE (for Logical English). LE has constants corresponding to all lexical items of English, in particular predicate constants for all verbs, adjectives and nouns. What would it mean to give a model for LE? Recall that a model is the basis for assigning truth values to all formulae of the logical language. Since these comprise the translations of all English sentences, the model must provide the relevant information for assigning TRUE or FALSE to every possible English sentence. Now, sentences are not simply true or false (except for logically true or false sentences, 4.2). Rather, their truth values depend on, and change with, the CoU. For example, the sentences in (34) keep changing their truth values through time; at some times one is true and the other false, at others both are true or both false.

(34) a. *Mary is tired.*
     b. *Mary was tired.*

The time dependence is due to the fact that the VPs carry tense. That is why the time of utterance is one component of the CoU (1.1.2). In addition, the truth values of the sentences also depend on who is referred to by the name *Mary*, again a feature of the CoU. And even if time and person reference is fixed, the truth values depend on the particular facts given in the CoU, on what Mary has been doing and how much and well she has slept. That is why the given facts must also be considered a component of the CoU. When we defined the model for PL-F, we implicitly fixed all these components of a possible CoU. We assigned referents to the proper names, we assumed certain facts as given, such as Fritz being fat and John being a fat, wicked, busy smoker. We also implicitly fixed a reference time and interpreted all predications as relating to this time of utterance.

What we have been calling a CoU is called a **possible world** in formal semantics. A possible world is the sum of all facts, or conditions, on which the truth value of any sentence may depend. A possible world fixes a time and place of utterance, the circumstances such as who is the speaker and who are the addressees, it fixes reference and a 'universe' of individuals and it fixes all the relevant facts. There are possible worlds that correspond to reality in sharing all their facts with what we consider our real world, while other worlds represent alternative ways of how things might be. There is not only one 'real' world but many, since even if the facts are real, different CoUs could be fixed within reality.[8] Alternative, non-real worlds will not be completely different, but differ only in some details. For example, Mary may be tired in a real world w_1, but might just have had a nap in some other world w_2 which is otherwise not so different from w_1. This is the kind of world one would refer to in a statement like (35):

(35) *If Mary had had a nap, she would not be so tired.*

The verb forms in the *if*-clause and the main clause indicate a shift of reference from the real world into an alternative world. In this world Mary is said to be not as tired as in the real one. The alternative world is construed as one which differs in what the *if*-clause states but otherwise is like the real world.

In actual applications of possible-world semantics (PWS), i.e. the branch of formal semantics that employs this notion, concrete possible worlds are never actually spelled out. This would, of course, be impossible. We are not omniscient. Possible worlds are simply assumed as given, and even the ingredients that make up a possible world such as time of utterance, speaker, addressee, location and circumstances are only made explicit to the extent that is required by the semantic data to be analysed. Possible worlds are theoretical constructs for what the truth value of a sentence may depend on. This construction enables us to describe how reference and truth values can be derived *if* we are given the necessary information in a particular CoU.

10.4.2 Intensions

With the notion of possible worlds, we are able to assign general interpretations to linguistic expressions. These interpretations are functions that assign the expression not just its referent, truth value, etc. but a referent, truth value, etc. *for every possible world*. Consider an arbitrary sentence, such as the above *Mary is tired*. In each possible world, the sentence is either true or false.[9] Let $\mathcal{W}$ be the set of all possible worlds. Then a function can be defined that assigns to each possible world w in $\mathcal{W}$ the truth value of *Mary is tired* in that world. In PWS the usual notation for the function is double square brackets $[\![\ ]\!]$. $[\![Mary\ is\ tired]\!]$ is the function that assigns the sentence a truth value for every possible world. The truth value in a particular world w is $[\![Mary\ is\ tired]\!]^w$.

DEFINITION
For arbitrary sentences S, $[\![S]\!]$ is a function that assigns to every possible world w in $\mathcal{W}$ the truth value of S in that world, i.e. $[\![S]\!]^w$.

This function is considered the meaning, and called the **proposition**, of the sentence in PWS. You may think of the proposition of a sentence S as an infinite table that lists a truth value for every possible world, as illustrated in (36):

(36)   **proposition of S, $[\![S]\!]$**

world	w_1	w_2	w_3	w_4	w_5	w_6	w_7	w_8	...
truth value of S	1	1	0	1	0	0	0	1	...

Formally, for every sentence S its proposition is an m-predicate over the set of possible worlds. It is true of those worlds in which S is true and false of the rest. Insofar as m-predicates are analogues of predicates-as-concepts, this is well in accordance with the view taken in Chapters 6 and 9 that the descriptive meaning of a sentence is a predicate about the CoU.

Let us next consider the interpretations of natural language individual terms, for example the name *Mary*, taken as a proper name, or the pronoun *I*. For these, interpretations are defined that yield a (potential) referent for every possible world. We will assume that part of what makes up a particular possible world w is a 'universe' U^w of its own. Thus, an individual term in each world w is assigned an individual in that universe.

> DEFINITION
> For arbitrary individual terms T, $[\![T]\!]$ is a function that assigns to every possible world w in $\mathcal{W}$ $[\![T]\!]^w$, the individual in U^w that is the referent of T if T is used referentially.

For the pronoun *I*, $[\![I]\!]^w$ is the speaker who utters the sentence in world w. For *Mary*, the interpretation assigns to each possible world the person referred to as 'Mary' in that world. If a possible world were to have more than one such person Mary, we would have to distinguish different names *Mary*$_1$, *Mary*$_2$, etc. in the lexicon and assign them different interpretations. The interpretations for individual terms in PWS are called **individual concepts**. Again, you may think of an individual concept as an infinite table like that in (36) that lists an individual for every possible world.

Propositions and individual concepts are generally called **intensions**. The intension of an expression assigns it its **extension** for, or in, every possible world. Thus the intension of a sentence S is a proposition and the extension of S in a particular world is its truth value there. The intension of an individual term is an individual concept, its extension in w is an individual in U^w.

> DEFINITION
> For arbitrary expressions E, the **intension of E**, $[\![E]\!]$, is a function that assigns to each possible world w in $\mathcal{W}$ an entity in w of appropriate type (see definitions). $[\![E]\!]^w$ is the **extension of E in the world w**.

For a predicate term, its extension in a world w is, of course, an m-predicate over the respective universe U^w. We will therefore define the intensions and extensions of predicate terms as follows.

> DEFINITION
> For arbitrary predicate terms P, $[\![P]\!]$ is a function that assigns to every possible world w in $\mathcal{W}$ an m-predicate over U^w as its extension $[\![P]\!]^w$.

Intensions of one-place predicate terms are called **properties**. Table 10.3 gives a survey of the three types of intensions and extensions introduced.

Table 10.3 Intensions and extensions

Expression E	Its intension $[\![E]\!]$	Its extension in world w $[\![E]\!]^w$
sentence	proposition	truth value
individual term	individual concept	individual
predicate term *(1-place)*	property	function that assigns truth values to individuals

10.4.3 Intensional models

In application to formal languages, a possible world corresponds to a model: it fixes reference and truth values. Hence, the value of an expression E in a particular model corresponds to the extension of E in the corresponding possible world w: [E] (in that model) is $[\![E]\!]^w$. We will therefore call the type of models introduced in 10.3.1 **extensional models**.

In an **intensional model** for a formal language, the basic expressions receive intensions as interpretations. Individual terms and predicate terms receive interpretations of the following forms (for individual terms T and one-place predicate constants P1):

(37) a. $[\![T]\!]$ = a function that assigns to every possible world w in $\mathcal{W}$ an individual $[\![T]\!]^w$ in U^w.

   b. $[\![P1]\!]$ = a function that assigns to every possible world w in $\mathcal{W}$ a one-place m-predicate $[\![P1]\!]^w$.

What we then need are intensional interpretation rules for deriving the intensions of complex expressions. This too is straightforward. Recall the extensional rule for prime formulae of the form 'P1(T)' (we attach the subscript *e* for *extensional*):

I1$_e$ [P1(T)] = 1 *iff* [P1]([T])=1

The *in*tensional interpretation rule must ensure that I1$_e$ remains valid at the extensional level. We can ensure this if we simply define I1$_i$ (*i* for *intensional*) as follows:

I1$_i$ for every possible world w $[\![P1(T)]\!]^w = 1$ *iff* $[\![P1]\!]^w([\![T]\!]^w) = 1$

The use of intensions as interpretations brings us an important step further in coping with the problems pointed out at the end of 10.3.4. First, the interpretations are no longer restricted to one particular CoU (possible world). Rather, they cover the range of all possible CoUs. Second, the interpretations no longer massively coincide for expressions with intuitively different meanings. For example, the adjectives *fat* and *wicked* may happen to be true for the same set of individuals in some possible worlds. But there will always be other worlds where they differ, because it is *possible* that someone is fat and not wicked or wicked and not fat. Thus, there is at least one world w and one individual i in U^w such that $[\![fat]\!]^w(i) \neq [\![wicked]\!]^w(i)$. Therefore $[\![fat]\!]^w$ and $[\![wicked]\!]^w$ are different and hence also the intensions $[\![fat]\!]$ and $[\![wicked]\!]$.

10.4.4 Logical properties and relations

When an intensional model is supplied for the formal language into which the sentences of natural language are translated, this yields an intensional interpretation system for the latter. Such a system provides general truth conditions for all sentences. For example, for the truth conditions of *a fox dislikes John* we obtain formally (38a), and less formally (38b) (see (33) for the derivation):

(38) a. for every possible world w in $\mathcal{W}$, *a fox dislikes John* is true iff there is at least one individual u in U^w such that $[\![fox]\!]^w(u) = 1$ and, given John = $[\![John]\!]^w$, $[\![dislike]\!]^w(u,John) = 1$.

   b. for every possible world w in $\mathcal{W}$, *a fox dislikes John* is true iff there is at least one individual in U^w, for which, in w, the predicate *fox* is true as well as the predicate *dislike* with respect to the person John in U^w as the object of dislike.

The availability of general truth conditions allows a very important step: the formal definition of the logical notions introduced in Chapter 4:

DEFINITION

a. A sentence S is **logically true** iff S is true in every possible world.

b. Sentence S_1 **logically entails** sentence S_2 iff for no possible world S_1 is true and S_2 is false.

c. Two expressions E_1 and E_2 are **logically equivalent**, iff they have equal extensions, i.e. equal extensions in all possible worlds.

We can therefore check the results of a PWS analysis by testing if the formal interpretations produce intuitively correct logical properties and relations. For example, the A+N combination *fat fox* intuitively entails both *fat* and *fox*: fat foxes are foxes and fat foxes are fat. This observation is correctly carried out by our analysis, because it yields the following translations for the respective test sentences with a free individual variable x:

(39) a.   *x is a fat fox* $\mathbf{fox}(x) \wedge \mathbf{fat}(x)$
   b.   *x is a fox* $\mathbf{fox}(x)$
   c.   *x is fat* $\mathbf{fat}(x)$

Given the intensional model sketched in 10.4.3, we can easily verify the entailments. According to what would be I4$_i$, in every possible world w the formula '$\mathbf{fox}(x) \wedge \mathbf{fat}(x)$' is true iff '$\mathbf{fox}(x)$' and '$\mathbf{fat}(x)$' are both true in w. Thus, whenever (39a) is true, (39b) and (39c) are true too.

However, the intensional interpretation given so far only captures those logical relations that originate from the application of the composition rules. The system is not able to derive entailments based on meaning relations between lexical items, for example, that *x is a dog* entails *x is an animal*. There are two ways to handle this kind of phenomenon.

First, one can set up a collection of meaning postulates such as *dogs are animals, children of the same parents are siblings, pork is meat from pigs, etc.* (cf. 7.3.4). These are declared axioms of the interpretation system, i.e. sentences that must come out true in every possible world. The possibilities of defining the overall intension function $[\![\ ]\!]$ would thereby be considerably constrained. Note that, up to now, we have only given a general characterization of intensions. In principle, $[\![\ ]\!]$ can be defined in a way such that, for example, for some world w $[\![duck]\!]^w$ and $[\![human]\!]^w$ both assign 1 to some individuals which would then be both ducks and human beings. If we want to exclude this kind of contradiction, we can take care of the matter by appropriate meaning postulates.

Alternatively, we can incorporate lexical decomposition into this kind of approach. In fact, Dowty's theory of decomposition (7.4.1) was developed within the framework of PWS. Lexical items to be decomposed are then translated not directly into corresponding predicate terms (*fox* = $\mathbf{fox}(\_)$) but into decompositional formulae. For example, the nouns *woman* and *man* could be translated as follows:

(40) a.   *woman*   = $\mathbf{human}(\_) \wedge \neg\, \mathbf{male}(\_)$
   b.   *man*   = $\mathbf{human}(\_) \wedge \mathbf{male}(\_)$

We can then immediately derive that *x is a woman* logically contradicts *x is a man*. This procedure does not constrain the intension function $[\![\ ]\!]$. Rather it reduces the number of predicate constants in LE for which intensions have to be defined. But ultimately we would of course want to constrain the interpretations of the remaining semantic primitives, i.e. the irreducible basic expressions of LE.

10.5 The scope and limits of possible-world semantics

10.5.1 Scope and potential

Above all, PWS is a theory that provides a precise theoretical notion of meaning: in PWS, the meaning of a lexical or non-lexical expression is its intension in an intensional model. For sentences, intensions are functions that assign the sentence a truth value for every possible world, where *possible world* is a theoretical construct for the CoU. The semantic description of a sentence in PWS is a definition of its truth conditions. For all kinds of expressions, the approach provides not only a notion of meaning (intension) but also a notion of reference: for a given possible world w, the extension of an expression E can be considered its actual or potential referent in that world. Thus, PWS can claim to provide theoretical definitions for the following central semantic notions:

- the meaning of a lexical or syntactically complex expression: its intension;
- the context of utterance: a possible world;
- the (potential) referent of an expression: its extension in a given world;
- the truth conditions of a sentence: a description of its intension.

As a semantic framework, PWS is primarily aimed at describing semantic composition. As we saw in the fragment, lexical meanings are essentially treated as simply given; by translating them into corresponding constants of the formal language, e.g. *know* = **know**$(\_,\_)$, they are themselves not analysed. This corresponds to the aim of sentential semantics to address questions such as: *given* the meanings of the adjective *fat* and the noun *fox*, what is the meaning of the A+N combination *fat fox*? Neither structuralist semantics nor cognitive semantics have so far managed to come up with a theory of composition. This is the main asset of PWS. PWS describes composition by translating natural language expressions into a formal logical language. The two-step procedure yields explicit meaning representations in the form of semantically transparent and explicit logical translations. It further allows the description of logical properties and relations. Thus, as a descriptive apparatus, PWS provides the following:

- meaning representations in a logical language;
- a description of composition rules for sentences and complex expressions in general;
- the description of logical properties and logical relations such as entailment.

In addition, as we saw in the last section, PWS provides a suitable framework for decomposition and thereby for describing, to a certain extent, word meanings and meaning relations between lexical items.

10.5.2 Limits

While the basic notion of intension opens up all the possibilities PWS offers, it also demarcates its limits. First of all, meaning in PWS is defined in terms of reference to truth conditions. Consequently all the restrictions apply to PWS that were outlined in 4.6 for the logical approach to meaning in general:

- PWS cannot account for non-descriptive meaning, in particular social and expressive meaning and the meaning of sentence type (cf. 2.2.3).
- Even descriptive meaning is only captured indirectly.

In terms of the semiotic triangle, PWS exclusively describes the relation between an expression and its extensions, i.e. the right side of the triangle (Figure 10.6):

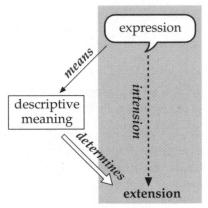

Figure 10.6 Semiotic 'triangle' for possible world semantics

In fact, it is not that PWS just focuses on the right side of the triangle, rather it eliminates the rest of it. The two-step link from an expression via its meaning to its extensions or denotation is bypassed, as it were, by the intension, i.e. by the direct assignment of extensions to the expression. Since to PWS the intension is the meaning, there is nothing in the PWS model that corresponds to the component 'meaning' in the semiotic triangle. To PWS it does not matter how the truth conditions of a sentence come about. What counts is what the truth conditions objectively are. But can we do without meaning? Can we account for the semantic data on the basis of direct expression → intension → extension assignments? The answer is: partly, but not totally.

In PWS, two expressions with the same intension must be considered synonymous, because synonymy is defined as meaning identity and the intension is the meaning. However, as we saw in 4.6.1, logical equivalence does not even amount to descriptive synonymy (let alone total synonymy, which would also include non-descriptive meaning). In particular, sentences with identical truth conditions need not have the same descriptive meaning. One extreme consequence of the PWS approach is that all logically true sentences receive the same meaning, because they all have the same intension, namely the one and only function that assigns the value to every possible world. Thus, contrary to our semantic intuitions, the following sentences all have the same meaning in PWS:

(41) a.   *Donald is a duck or Donald is not a duck.*
    b.   *All dogs are dogs.*
    c.   *Two plus two equals four.*

The list grows considerably, if meaning postulates are added as axioms. All meaning postulates would mean the same because they all would come out as logically true in the resulting interpretation system.

It is not only logically true sentences whose meanings coincide, contrary to intuition, in a PWS approach. Likewise pairs of sentences such as the following turn out semantically indistinguishable (recall the discussion in 4.6):

(42) a.   *Today is Sunday.*
    b.   *Tomorrow is Monday.*

What holds for natural language expressions also applies to the meaning representations in the formal language: they may look like having (and thereby representing) different meanings, but actually fail to do so. For example, one might prefer a translation system that produces (43a) rather than (43b) as the translation of *Mary squints,* i.e. an analysis that treats proper name NPs as directly inserted into predicate slots:

(43) a.   **squint(m)**
    b. $\exists x(x=m \land \textbf{squint}(x))$

When we interpret the formulae, as we inevitably do, in the same way as we interpret natural language sentences, the two formulae are semantically different. One is a simple predication with a one-place predicate applied to one definite argument. The other is much more complex, an existential quantification applied to a conjunction of two different predications. But as long as the formulae receive the PWS interpretations they do, the difference is an illusion: the formulae have the same meaning. At best, they can be seen as representing the meaning of *Mary squints* in different ways. But they do not represent two different meanings.

10.5.3 Possible-world semantics vs mentalistic semantics

The shortcomings of PWS with respect to the distinction between logically equivalent expressions are immediately due to eliminating meanings proper from the semiotic scheme by equating sentence meaning with truth conditions. To PWS, meanings are but assignments of extensions to CoUs (possible worlds). Thus, PWS provides a model for capturing the context dependence of truth and reference. But it does not provide an answer to the question of how all this works at the cognitive level. Clearly, we do not have ready-made intensions in our minds that produce the relevant extensions (truth values, referents, m-predicates) for any context we might encounter. Intensions are infinite, because there are an infinite number of logically possible CoUs. Of course, PWS does not claim that we have intensions in our minds. Rather, the approach does not aim at all at the cognitive level. But the cognitive level exists and we would like to understand how it works.

From the mentalistic perspective on meaning which has been advocated throughout the book, truth conditions and reference are but an *effect* of meaning, not meaning itself. For example, the meanings of (42a) and (42b) are two situation concepts that hold true of the same situations in the same CoUs, but they do so for different reasons. They are different concepts. Ultimately, the task of semantics is a description of the concepts that constitute the meanings of the expressions we use. PWS contributes to this task in describing what these concepts must yield in terms of truth and reference.

Let us compare the situation of a semanticist with that of someone who is to describe a computer program. Essentially, computer programs are entities that produce certain outputs when fed with certain inputs. With a PWS-like approach one would give a complete account of the input–output characteristics of the program, a table which for each input gives the resulting output, similar to the table given in (36) for propositions in a PWS approach. An approach in the vein of mentalistic semantics would aim at a description of the program itself, its structure and the way it works. Given such a description, the input–output characteristics of the program can be predicted and explained. Clearly, differently written programs may have the same input–output characteristics. And since this is so, we would not agree that we know what is essential about a program as long as we just know its input–output characteristics. Analogously, we can consider sentence meanings as mental software that when fed with the description of a CoU produces the output TRUE or FALSE. PWS tries to capture the input–output characteristics of the software, but mentalistic semantics would try to describe the software itself, how it works and why it produces the truth values it does. We do not know what is essential about the meaning of a sentence as long as we only know its truth conditions. The crucial thing about meaning is the kind of software of which it is constituted.

10.5.4 The development of possible-world semantics

The notions of *possible world*, *intension* and *extension* were developed in the early 1940s by the philosopher Rudolf Carnap (1891–1970), a pupil of Frege. The one who introduced the formal apparatus of PWS was another non-linguist, the mathematical logician Richard Montague (1930–1970). He was the first to develop a compositional analysis of fragments of English in systems that jointly describe the parallel formation and interpretation of complex expressions, as shown in Figure 10.2. Systems of this kind, like our three little examples for Japanese numerals, the English fragment and PL-F, came to be called *Montague grammars*. In the first of three papers on English fragments, 'English as a formal language' (1970a), Montague supplied a fragment of English directly with an intensional model. The two-step technique (Figure 10.5) of translating the fragment into a formal language, which is then given a model-theoretic interpretation, was introduced in his second paper, 'Universal grammar' (1970b). The third paper, 'The proper treatment of quantification in ordinary English' (1973), became a milestone that was to trigger off formal semantics as a major semantic approach throughout the last three decades. In this period, Montague's work was considerably extended to cover more and more phenomena of sentence semantics. Several alternatives were developed, all working with the same rigid type of descriptions. Formal semantics is a firmly established discipline with a lot of work going on in various languages – within different frameworks that keep being elaborated and refined in order to capture more and more semantic phenomena.

Checklist

compositional semantics
    formation base
    formation rules
    interpretation base
    interpretation rules
formal semantics
fragment
PL-F
    prime formulae
    existential quantifier
        scope
        bound variable
        free variable
translation into PL
    translation base
    translation rules
    model-theoretic semantics
    model (extensional)
        universe
        individual

domain of quantification
interpretation in a model
function
    m-predicate
interpretation rules for PL
possible worlds semantics
    possible world
    intension
    proposition
    individual concept
    property
    extension
    extensional model
    intensional model
    truth conditions
    logical properties
    logical relations
    meaning postulates
    decomposition
    Montague grammar

Exercises

1 Describe the structure of a compositional interpretation system in your own words.

2 The Japanese word for 100 is *hyaku*. The word for 200 is *nihyaku* (lit. 'two hundred'), and so on, up to *kyûhyaku* for 900. (Actually, some terms for the hundreds are slightly irregular due to phonological effects of concatenation, e.g. *sanhyaku* → *sanbyaku*. These irregularities are to be ignored in the exercise.) To the terms for the hundreds as first parts the terms for the numbers from 1 to 99 are directly concatenated. For example, the term for 539 is *gohyaku sanjûkyû*.
   (a) Define the two additional formation rules for the terms for 101 to 999.
   (b) Define the interpretation of *hyaku* and the two additional interpretation rules for the terms for 101 to 999.
   (c) Give a parallel account of the formation and compositional interpretation of the numeral *nanahyaku nijûichi* in the style of Figure 10.1.

3 Introduce categories in the original system for Japanese numerals. Note that a category is needed for each set of expressions, basic or complex, that figures as input of a formation rule. For example, the terms for 2 to 9 form a category because they constitute the possible first terms in F1; the terms for 1 to 9 form another category, the possible second terms for F2. The example shows that some expressions may belong to more than one category. Categories are also needed for the outputs of the rules. Assign categories to the basic expressions and reformulate the formation and interpretation rules in the style of those for the English fragment.

4 (a) Give a full account of the formation of the fragment sentence *A wicked person squints* in the way illustrated in (7).
   (b) Derive, step by step, the translation of the sentence as is done in (17), (18).
   (c) Derive, step by step, the truth value of the sentence in the given extensional model of PL-F (cf. (33)).

5 (a) Derive the translation of *A wicked person is Mary* (the sentence is odd, but do it for the sake of the exercise).
   (b) Reduce the formula by quantifier elimination.

6 Consider the PL-F formula **wicked(m)**.
   (a) Derive the truth conditions of the formula in the given model for PL-F.
   (b) Find a fragment sentence that has the same truth conditions.
   (c) Translate the sentence into PL-F.
   (d) Derive its truth conditions.
   (d) Explain why the formula **wicked(m)** and the translation of the sentence have the same truth conditions.

7 (a) Define an extensional model for PL-F with only three individuals, where Mary is a fat squinting fox, John a wicked dog, x is Mary and y is Sheila, a busy smoker. Each individual knows each other individual and dislikes Mary (including Mary herself). Give complete definitions of the interpretation of all basic terms of PL-F in that model. Which m-predicates receive equal interpretations?
  (b) Determine the truth values in this model for the formulae in (28), (29), (30), (32), (33), making use of the derivations given there.
8 Explain the notions *possible world*, *intension* and *extension* and how they are related.
9 Describe the overall scheme of possible-world semantics. How is meaning defined in PWS? What is the method of semantic description in PWS?
10 Explain why extensional models are insufficient for a semantic description of natural language sentences.
11 Explain why meaning cannot be fully described in terms of truth conditions and reference.
12 What is the difference between m-predicates and predicates?
13 In which respect is PWS superior to cognitive semantics? In which respect is cognitive semantics superior to PWS?

Further reading

There are several introductions to formal semantics. Some of the more recent ones are, in alphabetical order: Cann (1993), Chierchia and McConnell-Ginet (1990), de Swart (1998), Heim and Kratzer (1998). Bach (1989) offers an informal introduction to central topics of formal semantics.

Notes

[1] Compared to the general scheme of semantic composition given in Figure 1.1, the intermediate level of grammatical meaning is missing here. It will be neglected throughout this chapter.

[2] We use the more general term *interpretation* instead of *meaning*. Interpretations are whatever the expressions are assigned in such formal systems. How far these interpretations can be considered meanings in the proper sense will be discussed later.

[3] All VPs of the fragment are to be taken in their habitual reading. *Smokes* means as much as *is a smoker*, *squints* is to be taken as *has eyes that look in different directions*. The restriction enables us to use the verbs in the simple present tense and assume present time reference.

[4] It would be nice to include the definite article as well, but its semantics is too complex to be discussed here.

5   Strictly speaking, the meanings of *a fox* and *is a fox* are not the same, as only the latter carries present tense. The difference is not relevant in the fragment, because tense is neglected in our analysis.

6   In the literature you will often find that predicate constants are given sets of individuals as values instead of functions (m-predicates). Given a universe, there is an obvious correspondence between an m-predicate and the set of individuals to which it assigns the value 1. In such set-models, the value of **fox** would be the set consisting of Fritz alone, the value of **wicked** would be the set consisting of Fritz and John and so on.

7   Each time when I4 is applied, a new variable must be chosen, hence v instead of u.

8   In some variants of formal semantics, what we call a possible world is divided into two components. One called *context* comprises the parameters of the situation of utterance, while a *world* consists of those facts that are independent of the utterance event. In such frameworks, there is only one 'real' world, which, however, can be paired with different 'contexts'.

9   Strictly speaking, the sentence is only true or false in those possible worlds where there is a person called *Mary*. That there is such a person is what is called a presupposition of using the proper name NP *Mary* referentially. In general, natural language sentences may carry several such preconditions for being true or false. As a consequence, they receive a truth value only in those possible worlds where all presuppositions are fulfilled. See also note 6, Chapter 9.

References

Aitchison, Jean. 1987: *Words in the mind*. Oxford: Blackwell.

Andersson, Lars-Gunnar and Trudgill, Peter. 1990: *Bad language*. Oxford: Blackwell.

Aristotle. [1958]: *Metaphysics*: A revised text with introduction and commentary by W.D. Ross. Oxford: Clarendon Press.

Bach, Emmon. 1989: *Informal lectures on formal semantics*. Albany, NY: State University of New York Press.

Barsalou, Lawrence W. 1992: *Cognitive psychology. An overview for cognitive sciences*. Hillsdale, NJ: Erlbaum.

Berlin, Brent and Kay, Paul. 1969: *Basic color terms. Their universality and evolution*. Berkeley, CA: University of Los Angeles Press.

Bierwisch, Manfred. 1982: Formal and lexical semantics. *Linguistische Berichte* **80**, 3–17.

Bierwisch, Manfred. 1983: Semantische und konzeptuelle Repräsentation lexikalischer Einheiten. In Růžička, R. and Motsch, W. (eds), *Untersuchungen zur Semantik*. Berlin: Akademie-Verlag, pp. 61–100.

Bierwisch, Manfred and Lang, Ewald (eds). 1989: *Dimensional adjectives: Grammatical structure and conceptual interpretation*. Berlin: Springer.

Brown, Penelope and Levinson, Stephen. 1978: Universals in language usage: politeness phenomena. In Goody, E. (ed.), *Questions and politeness: Strategies in social interaction*. Cambridge: Cambridge University Press, pp. 56–311.

Brown, R. and Gilman, A. 1960: The pronouns of power and solidarity. In Sebeok, T. (ed.), *Style in language*. Cambridge, MA: MIT Press.

Cann, Ronnie. 1993: *Formal semantics: An introduction*. Cambridge: Cambridge University Press.

Chierchia, Gennaro and McConnell-Ginet, Sally. 1990: *Meaning and grammar: An introduction to semantics*. Cambridge, MA: MIT Press.

Cruse, D. Alan. 1986: *Lexical semantics*. Cambridge: Cambridge University Press.

de Swart, Henriëtte. 1998: *Introduction to natural language semantics.* Stanford, CA: Center for the Study of Language and Information.

Dillon, George L. 1977: *Introduction to linguistic semantics.* Englewood Cliffs, NJ: Prentice-Hall.

Dowty, David R. 1979: *Word meaning and Montague grammar.* Dordrecht: Reidel.

Foley, William A. 1997: *Anthropological linguistics: An introduction.* Oxford: Blackwell.

Givón, Talmy. 1993: *English grammar: A function-based introduction.* Amsterdam and Philadelphia, PA: John Benjamins.

Goddard, Cliff. 1998: *Semantic analysis: A practical introduction.* Oxford and New York: Oxford University Press.

Gussenhoven, Carlos and Jacobs, Haike. 1998: *Understanding phonology.* London: Arnold.

Harris, Roy. 1983: *F. de Saussure: Course in general linguistics.* Transl. Roy Harris. Oxford: Gerald Duckworth.

Haspelmath, Martin. 2002: *Understanding morphology.* London: Arnold.

Heim, Irene and Kratzer, Angelika. 1998: *Semantics in generative grammar.* Oxford: Blackwell.

Hughes, Geoffrey. 1992: *Swearing: A social history of foul language, oaths and profanity in English.* Oxford: Blackwell.

Jackendoff, Ray. 1990: *Semantic structures.* Cambridge, MA: MIT Press.

Kay, Paul and McDaniel, Chad K. 1978: The linguistic significance of the meaning of basic color terms. *Language* **54**: 610–46.

Kuroda, S.-Y. 1973: Where epistemology, style and grammar meet: a case study from Japanese. In Kiparsky, Paul and Anderson, Stephen (eds), *A Festschrift for Morris Halle.* New York: Holt, Rinehart & Winston, pp. 377–91.

Lakoff, George. 1987: *Women, fire, and dangerous things. What categories reveal about the mind.* Chicago, IL: The University of Chicago Press.

Levinson, Stephen C. 1983: *Pragmatics.* Cambridge: Cambridge University Press.

Lee, Penny. 1996: *The Whorf theory complex. A critical reconstruction.* Amsterdam, Philadelphia, PA: John Benjamins.

Lucy, John A. 1992: *Language diversity and thought.* Cambridge: Cambridge University Press.

Lyons, John. 1977: *Semantics.* Cambridge: Cambridge University Press.

Lyons, John. 1995: *Linguistic semantics. An introduction.* Cambridge: Cambridge University Press.

Martin, Samuel E. 1975: *A reference grammar of Japanese.* New Haven, CT and London: Yale University Press.

Matthews, Peter. 2001: *A short history of structural linguistics.* Cambridge: Cambridge University Press.

Montague, Richard. 1970a: English as a formal language. In Thomason (ed.) (1974), pp. 188–221.

Montague, Richard. 1970b: Universal Grammar. In Thomason (ed.) (1974), pp. 222–46.

Montague, Richard. 1973: The proper treatment of quantification in ordinary English. In Thomason (ed.) (1974), pp. 247–70.

The New Oxford Dictionary of English. 1998: Oxford: Clarendon Press.

Palmer, F.R. 1994: *Grammatical roles and relations.* Cambridge: Cambridge University Press.

Palmer, F.R. 2001: *Mood and modality.* Cambridge: Cambridge University Press.

Palmer, Gary B. 1996: *Toward a theory of cultural linguistics.* Austin, TX: University of Texas Press.

Partee, Barbara H., ter Meulen, Alice and Wall, Robert E. 1993: *Mathematical methods in linguistics.* Dordrecht: Kluwer Academic Publishers.

Pustejovsky, James. 1995: *The generative lexicon.* Cambridge, MA: MIT Press.

Radford, Andrew. 1988a: *Transformational grammar.* Cambridge: Cambridge University Press.

Radford, Andrew. 1998b: *Syntax: A minimalist introduction.* Cambridge: Cambridge University Press.

Saeed, John I. 1996: *Semantics.* Oxford: Blackwell.

Salzmann, Zdenek 1993: *Language, culture and society: An introduction to linguistic anthropology.* Boulder, CO: Westview Press.

Sapir, Edward. 1921: *Language: An introduction to the study of speech.* New York: Harcourt, Brace & World.

Suzuki, Takao, 1978: *Japanese and the Japanese: Words in culture.* Tokyo: Kodansha.

Tallerman, Maggie. 1998: *Understanding syntax.* London: Arnold.

Thomason, Richmond H. (ed.) 1974: *Formal philosophy: Selected papers of Richard Montague.* New Haven, CT and London: Yale University Press.

Ungerer, Friedrich and Schmid, Hans-Jörg. 1996: *An introduction to cognitive linguistics.* London and New York: Longman.

Verschueren, Jef. 1999: *Understanding pragmatics.* London: Arnold.

Wierzbicka, Anna. 1996: *Semantics: Primes and universals.* Oxford and New York: Oxford University Press.

Whorf, Benjamin Lee. 1940: Science and linguistics. In Benjamin Whorf (1956), pp. 207–19.

Whorf, Benjamin Lee. 1956: *Language, thought and reality: Selected writings by Benjamin Lee Whorf,* ed. by John B. Carroll, Cambridge, MA: MIT Press.

Wittgenstein, Ludwig. 1958: *Philosophische Untersuchungen/Philosophical investigations.* Transl. G.E.M. Anscombe. Oxford: Blackwell.

Index